Cover

The cover shows the handwriting of a person with Parkinson's Disease. It consists of a part of the 'Essay on the Shaking Palsy', the article where Dr. James Parkinson first mentioned the disease (1817). The disease was later named after him.

Parkinson's Disease Selfcare Manual

**IF YOU REQUIRE THE CD-ROM WHICH
ACCOMPANIES THIS BOOK, PLEASE ASK
LIBRARY STAFF.**

MFS.

Parkinson's Disease

Editors:

E.H. Coene, M.D.
Professor R.K. Griffiths CBE

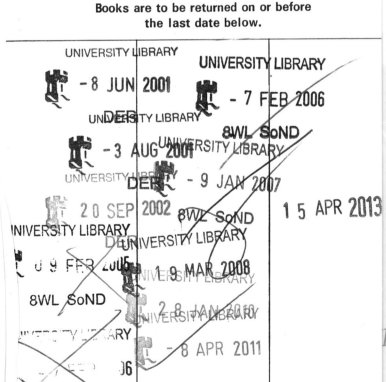

ptember
Foundation

...tion, 2000

Colophon

Published by the September Foundation, Amsterdam, the Netherlands, 2000

This manual was made possible thanks to subsidy granted by the NHS Executive West Midlands.

Final editor:	E.H. Coene. M.D., Professor R.K. Griffiths CBE
Artwork:	MattArt, Haarlem, the Netherlands
Illustrations:	P. Buchel, Amsterdam, the Netherlands
Production:	Giethoorn Ten Brink, Meppel, the Netherlands

ISBN 90-72248-48-1

Copyright: copyright of some parts of this text are ownded by the September Foundation and others by E.H. Coene. For further information please contact:

The September Foundation
Nieuwpoortkade 2A
1055 RX Amsterdam, the Netherlands
Tel.: ++31 20 60 60 745
Fax: ++31 20 60 60 798
e-mail: info@stichtingseptember.nl

Liability agreement

Foreword

Dear Reader,

It gives me great pleasure to introduce you to the Parkinson's Disease Self-Care Manual that is a very special publication for a number of reasons.

Firstly, the contents. As you may know, Parkinson's Disease affects every aspect of daily life and this manual provides extensive and accessible information about how to manage the many challenges of living with this chronic neurological condition. The manual describes the help that is available to do this, yet it also focuses on what people with Parkinson's, their families and friends can do for themselves in order to create an independent and enjoyable lifestyle which means that people with Parkinson's and their carers become 'Partners in Care'.

Secondly, the reason why this manual is so special is because of the initiative undertaken by the NHS Executive West Midlands who provided the financial backing. It is based on a successful Dutch self-care manual, produced by the September Foundation, financed by the Dutch government and made in collaboration with the Dutch Parkinson's Disease Society. With the September Foundation as project coordinator, this edition has been adapted by a team of experts in close consultation with both the European Parkinson's Disease Association (EPDA) and the Parkinson's Disease Society of the United Kingdom (PDS).

This approach has enabled an international project to use proven existing materials and has allowed us to build on the experience of Parkinson's care in the Netherlands. This has meant that we have not had to 'reinvent the wheel' and illustrates how national and international co-operation can result in a product that individually, because of time and cost, the national organisations would have been unable to develop.

Thirdly, this manual is special because it exploits the latest developments in the field of Information Technology. It is published alongside a CD-ROM that draws on multi-media's full potential: text, sound, video, photographs and animation. This means that information can be provided not only in the old, tried and trusted form but, also by using the latest form of communication. This project marks the transition to a new millennium!

This initiative, which has been developed through partnership and collaboration, shows that there is hope. It demonstrates not only that it is possible to retain independence whilst living with Parkinson's, but also what can be achieved by working together at a national and international level.

I sincerely hope that this initiative will inspire other organisations dealing with chronic conditions to develop similar self-care manuals and CD-ROMs to encourage independence, and will highlight what can be achieved by working together.

The NHS, the PDS, the EPDA and the September Foundation will do their very best to achieve this aim.

Mary G. Baker MBE
Chief Executive Parkinson's Disease Society
President European Parkinson's Disease Association

How to use this self-care manual

This is the 'Self-Care Manual for People with Parkinson's Disease'. This book is intended first and foremost for people with Parkinson's, but it may also prove useful to partners, families, friends and professional carers.

Why this manual?

If you have Parkinson's, you can choose to remain independent and in charge of your own life for as long as possible. This means that your goal is to stay at home where you can look after yourself. You may also be helped by the people you know and by professional carers. This manual supports you in that aim, but is not intended to oblige you to take care of yourself.

Looking after yourself can mean that you are confronted with many unknown situations and problems. This self-care manual provides *practical information* about a great number of these difficulties and emphasises what you yourself can do about them. Information is also provided on the help that can be made available to you.

The recommendations included are simply intended as suggestions. You should decide for yourself whether or not to apply them to your particular situation.

What is included in this manual?

This manual provides a survey of the ways in which the problems caused by Parkinson's can be coped with. You will decide which of these possibilities you want to opt for.

At present, there is no treatment that can cure Parkinson's Disease. But there are ways to improve the quality of your life. This includes medication, special resources, social security, benefits, complementary treatments, physiotherapy, etc.

Warning

Do not be put off by the fact that this manual has so many pages. It is not a novel you have to read from beginning to end. We suggest that you read only the chapters that relate to your particular situation.

The manual contains information about many problems and symptoms. You will only have to deal with *some* of these problems; there are other symptoms that you will never encounter. For that reason we again advise that you read only those sections that are important to you.

You can use the manual as a *reference* work in which you look up information as you need it.

Instructions for use

The *table of contents* gives you an idea of the subjects that are discussed in this self-care manual.

In addition, most chapters are preceded by a *summary*. This summary contains the most important information, so that (initially) you do not have to read through the entire chapter.

There is also an *index of key* words in the back of the manual in order to make it easier to look things up.

Furthermore, there is a *glossary* in which the medical and technical terms used are explained.

Updates

Much is changing in the field of Parkinson's, and for this reason there are plans to revise and supplement this book regularly on the Internet. For more information contact: the Parkinson's Disease Society (PDS), tel. 020 7931 8080, or the NHS Executive West Midlands, tel. 0121 224 4676.

CD-ROM

This manual is also available on CD-ROM, where full use is made of the possibilities multimedia can offer to illustrate and present the text of this book. For more information contact: the PDS,
tel. 020 7931 8080, or the NHS Executive West Midlands, tel. 0121 224 4676.

Following this introduction, we would like to wish you good luck and we sincerely hope that the manual may prove useful to you.

Professor Rod Griffiths CBE,
Regional Director of Public Health, NHS Executive West Midlands, UK

Dan Coene,
M.D., Director of the September Foundation, Amsterdam, The Netherlands

Acknowledgements

First and foremost we would like to express our gratitude to the NHS Executive West Midlands who initiated this project and provided the necessary financial support.

This manual is the result of a project involving the close collaboration of the NHS Executive West Midlands of Birmingham, UK, and the September Foundation of Amsterdam, the Netherlands.
It was based on the example of an existing and successful Dutch manual, produced by the September Foundation.
The text has not only been translated, it has also been rewritten by a large group of British specialists, so that it relates specifically to the current situation in the UK.
The rewritten text was then checked in terms of its contents by an Advisory Board/Expert Panel consisting of professional experts from the UK. A Pretest Panel (Consumers Panel), consisting of people with Parkinson's Disease and their partners, has also examined it for user friendliness.
A journalist subsequently edited it before the September Foundation completed the final editing.

Throughout its entire duration, this project involved the close co-operation of both the Parkinson's Disease Society of the UK (the PDS) and the European Parkinson's Disease Association (the EPDA). For further information about the project and the participating organizations, see pages 275, 277, 279 and 282.

We would like to thank the following people for their dedication and expertise:

NHS Executive West Midlands
Professor Rod Griffiths CBE, Regional Director of Public Health, Editor
Karen Saunders, Business Manager, Project Coordinator
Janice Cunningham, Deputy Head of Communications (Development)
Karen Fellows, Secretarial Support
Sue Yaman, Secretarial Support
Gráinne MacRae, Temporary Secretarial Support

The September Foundation
Dan Coene, M.D., Director, Project Leader, Editor
Debbie Lups, Staff Member, Project Coordinator
Sander Kollaard, Staff Member, Editor
Claudia van Kessel, Staff Member, Communication
Suzanne Gerits, Staff Member, Content Manager
Kirsten Wilbrink, Staff Member, Production
Carolien Leeuwenburgh, Staff Member, Production

Parkinson's Disease Society, UK (PDS)

Mary G. Baker MBE, Chief Executive
Lizzie Graham, Projects Development Manager
Marilyn Caven, Projects Development Officer
Gregg Vines, PR Officer
Eddie Falvey, Care Services Manager
Simon Hope, PR Manager
Barbara Cormie, Publications Manager
Bridget McCall, Information Manager
Clare Jones, Secretarial Support

European Parkinson's Disease Association (EPDA)

Mary G. Baker MBE, President
Lizzie Graham, Liaison

Advisory Board/Expert Panel

John Bucknall, Welfare & Employment Rights Advisor, PDS
Dan Coene, M.D., Director, September Foundation
Professor Rod Griffiths CBE, Regional Director of Public Health, NHS Executive West Midlands
Terry Lawrence, Department of Public Health & Epidemiology, University of Birmingham
Debbie Lups, Project Coordinator, September Foundation
Karen Saunders, Business Manager, NHS Executive West Midlands
Pauline Smith, Parkinson's Disease expert, Project Consultant Overbridge Training, former Director of Operations, PDS
Professor Adrian Williams, department of Neurology, Queen Elizabeth Hospital, Birmingham

Authors/advisors/contributors:

Professor Mike Barnes, UK
Alison Beattie, Occupational Therapist, Independent Occupational Therapy Services, Glasgow, UK
Rev.Peter Bellamy, UK
Emma Bennion, Chairman of YAPP&Rs, the young on-set special interest group of the Parkinson's Disease Society and Trustee of the Society, UK
Mala Bhinda, Senior Dietician, The National Hospital for Neurology & Neurosurgery, London, UK
Dr Carl Clarke, Consultant in Neurology and Honorary Senior Lecturer, Hull Royal Infirmary, UK
Marit Eikaas, UK
Professor E.Ernst, Director, Department of Complementary Medicine, Postgraduate Medical School, University of Exeter, UK
Professor L.J. Findley, T.D., O.L.J., M.D., F.R.C.P., F.A.C.P., Consultant Neurologist 'Avenue House', Romford, UK
Dr Caron Grainger, Consultant in Public Health Medicine, NHS Executive West Midlands, UK
Marion Grimwood, UK
Peter Harvey, UK
Rosie Hayward, Placement Advisor, Parkinson's Diseae Society, UK
Jean Hearne, Parkinson's Disease Nurse Specialist, Department of Neurology, Queen Elizabeth Hospital, Birmingham, UK
Liz Hoyle, physiotherapist, Penrith Hospital, UK
Rosemary Maguire, UK

Jo Marcus, UK
Lady Jill Pitkeathley, UK
Sue Preston, former Parkinson's Disease Nurse Specialist, Ealing & Hammersmith Health Authority, UK
Sheila Scott, Speech and Language Therapist, Scottish & Northern Regional Manager Parkinson's Disease Society, UK
Beverly Shember, Parkinson's Disease Society, UK
Sue Thomas, Nursing Policy and Practice Advisor, the Royal College of Nursing, London, UK
Keith Williams, Director of Public Health, Coventry Health Authority, Coventry, UK

Pretest Panel (consumers/patients/partners)
Mr L. Essex
Mr & Mrs B. Wall
Mr & Mrs T. Lewis
Mr & Mrs N. Howard
Mrs A. James
Mr & Mrs A. Burgess
Mr D. Smith

Other Project input
Victoria McNeile: Journalist, Editor, London, UK
Norman McIntosh Raitt, Translator, Goes, the Netherlands
Annie Wright, Translator, Amsterdam, the Netherlands
Daniel Carroll Language Service, Translator, Amstelveen, the Netherlands
Peti Buchel, Illustrations, Amsterdam, the Netherlands

Thanks to Professor Adrian Williams and Marie Oxtoby for permission to include the Glossary from 'Parkinson's at your Fingertips'.

author: - E.H. Coene, M.D., September
Foundation, the Netherlands

advisors: - Professor L.J. Findley, T.D., O.L.J., M.D.,
F.R.C.P., F.A.C.P., consultant neurologist
'Avenue House', Romford, UK
- Dr C.E. Clarke, Consultant in Neurology
& Honorary Senior Lecturer, Hull Royal
Infirmary, UK
- Professor J.P.W.F. Lakke, chairperson of
the Medical Advisory Counsel of the
Dutch Parkinson's Disease Society,
the Netherlands
- Dr. J. van Manen, neurologist, advisor to
the Dutch Parkinson's Disease Society,
the Netherlands

1

What is Parkinson's Disease?

Summary

Parkinson's Disease affects the part of the brain responsible for control of movement, which in turn can cause difficulties such as tremor, stiffness and slowness of movement. Symptoms vary from person to person, and can change from day to day.

Symptoms are initially vague; therefore it can be difficult to diagnose Parkinson's Disease, also because there are no special examinations or blood tests that can prove whether or not a person has Parkinson's Disease. In the course of time, symptoms tend to get worse, leading to difficulties with daily activities.

The cause of the disease is not yet known. Parkinson's usually affects older people but younger people can get it too. Mental faculties are usually not affected. With medication, people can lead normal lives for years.

Introduction

This chapter deals with Parkinson's Disease: the symptoms and causes, who gets it, the way in which it is diagnosed and how it develops.

This chapter introduces the following subjects:
- What is Parkinson's Disease?
- What are the symptoms?
- Who gets it?
- What is the cause?
- Examination and diagnosis
- How does Parkinson's Disease progress?

"We have known for three years now that my husband has Parkinson's. It was difficult to accept, and in the last three years we've gone through a lot of rough patches. It may sound strange, but we have come a lot closer because of it, as though we've grown together more..."

What is Parkinson's Disease?

Parkinson's Disease (often referred to as 'Parkinson's' or 'PD') affects the part of the brain that is responsible for the control of movement.

Normally the brain acts like the automatic pilot on a plane, organising and controlling our movements without our being aware of it. All aspects of movement are carefully attuned to each other as a matter of course. With Parkinson's, something goes wrong with the automatic pilot, which means that movement is no longer simple and straightforward. As yet, there is no cure for the disease, but much can be done to limit its symptoms.

What are the symptoms?

The symptoms vary from person to person. The most common are *tremor* (trembling or shaking), *stiffness* and *slowness of movement*. These symptoms lead to difficulties with daily activities such as walking, getting in and out of bed, sitting down in a chair and then standing up again.

People also find that they need a greater degree of concentration to do things like walking or eating. They may experience difficulty in getting dressed, writing or doing simple tasks such as repairs or ironing. This is because the brain cannot effectively direct the movements needed. There may, in the long-term, be problems with maintaining posture and balance which can result in falls.

People with Parkinson's become less supple. They also tend to apply too little force so that movements become slower, too small and executed with difficulty. Eventually, they can carry out only the most basic movements.

Other symptoms involve problems with urinating, slow bowel movements and a greasy skin. These and other Parkinson's symptoms are described in detail in Chapter 2 '*General Symptoms*' and Chapter 27 '*Particular Symptoms*'. Information is also included about what can be done to alleviate these conditions.

Generally, Parkinson's does not affect a person's powers of comprehension. Although Parkinson's affects a small part of the brain, people with the disease have only a ten per cent higher chance of developing dementia than their contemporaries without this disease.

Symptoms can vary from day to day

A characteristic of Parkinson's is that symptoms can change from day to day and sometimes even from hour to hour. For example, a person may find it very difficult to move to the front door and then, perhaps only thirty minutes later, he will be going for a walk. These changes are very common. They are a part of Parkinson's Disease or may also be a result of drug treatment. Other people may find it difficult to understand and may even think the person is being difficult or lazy. That is certainly not the case.

Who gets it?

Parkinson's generally affects older people. The average age at which symptoms first appear is between 58 and 62 years. Younger people, however, also develop Parkinson's: one in twenty of the people who is diagnosed is under the age of 40. Parkinson's affects about 120,000 people in the UK alone. Statisticians estimate that about one in every 100 people over the age of 65 will develop the disease.

Parkinson's occurs throughout the world in every culture and race.

What is the cause?

In Parkinson's, a small part of the brain known as the 'black nucleus' or *substantia nigra* is damaged. This nucleus of nerve cells plays an important role in enabling a smooth flow of movement. This takes place by means of a chemical substance called *dopamine* which is manufactured in the substantia nigra. Dopamine is a chemical messenger (neurotransmitter). Parkinson's damages the cells of the substantia nigra, so that insufficient dopamine is produced. This results in movement difficulties, muscular stiffness and tremor.

No one knows what causes the brain damage that results in Parkinson's but there are a number of possibilities. Parkinson's might be caused by a virus or it may be an immunological disease. It might also be a degenerative disease occurring as the body wears itself out with age. Another theory is that Parkinson's may be caused by chemicals in the food and fluid we consume or by their by-products following digestion.

We know that Parkinson's is not an infectious disease, so you cannot catch it through physical contact. We also know that Parkinson's is not caused by consumption of alcohol or by stress, although these factors can have an adverse effect on symptoms at a particular time. There is also no proven link with particular diets or occupations.

Recent re-evaluations of twin studies in Parkinson's suggest there is a genetic component to the illness. This does not mean to say the children of someone with Parkinson's have a high risk of developing the condition but they are slightly more predisposed to it than the rest of the population.

Examination and diagnosis

The initial signs of Parkinson's are frequently vague and confusing. It often starts with a slight trembling of an arm. Other people feel tired or experience slight cramps such as pain in an arm. Sometimes these symptoms are not noticed by the individuals themselves but are spotted by their friends or families. The symptoms often develop so gradually that it can be hard to remember when they began.

Because the symptoms are initially vague, a doctor may find it difficult to discover their cause: tiredness, pain in an arm or frequent falls might suggest a number of possible illnesses. Tremor also has a number of causes and, as it is common in the elderly, can sometimes be wrongly diagnosed as Parkinson's (for further information on this, see page 19). Sometimes the symptoms of Parkinson's are mistakenly attributed to old age or depression.

A doctor will base his diagnosis on talking with you and looking at the symptoms you present. There are no special examinations or blood tests that can prove whether or not a person has Parkinson's. There will always be some degree of slowness of movement in established Parkinson's and this may involve tremor, rigidity and problems in maintaining balance. Parkinson's is always progressive so a Parkinson's diagnosis is unlikely if there is no progression over a period of three years or more.[1]

For many people, it may have taken a long time to discover that their symptoms were caused by Parkinson's. This might have involved a period of great uncertainty. If the symptoms become clearer - muscles stiffer, tremor more pronounced and movements slower - the diagnosis is generally quite straight-forward. Two of the three symptoms must be present to establish Parkinson's.

"I found it difficult to accept that it took so long to diagnose Parkinson's Disease. First it was 'possibly Parkinson's', then 'probably Parkinson's' and later 'definitely Parkinson's'. Now that I know more about it, I can understand why they were cautious, but it was difficult to live with the uncertainty. I like things to be clear, don't like 'maybe' or 'possibly'. Actually I was quite relieved when the neurologist told me it was certain I had Parkinson's, even though it's not a very nice thought."

How does Parkinson's Disease progress?

If you're diagnosed as having Parkinson's, you will want to know about how this is going to affect you. It is impossible to answer this question accurately, because the condition develops differently in each individual and treatment is also individual.

Parkinson's tends to begin gradually, with the symptoms becoming more serious as time passes. That is why the course of this disease is referred to as progressive. The symptoms can sometimes remain slight for years, however, and it is a mistake to suppose that everyone with Parkinson's becomes seriously disabled. With medication most people with Parkinson's manage to lead normal lives for many years. However, symptoms can develop rapidly in a small number of people.

Parkinson's is not a directly fatal disease, but mortality rates in the condition are higher than in the normal population. People can die from the indirect consequences of the disease. For instance, someone might be more susceptible to pneumonia because of the deterioration of his or her general condition.

author: - E.H. Coene, M.D., September
Foundation, the Netherlands
advisors:- Profesor J.L. Findley, T.D., O.L.J., M.D.,
F.R.C.P., F.A.C.P., Consultant neurologist
'Avenue House', Romford, UK
- Dr. C.E. Clarke, Consultant in Neurology
& Honorary Senior Lecturer, Hull Royal
Infirmary, UK
- Dr. J.D. Speelman, neurologist, Academic
Medical Centre, University of Amsterdam,
the Netherlands
- Dr. J. van Manen, neurologist, advisor to
the Dutch Parkinson's Disease Society,
the Netherlands

2

General symptoms

Summary

This chapter will address some of the complaints associated with Parkinson's: tremor, stiffness, and slowness of movement and tiredness. The symptoms of each complaint will be described. Then you will be advised as to what you can do to reduce the complaint, and informed about the help available for it.

Tremor is often the first symptom of Parkinson's to show. It usually begins very slightly, in an arm or hand on one side of the body.
The *stiffness* or rigidity is caused by excessive muscular tension. It usually begins in the neck or shoulders.
Movements will become *slower*. 'Automatic movements', like walking may also become difficult.
The stiffness and tremor are a severe strain on the muscles. This often causes people with Parkinson's to feel extremely *tired*.

Much can often be done to alleviate these complaints, with for example medication or physiotherapy.

Introduction

In this chapter, a number of the symptoms that occur regularly with Parkinson's Disease are described. These include:

- shaking
- stiffness (rigidity)
- slowness and poverty of movement
- tiredness.

This chapter does not describe all the symptoms of Parkinson's, however. More information appears in Chapter 27 *'Particular Symptoms'*. Practical advice on how to cope appears in both chapters.

You may not experience many of the symptoms described in these two chapters. No two people with Parkinson's are alike. One way to treat the information would be to use the chapters as reference books and just read parts of them if you want to look up a symptom. Reading from beginning to end may frighten you with symptoms that may never trouble you! Fortunately a lot can be done for most of the symptoms described.

Consult your GP
We advise you always to consult your GP about your symptoms if you are worried about them. Be certain to seek advice if they get worse, if they change or if new ones appear. Remember that a symptom discussed in this chapter need have nothing to do with Parkinson's. There could be another cause that should be investigated. A new symptom might, for example, be a side effect of drug treatment. You could also consult a Parkinson's Disease Nurse Specialist or a practice nurse about your health.

The medications mentioned in the text are given as examples only. Perhaps you will use different ones: there are others available. A number of the medications mentioned here are described in more detail in Chapter 3 'Treatment and medication', in Chapter 29 'Medication that contains levodopa' and chapter 27 'Other medications'. When a medication (often referred to as a treatment drug) is referred to by its trade or brand name, an initial capital letter is used e.g., Madopar. When the generic name is given, a small first letter is used e.g., co-beneldopa.

Shaking

Symptoms and signs
Shaking, or tremor as it is sometimes called, is in many cases the most obvious symptom of Parkinson's. In two thirds of cases it is the first symptom. If the shaking is slight, it can be a long time before Parkinson's is suspected. Sometimes it is so slight that it is not noticed by other people although the person concerned may be aware of it. Not everyone with Parkinson's will have a tremor.

Where tremor exists, shaking usually begins in the hands and arms, on one side of the body. Later, the other side may be involved. This can happen after some years or not at all. Often the thumb and forefinger move against each other, the so-called 'counting money' or 'pill rolling tremor', or the wrists move as if the person is beating an egg. The shaking can also occur in the foot, less often in the mouth and jaw (not the whole head). Sometimes the trunk moves. The tremor can also be felt internally. It is strongest when someone is not moving, hence the term 'rest' tremor. If a movement is made, the shaking is reduced. Shaking stops during sleep. Emotional states (sorrow, anger, joy, nervousness) or tiredness often make it worse. To begin with, the shaking may only be noticeable at such times.

What can you do to help yourself ?
Some people don't have too many problems with tremors, particularly if they are having treatment. Even if it is obvious, they might not choose to do anything about it. For some people though, to have an obvious tremor is embarrassing.

If someone is embarrassed about his tremor, he may avoid contact with other people and become isolated. Situations such as going out for a meal can feel threatening. Perhaps it could help to remember that, although other people notice the tremor, they are generally not worried by it. They will be much more interested in you and your conversation than a shaking hand. Putting your cards on the table and explaining what is going on can be very good for both parties. In any case, the more you get anxious about it and try to hide it, the worse it will become. Stress makes the tremor worse, but it is not the cause.

If you suffer from nerves and stress, relaxation can help. (For more information, see Chapter 32 'Coping with Stress').

Some people may have problems with tremor at work, because they notice that other people, perhaps colleagues or clients, have less confidence in their abilities. Explaining what Parkinson's is, and the fact that the tremor generally does not have an adverse effect on your work, can prevent this.

Tremor is reduced during movement, so some people with Parkinson's make more gestures with their hands while they are talking. Holding the arms in a particular position or holding on to something solid while walking can also help. Some people are able to temporarily suppress the tremor by their own will power but this takes a lot of energy and is exhausting in the long run.

What help is available?
A lot of different forms of help are available.

The doctor can prescribe various medicines for Parkinson's. These usually help to reduce the tremor. More often than not, a doctor will make no attempt to get rid of it altogether, because the dose would have to be so high that there would be many side effects. Examples of drugs that help are:
- levodopa preparations (see Chapter 29 'Medication that contains levodopa')
- anticholinergic drugs (see Chapter 30 'Other medication')
- benzodiazepines (for example diazepam or oxazepam)
- beta-blockers (for example propranolol).

Occupational therapists can help you (see Chapter 18 'Occupational Therapy') as can physiotherapists (see Chapter 17 'Physiotherapy'). In certain rare cases, an operation can help (see Chapter 31 'Surgical Treatment').

Further information
Shaking is not only caused by Parkinson's. There is a form that often occurs called *essential tremor*, which has nothing to do with Parkinson's. Essential tremor is more common than Parkinson's Disease.[1] It occurs in many, usually older, people and can be hereditary. Because Parkinson's also occurs in older people the two are often confused. As a result, a number of people with an essential tremor are mistakenly treated for Parkinson's and vice versa. This is why it is important to have your diagnosis confirmed by a specialist.

There are a number of clear distinctions between the different sorts of tremor. Essential tremor is absent at rest, but appears when the arms are held out in posture. It may be described as an 'action tremor'. With a tremor such as this, the head can also be involved. Essential tremor may often also become less with the intake of alcohol and the tremor is slightly more rapid than with Parkinson's. Other Parkinson's symptoms such as stiffness and slowness are absent with essential tremor.

> *"At first I thought the tremor came from old age. My children used to tease me a bit. They used to say: 'You're getting old, Dad' and laugh a bit...*
> *It was only later that I knew that it came from the Parkinson's.*
> *Of course it's annoying, all that shaking, but I still feel better knowing that it's not because of old age. Strange, isn't it? I do shake, but I do not feel old at all!"*

Other causes of tremors are an over-active thyroid, anxiety, smoking too much and long-term misuse of alcohol and drugs. The differences between such tremors and Parkinson's are clear to a specialist.

Stiffness (rigidity)

Symptoms and signs

In Parkinson's the muscles become stiffer because they are always a little tense. This is also known as 'hypertonus' (hyper = excessive, tonus = tension) or *rigidity*. Rigidity mostly begins in the neck/shoulder or in an arm. It can be felt as real stiffness in the joints (in the elbow, wrist or knee) but also as a tired, heavy or nagging bruised feeling in the muscles. The stiffness is one of the symptoms of Parkinson's that can be the most trouble to people. Everyday tasks may become more difficult, for example, rolling over in bed, getting out of a chair, looking over your shoulder, etc.[3]

When rigidity is present, there is usually a degree of slowness of movement (bradykinesia, see page 21). Both of these symptoms contribute together to increase the difficulties a person with Parkinson's experiences.

Rigidity is usually not the first symptom that someone notices. It is often some time before someone becomes aware of it because it begins slowly. In that case it can be the doctor who diagnoses the stiffness. He or she does this by bending an arm or a leg while you hold it relaxed. The doctor then feels a shock-like resistance during the movement. This is called the lead pipe or cogwheel rigidity.

Involvement of the back muscles leads to postural change and to a tendency to sit, stand and walk bent forward. The arms are then held close to the body, bent at the elbow. If the position of the back, arms or legs remains like this for a long time, the muscles and joints can become painful.

If the face muscles become stiff, a person has a fixed look with little possibility of facial expression. This is sometimes called the *Parkinsonian mask* (or: *poker face*). The tongue may also be affected by muscle rigidity, which will result in speech difficulty. Internal organs such as the bowel and the bladder can be affected as well (see Chapter 27 '*Particular symptoms*').

What can you do to help yourself?

If your facial expression is reduced and you have difficulty smiling, frowning or raising your eyebrows, it may be that other people are unable to read your 'body language' and your feelings in the usual way. You can try to explain what is going on, because it could be useful to both you and them.

You could also try to train your facial muscles. Pulling funny faces can help. Perhaps you can start doing it in front of the mirror. For example, you can purse your lips, smile, open your mouth and shut it again tightly, raise and lower your eyebrows, blow out your cheeks and suck them in again, bare your teeth, stick out your tongue and move it around. Make all these movements in an exaggerated way.

Problems with handwriting are described in the next part of this chapter ('Slowness of movement'). Speech problems are discussed in Chapter 19 '*Speech and language therapy*'; problems with pain in Chapter 27 '*Particular Symptoms*'. In Chapter 7 '*Tips for everyday living*' and Chapter 8 '*Help with movement*', information is given about how to cope with the consequences of stiffness, for example when walking, keeping your balance, or turning over in bed.

What help is available?

Stiffness can best be controlled with medicines, for example levodopa preparations which are converted in the body into dopamine (see Chapter 3 '*Treatment and medication*' and Chapter 29 '*Medication that contains levodopa*').

Physiotherapy can be useful against stiffness and a bent posture (see Chapter 17 '*Physiotherapy*'). Do not delay too long before asking for help, because that could result in the symptoms getting worse. Speech and Language Therapy can help with all forms of communication difficulties, including loss of facial expression and the Parkinson's Disease Society has a video of facial exercises called "Face to Face". See Chapter 19 '*Speech and language therapy*'.

Slowness and poverty of movement

Symptoms and signs

In Parkinson's, movement becomes slower, so-called bradykinesia (brady = slow, kinesia = movement) and reduced, so-called hypokinesia. Slowness of movement often occurs together with the muscle stiffness described earlier in this chapter.

People often comment at the beginning that they have 'weak muscles' or that their limbs feel rubbery, rather than their movements are slower. The strength of the muscles doesn't actually decline, but the muscles do not react so quickly and this gives a feeling of uncertainty.

Automatic movements that previously happened unconsciously now have to be made consciously. For example, clearing the throat or changing position happen unconsciously less often than they once did. The same goes for blinking, which causes dry eyes. Swallowing is reduced so more saliva remains in the mouth, which can cause someone to dribble especially if the posture is bent. A reduced swinging of the arms during walking is also noticeable. This sometimes happens on one side with the stiffer arm moving less. People with Parkinson's often sit 'stiller' than other people.

Doing all kinds of things, especially those involving fine movements, takes more time and effort: for example, tying shoelaces, turning pages, doing up shirt buttons. This is often frustrating because people want to do them as quickly as they used to in the past. Handwriting can change, with the letters becoming unsteady and smaller, sometimes in the course of a line. In the long term, writing can become difficult to read. This is called micrographia (micro = small, graphia = writing).

In the course of the disease, not only fine movements but coarser movements can decline and not happen automatically. Sitting down in a chair, getting out of the car, putting on a jumper, turning over in bed, have to be done consciously and step by step.

It also becomes more difficult to change movements, because the muscles react more slowly. Examples of this include back and forth movements such as beating an egg, brushing teeth or stopping if the person has started walking. It also becomes difficult to do two things at the same time.

While automatic movements can become more difficult, acquired movements are less affected. This means, for instance, that it is not unusual that someone with Parkinson's can still play the piano.

The sudden onset of tiredness and problems with balance are consequences of the slowness of movement. Another result is that walking can become more difficult. Slowness of movement can vary a great deal during the course of a day. One moment you can do something that is impossible the next.

> *"For a time I had a lot of problems walking. There was even one time... we were walking through town and a policeman stopped us because he thought I was drunk. Such a young lad he was. He wasn't unfriendly – just a bit concerned. He said: 'Are you feeling OK?' My husband was furious, but I had to giggle. It was a crazy situation. The poor lad blushed like fury when we told him what was the matter."*

What can you do to help yourself?
Keeping active is highly recommended, although things you used to do quickly

will seem more difficult. The more you keep trying, the more you will find you can do.[4]

Although the symptom itself does not go away, the unpleasant consequences of it can be limited. Chapter 7 '*Tips for everyday living*' and Chapter 8 '*Help with movement*' give information and tips about this, covering problems with walking, balance, turning over in bed etc. For instance, writing with a thicker pen can help with problems with handwriting.

Dribbling is discussed in Chapter 27 '*Particular symptoms*'.

The variation that can take place suddenly in the speed of movement can be very difficult to cope with. Other people can find it difficult to understand and can think the person is putting on an act or being lazy. You may have to explain this variation again and again. If the slowness is very extreme, however, there is the possibility that things will improve later.

What help is available?

Medicines often help with slowness of movement: for example, levodopa preparations, and dopamine agonists (see Chapter 3 '*Treatment and medication*', Chapter 29 '*Medication that contains levodopa*' and Chapter 30 '*Other medication*').

When blinking is too infrequent, the eyes become very dry, burning or red. There is then a danger of infection. The doctor can prescribe artificial tears (methyl cellulose eye drops).

Occupational therapy and physiotherapy can help with movement problems (see Chapters 18 and 17) and speech therapy (Chapter 19) can help with swallowing difficulties.

Tiredness

Tiredness often occurs with Parkinson's. The explanation is that the stiffness and tremor heavily tax the muscles, which then become tired. The tiredness often fluctuates; sudden periods of tiredness alternate with periods of more energy. For instance, someone may have to give up vacuum cleaning after a couple of minutes, because he is too tired and has to lie down for the afternoon in order to recover.

It is often difficult for other people to accept that someone is tired. They cannot always see the reason and it can be confusing that someone can do something one day and not the next. If they do not understand, they can be critical.

"I was sleeping well enough and was getting up in the mornings with no trouble. While I was having breakfast I'd make all sorts of plans, what I was going to do that day. Nice plans they were, too, only things that I really wanted to do. But once I'd made the bed I felt so tired that all I wanted to do was crawl back in."

24

What can you do to help yourself?

The first step is to accept that you are sometimes tired and that you must adjust your lifestyle. Contact with other people with Parkinson's can help you to understand this.

Take the tiredness seriously: if you begin to feel tired, get some rest straight away and only carry on when you are really refreshed. It usually is the case that the tiredness is over soonest if you do this. If you force yourself, the tiredness will become worse and more persistent. It can happen that you have slept well and yet wake up tired. You may have forced yourself the day before, but you can also be tired for no apparent reason. Take that day quietly.

If you make plans to do something strenuous, then plan places or moments to take a breather. You can divide a heavy task into sections and spread it over several days. Tiredness is usually greatest at the end of the day so try to adapt your daily programme and take account of the moments when you are fit or less tired. Do strenuous things at a favourable time and make sure that in your less good moments you have a chance to rest. For example, you could try to work part time or have a nap every afternoon. Perhaps you can organise your life in such a way, that you do not have to do too much all at once.

Household appliances can save you a lot of work: a deep freeze so that you don't have to go shopping every day, a microwave, equipment with remote control, lighting that reacts to your movements etc. Other equipment can also help: an office chair on casters in the kitchen, a low hung washing line, more than one telephone, and so on.

Perhaps other people can take over tasks that are very tiring, while you do other things for them in return. At home, for instance, you could do the accounts while your partner does the housework. A division of labour is perhaps also possible at work. You need to explain - and perhaps repeat the explanation - that you are tired and that this is because you have Parkinson's, but you can still make a valuable contribution in different ways.

Many people benefit from regular movement and exercise (see Chapter 9 'Exercises'). In this way you can keep as fit as possible in spite of your tiredness. Other people benefit from yoga or other relaxation exercises (see page 251). You can relieve extreme tiredness for a couple of hours by having a shower and letting the water run gradually colder. It has been found that a lot of coffee and other stimulants do not help.

What help is available?

- A doctor can investigate whether there is a reason for your tiredness apart from Parkinson's: for example a virus infection or anaemia.
- Medication for Parkinson's can have a beneficial effect.
- A physiotherapist can help you with exercises that will keep you in good condition. See Chapter 17 'Physiotherapy' and Chapter 9 'Exercises'.
- An occupational therapist can advise you on special equipment and safety in the home,and breaking down tasks to make them easier at home and at work (see Chapter18 'Occupational therapy').

- You may be able to have a domestic help for a number of hours a week, which will relieve you of some of your work (see Chapter 16 '*Outline of professional help*').

author: - E.H.Coene, M.D., September Foundation,
the Netherlands

advisors: - Professor L.J. Findley, T.D., O.L.J., M.D.,
F.R.C.P., F.A.C.P., Consultant neurologist
'Avenue House', Romford, UK

- Dr C.E. Clarke, Consultant in Neurology
& Honorary Senior Lecturer, Hull Royal
Infirmary, UK

- Dr. J. van Manen, neurologist, advisor to
the Dutch Parkinson's Disease Society,
the Netherlands

- Dr. J.D. Speelman, neurologist, Academic
Medical Centre, University of Amsterdam,
the Netherlands

- Professor J.P.W.F. Lakke, chairperson of
the Medical Advisory Council of the
Dutch Parkinson's Disease Society,
the Netherlands

3

Treatment and medication

Summary

Parkinson's Disease is almost always treated with medication. Parkinson's cannot be cured with medication, but its symptoms can usually be treated with medication for a long time. Many types of medication are used to fight Parkinson's. Sometimes a person with Parkinson will be using several different types of medication at any one time. And it often takes some time to find the right medication and the right dose for each individual.

It is important that the medicines are taken as prescribed. Moreover, the doctor must be kept informed of all the types of medication used, including those used for other illnesses. This will prevent wrong combinations of medication being taken. Medication for Parkinson's can have side effects and older people are more sensitive to these side effects.

Introduction

Medication cannot cure Parkinson's Disease, but it can considerably reduce the symptoms. This chapter introduces the following subjects:

- What is involved in the treatment of Parkinson's Disease?
- What kind of medication is used?
- Using medication for Parkinson's
- Medication and the elderly
- What medication should not be used if you have Parkinson's?
- Finding out more about medication
- Scientific research (trials)

Chapter 29 'Medication that contains levodopa' and Chapter 30 'Other medication' provide detailed information on the medications themselves (their effects, side effects, etc.).

What is involved in the treatment of Parkinson's Disease?

The smooth working of movement is regulated in the brain by a number of substances called neuro-transmitters. In Parkinson's, there is a shortage of one of the neuro-transmitters, a substance called dopamine. This can be replaced by a drug called levodopa or with drugs that mimic dopamine called dopamine agonists. Different forms of these drugs have been developed for use in different circumstances. Doctors have found that it is easier to treat slowness of movement and stiff muscles than to combat tremor.

Parkinson's cannot be cured or its progression halted, but medication (i.e., drug treatments) can do a great deal for the symptoms and improve people's quality of life. Treatment can be adjusted to your own symptoms and wishes. Different drugs might be tried, sometimes in combination, to see which give the best results. Some adjustment of dosages may be necessary for the same reason. Sometimes further medication may be required. This process of adjustment can last some time and may test your powers of perseverance! It usually takes place in an outpatients' clinic but sometimes, although only rarely, a person has to be admitted to hospital to get the medication right.

Over the course of time, the symptoms of Parkinson's may become more extreme and the effect of medication reduced. From time to time, therefore, medication is reviewed to see whether it should be adjusted further.

Side effects

Medication reduces the symptoms of Parkinson's but can give unpleasant side effects. A high dose will deal with the symptoms but can also produce more side effects. Usually the doctor does not try to make all the symptoms disappear completely, but prescribes a dose sufficient to reduce your symptoms adequately. Some doctors advise people with mild symptoms not to take medication, since there are no drugs without side effects. Their advice is to maintain a healthy lifestyle and to keep the drugs for later use.

If you notice new symptoms, consult your doctor. He will be able to tell you if they are the side effects of medication. Bear in mind that if you experience side effects something can often be done, perhaps, for example, by adjusting the dose or prescribing medication that counteracts them.

When medicines are prescribed, read and follow the instructions carefully, and note which sideeffects may occur. The information leaflet supplied with the medication by the chemist gives full information on possible side effects, even the very rare ones. You will certainly not experience all of them.

What kind of medication is used?

The medication that is used in the treatment of Parkinson's Disease can be divided into six categories:
1. medication that contains levodopa
2. medication that imitates the action of dopamine: dopamine agonists (e.g. ropinerole, pergolide, bromocriptise, cabergoline)
3. anticholinergics (benzhenol and orphenadrine)
4. amantadine

5. medication that prolongs the action of dopamine
6. medication used for other diseases and conditions

These medicines are described in more detail in Chapters 29 and 30.

Using medication for Parkinson's

Medication is usually taken in the form of tablets or capsules. Some drugs are available in liquid form for people who have difficulty in swallowing. One drug (Apomorphine) is given by injections under the skin or by means of a small pump for continuous infusions.

The different medications used in the treatment of Parkinson's can be used alone or in combination. The disease takes a different course in each person, so it is possible that you would take medication in a different combination from someone who has similar symptoms.

Medications have a *brand name or trade name*, which use an initial capital letter, e.g., Madopar. When the *generic name* is given, a small first letter is used, e.g. co-beneldopa.

Make sure to take medication at the *prescribed time*. If you are half an hour late it can mean a deterioration for the whole day. This is especially the case if you have been taking medication for a long period.

Take the medication as prescribed (see the information leaflet and the label). If you want to change the medication you are taking, or are going to take non-prescription medication, then consult your doctor. Drugs that do not go well with Parkinson's medication are described at the end of the chapter. Take advice from your doctor on the amount of alcohol you can safely consume with your medication.

"Now I can say that my medication is right. But it took some time, and patience brought its own rewards. You have to try a medicine for some time and not give up too soon. And you've got to take it on time - that's why I've got a medication alarm clock."

Certain anti-parkinsonian medication is not recommended during pregnancy or whilst breast feeding. You should consult your doctor, who will be able to advise you.

Many people, especially the elderly, take several medicines (also for other diseases than Parkinson's) that have perhaps been prescribed by different doctors. When you visit the doctor, you must take with you a list of all the medication you use and the quantity. Mention too the medication that you use without prescription, for example pain killers or complementary medicines. The doctor can judge whether they can be used together. You can also ask whether a particular medication is really necessary or whether the amount can be reduced.

If you take a lot of medicines for your Parkinson's, it can be useful to have a medication alarm clock. This warns you with a bleep when it is time to take your medicine. You can also get dose containers in which you can set out all your medication for a week. There are a number of pillbox/timer devices on the market. Details are available from The Disabled Living Foundation, The Parkinson's Disease Society of the United Kingdom and from some pharmacists.[1]

Medication and the elderly

In general, elderly people are more sensitive to the effects of medication than younger people, although it takes longer for the drugs to start working. This is because with elderly people medication is absorbed more slowly into the blood-stream. Relatively more blood flows to the brain and therefore more drugs end up there. People can for that reason become sleepy with some medication. In older people, medication remains longer in the body, because it is broken down and eliminated more slowly. The elderly can therefore have more problems with side effects. A doctor can solve this by adjusting the dose.

What medication should not be used if you have Parkinson's?

Medication for Parkinson's can be dangerous if used in combination with some medications for other conditions. Some medications should not be used at all, others can only be administered under a doctor's supervision. Where possible, your doctor will look for safe alternative medication for you to take in conjunction with your Parkinson's medication.

It is a good idea to discuss with your doctor the safety of all the medication you take in addition to that prescribed for Parkinson's. If you are using any of the medications listed here, or if a doctor intends to prescribe them or if you are simply having doubts, you should speak to your doctor immediately.

1. Medications for serious mental disorders: neuroleptics and some tranquillisers, e.g.: Largactil (chlorpromazine), Stelazine (trifmoperazine), Serenace (haloperidol).

2. Some medications against nausea and vomiting: Maxolon (metoclopramide) and dizziness: Stemetil (prochlorperazine)

Finding out more about medication

The Parkinson's Disease Society can provide you with further information about medication and produce a useful booklet 'The Drug Treatment of Parkinson's Disease' which is free of charge. Further information is also available on the leaflet provided with your medication or from your doctor, neurologist or chemist. Chapter 29 'Medication that contains levodopa' and Chapter 30 'Other medication' provide detailed information on the anti-parkinsonian medication.

Scientific research (trials)

Scientific research is necessary to examine the effect and side ffects of new medications. Research usually takes the form of clinical trials. In these trials, new medications are compared with placebos (dummy pills) or medications that have been around for some time. People with Parkinson's may be asked to participate in these trials. Participation is entirely voluntary. (Also see page 164).

The Parkinson's Disease Society (see page 127) can provide further information about the state of current research.

> *"The first few years after I'd been told I had Parkinson's I kept on hoping that they'd invent a pill that'd cure me. I asked my neurologist every time I saw him. Any time I read about a new therapy I began to hope again. But I was continually disappointed. At the moment it means a lot less to me. Course, I do hope that they find something. But the important thing now is to learn to live as best I can with the symptoms. And even though I say it myself, I'm having quite a lot of success doing it."*

Notes

author: - Dr. F. van den Boom, Central Office of the
Dutch National Commission for Chronic
Diseases, the Netherlands
advisors:- Mrs M. Eikaas, UK
- Professor E. Schadé, the Institute for
General Practice, University of Amsterdam,
the Netherlands
- E. Falvey, Care Service Manager,
Parkinson's Disease Society, UK

4

Responding to the diagnosis

Summary

Hearing that you have Parkinson's, often arouses strong emotions: shock, disbelief, sorrow, anger, etc. It can be difficult to recognise that you have these feelings. They are, however, quite normal. Discussing and sharing these feelings with others can be a great source of relief.

It appears that many people, after hearing the diagnosis, go through a difficult period. The diagnosis heard sinks in little by little; often accompanied by intense emotions. Later too difficult moments can arise, for example when a complaint becomes more severe.

At the same time it turns out that most people do in time find a way to cope with their Parkinson's: they succeed in leading a more or less normal and enjoyable life, despite the Parkinson's. These people quite often take an active stance towards Parkinson's. This means that they:
- discuss their Parkinson's openly
- make sure they have adequate information (for example on (new) treatments or social and financial facilities)
- set themselves realistic objectives, ones they can meet without risk of disappointment.

When absorbing the diagnosis of Parkinson's is not successful, help is available from a psychiatrist, psychologist or social worker.

Introduction

The diagnosis can come as a shock. This chapter gives information on:
- Hearing the diagnosis
- Feelings after the diagnosis
- Who should be told that you have Parkinson's?
- What can you do to help yourself?
- Professional help
- Hope

Hearing the diagnosis

The news that your symptoms are caused by Parkinson's Disease can provoke a number of different reactions. Someone who does not know what Parkinson's is, may not be shocked initially. Others may be horrified at the diagnosis because they know what Parkinson's entails or they already know someone with Parkinson's.

For other people, the news may come as a relief. This is often because they've been suffering symptoms for a considerable period of time without there being any obvious cause. For them, the diagnosis means the end of a long and uncertain period of doctor's visits and medical examinations and, perhaps, a time when they may have wondered whether the problem was mental rather than physical.

Feelings after the diagnosis

Few people are instantly able to imagine the consequences of the statement "You have Parkinson's". After the diagnosis, many people wonder how they are going to carry on. They may respond in many different ways, but for each person life will no longer be the same.

For most people the diagnosis leads to a variety of strong feelings. Emotions can be extreme at this time. Some people initially panic, while others are frightened or grief-stricken. Some may find it difficult to react; it is as if they have been paralysed by the news. Many people are bewildered or disbelieving, 'it can't be true'. Some people react in a very unruffled and controlled way, but become emotional at a later stage.

People may subsequently experience periods of gloom and apathy, 'what's the point of it all?' They may also go through bouts of rage, for instance at the doctor who is unable to cure Parkinson's.

In time, the diagnosis begins to sink in. Many people become withdrawn during this period. They may avoid most people, spend a lot of time in bed or confide in almost no one. They may concentrate on the past, 'when things were still OK'. People may sometimes switch between admitting to themselves that they have Parkinson's and denying the diagnosis completely. All of these responses are ways of gradually dealing with bad news.

Strong feelings may also recur at times when they are reminded in a new way of the fact of Parkinson's, perhaps through having to change or stop work or be admitted to a nursing home. Events like this can throw people off balance.

"Some people experience it as a relief, whereas for others it comes as a shock. I was really shocked to hear that I had Parkinson's and this was followed by a great many other shocks."

Who should be told that you have Parkinson's?

It is always an emotional event to be told that you have Parkinson's. The question then is: who do you want to share this with, and who would you rather not tell? Sometimes you feel like telling everyone, sometimes you feel like withdrawing completely. This is quite normal. It is a good idea, however, to try to share your fear and worries with at least one other person.

Many people confide first in the person or people they trust most: a partner or one or more close friends. They can provide you with initial support. If Parkinson's scarcely affects you and if no one notices anything, then you don't have to tell anyone else.

You may choose to wait until you find the diagnosis easier to talk about or until others begin to notice changes, You may find at this point that your friends/colleagues already suspect that you have Parkinson's. Bringing it out into the open then becomes a relief to you and the people round you.

If you decide to tell someone, you should bear in mind that some people may not know how to cope with the news. This can mean that they are unable to provide you with the support that you need or had expected. They may even withdraw from you completely and this can be extremely hurtful. Other people may respond quite differently and become important to you in a way you might not have predicted.

As well as looking for support among the people in your immediate environment, you can make contact with other people who have Parkinson's through the Parkinson's Disease Society. For further information and the number of their telephone helpline, see Chapter 15 'Help from the Parkinson's Disease Society'.

What can you do to help yourself?

It is impossible to provide a recipe for how someone should deal with the fact of having Parkinson's and the turbulent feelings that this may bring. Everybody responds in an individual way and people can react differently from day to day. There are, however, a number of possibilities that need to be examined.

Talk about having Parkinson's

Being told you have Parkinson's may result in a great many strong feelings such as fear, doubt or anger. Sharing these feelings with someone else by talking about them may bring a feeling of relief. The other person may view the situation in a more dispassionate way so that some fears and worries may turn out to be unfounded. Just by listening, they can help you to unburden yourself. For more on this idea and on the importance of looking for practical support from other people, see Chapter 5 'Talking about your illness'.

> "My wife would never talk about me having Parkinson's. She just carried on as if it didn't exist. Sometimes I'd complain about something – I felt tired or stiff. And she'd say: 'Oh, everybody feels that way some time or other'. And then I felt even worse, even more alone. Once I really got angry and just spit it all out. It turned out that she thought she was helping me by not talking about it. I ask you! Fortunately things have changed now and we can talk about Parkinson's in a normal way. I hate arguments, but that time it was worth it, I think."

Take action against Parkinson's

After the initial shock, a number of people begin to deal with the condition in an active way. For instance, they start to collect information so that they know what they're up against. They check out what help is available, including alternative treatments. Others become active in the Parkinson's Disease Society (see Chapter 15) or adopt a healthier lifestyle such as smoking less, taking regular exercise or rest. By doing this, they are trying to maintain as much control as possible over their situation rather than throwing in the towel. Many people say that this helps them a lot.

Set limited and achievable goals

If you set yourself unrealistic goals, then you will not only fail in the short-term but will run the risk of becoming disillusioned and not want to try in the future. So set goals that are both worthwhile and that you know you can meet. You could decide to try the exercises the physiotherapist has set you or try a new recipe in the kitchen.

If you know your limits and recognise when you are getting tired, you will be able to stop half way through, if you need to rest, and finish off later when you have more energy. In this way you are balancing your immediate goal with your long-term aim of living well with Parkinson's.

Faith

A number of people find help through their faith. Parkinson's may be a reason to return to the church or to experience faith in a different way. Others benefit from talking to a priest or to a humanist counsellor. There is a discussion of these ideas in Chapter 33 'Spiritual Welfare'.

Contact with other people who have Parkinson's.

There are many other people with Parkinson's, who encounter situations similar to your own and that they have learned to deal with. Through contact with them you can discover that you have much in common. Everybody benefits from each other's solutions and from mutual support. People also benefit from the opportunity of speaking candidly about the illness and its effects. You can meet other people who are living with Parkinson's through the Parkinson's Disease Society. For more information, see Chapter 15 'Help from the Parkinson's Disease Society'.

Professional help

Many people find it easier to seek help for physical symptoms than for psychological or emotional problems. Anyone suffering from a serious illness such as Parkinson's may experience problems of this sort. They might have difficulties with thought, reasoning or memory. They might also experience depression or find it difficult to respond to people in the way they used to. These experiences are not uncommon.

Seeking professional help for these problems can prevent a lot of misery. This help is available through your general practitioner, nursing staff or your specialist; from a psychologist, a psychiatrist and through social services. There is information on some of the mental changes that can be involved in Parkinson's in Chapter 28 'Mental changes' and on the professional help available in Chapter 16 'Outline of Professional Help'.

> "During the first months after we'd heard that my husband had Parkinson's he had a lot of problems. The disease itself was OK, he didn't have too much trouble with it, but he had more trouble just thinking about it. He was dreadfully down, no energy, no interest in anything. You could see without looking that he felt useless. So I asked him to go and have a talk with a psychologist. And that was the last thing he wanted at first. 'D'you think there's something wrong in my head?', he asked. But once the GP – someone he trusted – had explained to him that it had nothing to do with 'being crazy', he went for an appointment. And he actually enjoyed it. The psychologist talked with him a couple of times and explained why it was that the news that he had Parkinson's had brought so much to the surface. It helped him to understand himself better and that was the big step in the right direction."

Hope

Parkinson's cannot be cured. The person with Parkinson's and their family and friends know that things will get worse, but nobody can tell exactly what will happen or how rapidly this will occur. This uncertainty makes it difficult to prepare for the loss of physical capabilities in the future.

An absence of deterioration may lead to a feeling of hope: hope that the progression of the disease has ceased, or hope that a miracle treatment or medication will be discovered. But hoping that a cure will be found may mean not being realistic about the future. It may also mean that people do not take the opportunities available to learn or relearn skills or make decisions about changes in lifestyle that may be needed.

This is not to suggest that you should give up hope. Hope is one of the essentials of life. The hope for a long and happy life can provide the inspiration you need to stay active and to look after yourself. It can function like a motor when you set yourself a goal or face up to difficulties. So be realistic, do not give up hope. This will mean that you can face the future positively.

author: - R.D. Coene, specialist in psychosocial skills, Groenelaan Nursing Home, the Netherlands

advisors: - Mrs J. Vliegenthart-Ladiges, (former) Board Member of the Dutch Parkinson's Disease Society, the Netherlands
- Mrs M. Eikaas, UK
- E. Falvey, Care Services Manager, Parkinson's Disease Society, UK

5

Talking about your illness

Summary

Parkinson's can change many aspects of your life. You will have to adjust to these changes. Talking with others about Parkinson's can help you with this.

Talking about Parkinson's can provide great relief. By expressing your anger at Parkinson's you will prevent yourself from bottling everything up inside and reinforcing your negative emotions.

By being open about Parkinson's, you can avoid the risk of becoming isolated. Because you are sharing your thoughts and feelings, you will not readily develop feelings of loneliness.

Parkinson's complaints may make contact with others harder. For example because talking becomes less easy or because your facial expression freezes. That is precisely when it becomes important to talk about Parkinson's.

You may also need to learn how to ask for help. For many people this is difficult. They believe that asking for help is a sign of weakness since it means that you can no longer manage alone. Asking others for help can however be a very positive experience. It means that you no longer have to face it alone. It is therefore by no means 'weak' to ask for help. On the contrary, it's a sign that you're taking charge of your situation.

Introduction

This chapter focuses on one of the ways by which you can come to terms and cope with Parkinson's disease. By talking and listening you can start to deal with the sense of loss, negative feelings and the sense of isolation that you may experience. Having Parkinson's may make you want to look for help and the second part of this chapter describes some difficulties you may experience.

This chapter covers:
- Recurring loss and letting go
- Negative feelings
- Isolation
- Talking about Parkinson's and sharing your feelings

- Carrying on together
- Asking for help: why is this so difficult?
- What can be positive about asking for help?
- How do you deal with the help that you ask for and receive?

> *"Of course I talk about having Parkinson's. The problem is that people don't always have the time to listen. But I find that usually I feel a lot better if there is someone to talk to when something's really bothering me. It doesn't improve my physical condition but it certainly helps with my feelings of anger and grief. I find that I can cope better and other people find it easier to understand what's going on."*

Recurring loss and letting go

Parkinson's may result in the loss of certain skills or abilities such as being able to write clearly or to take part in some sports. The loss may relate to something we have always taken for granted such as the ability to walk or to control our facial expression. Sometimes the loss is temporary but sometimes it is permanent. Each time the situation deteriorates, it means saying goodbye to certain actions and activities. The changes experienced in Parkinson's may also represent a loss of independence. Parkinson's therefore involves a recurring process of letting go and the sense of loss is frequently regarded as being one of the most difficult aspects of the condition to cope with. (Understanding loss and change is discussed further in Chapter 12 'Relationships'.)

Negative feelings

When you are confronted with Parkinson's and the problems it brings, negative feelings can occur. Letting go is an emotional business. The more you value what you are losing, the more intense your feelings. Different people, however, will react in different ways.

For instance, you may feel rage, "Having Parkinson's means that all my future plans will come to nothing" or, "That doctor's no good; he says that there's nothing he can do for me." Alternatively you may feel grief, "Why me?". Fear is another negative feeling, "So long as I don't end up as an invalid," or, "So long as she doesn't leave me." Doubt is also a common emotion, "Should I complete my course?" or, "Is there any point in continuing this relationship?"

If a person feels overwhelmed by negative feelings, he may withdraw from other people and begin to lose contact with the outside world. This will lead to isolation.

Isolation

The symptoms of Parkinson's can themselves lead to isolation. For instance, tremors can cause food spills, there may be a fear of falling or walking difficulties and freezing can make someone become suddenly rooted to the spot.

These symptoms can make you feel unsure of yourself particularly when you know that other people are aware of them. Embarrassment, uncertainty or fear may make you want to avoid people altogether and it can involve a great deal of effort and determination to make sure that you still get out and about. These same feelings may even make you become withdrawn from the people you live with or see regularly.

40

> *"At the beginning there were often awkward silences, because nobody dared to talk about 'it'. For instance when we had visitors. Then we'd talk awkwardly about everything and nothing. Me too, by the way, because I found it difficult to start a conversation about my illness. But it was still annoying, because you could see everyone thinking about Parkinson's. But slowly I've learned how to talk about it, even if nobody else starts. I wait for a chance, then I tell them very briefly how I'm feeling. That usually breaks the ice and we can carry on. But I always make sure that we go on to another subject, because there's no way I want to talk about Parkinson's all the time."*

Many people with an on-going illness experience the loss, negative feelings and isolation mentioned above. The next part of this chapter looks at a number of ways people can deal with these feelings.

Talking about Parkinson's and sharing your feelings

A person who is sick may feel separated from the rest of the world. Whilst you are involved in a process of change, and facing an uncertain future, your friends and family appear healthy and confident. It seems so unfair and can cause frustration or a sense of alienation. Talking about these feelings can help to relieve them and so remove the risk of isolation.

The first step in dealing with negative feelings is to acknowledge them - even though it may be easier to pretend that they simply do not exist. Nobody likes to admit that they're afraid or angry, but silence makes it impossible to share those feelings with other people and you are left trying to deal with them on your own.

Fear and worry increase if nothing is done about them and if they're not expressed. People who can talk about their illness, and about their feelings of loss and grief, have started to cope. Sharing feelings with other people often makes it easier to bear. Some people, of course, find this very difficult to do because they have no experience of sharing their feelings. Learning how to do this may be one of the most productive aspects of learning to live with the illness.

Some feelings such as rage, doubt or fear are hard to accept. But they are normal, natural reactions and are not bad or wrong. By talking about them, you allow yourself and someone else the opportunity of easing the burden. Afterwards you will probably find that you are more able to enjoy the aspects of your life that are going well. Not only people with Parkinson's, but also their partners and carers, may encounter negative feelings.

"There was a time when I was plagued with horrible thoughts. If only he'd die, I would think, and then I could be free. It gave me an awful shock. I felt so incredibly bad about it. And guilty, of course. For instance, if he was having more trouble with his legs, I would blame myself and think: that's because of what I've been thinking. I still find it difficult to talk about it now, even though I know that having thoughts like that every once in a while is 'normal'. It's a bit like being trapped. Without realising it you're looking for a way out. And then you start thinking things like that. I kept quiet about it for a long time, tried to suppress the thoughts. Until one day I was with a friend and burst into tears. It was like a waterfall. Everything came out. We were talking about it again recently and she said 'Don't worry about it'. I think things like that sometimes and my husband's as healthy as you could wish."

Carrying on together

The partner, friends and family of someone with Parkinson's are also unwillingly faced with a changing situation. They too may be fraught with concern. We all have our own particular problems but that does not mean that we should be dealing with them on our own. Sharing problems - so that everybody has the opportunity to air and communicate their feelings - makes many people feel closer to one another.

"My wife has Parkinson's. When I used to go out on the street with her I'd get embarrassed because she was stiff or shaky. Sometimes when we went out for a meal I'd be mortified because of the way she ate. And if she was in a shop and couldn't answer the assistant right away I used to answer for her, telling myself that I was only trying to make it easier for her. Now I realise that that was the wrong approach, it was my problem... Looking back I know I was the most embarrassed of the two of us, because I felt embarrassed about her."

It can be very supportive when someone is prepared to listen to your needs and feelings. It gives you the opportunity to express yourself. The other person shows respect by listening in a sincere and non-judgmental way. If you make the first move by confiding, you will often find that this was just what the other person wanted but did not (yet) dare to do. Your friends and family will also have feelings that they would like to discuss with you. It's important to remember that communication is a two way process: both sides need to listen as well as to talk.

Obviously communication does not always depend on discussion. Sometimes touching or an understanding silence can bridge the distance that separates people.

Asking for help: why is this so difficult?

Many people try to manage alone for as long as possible, but there may come a time when you realise you can't do this any longer. That's the moment to ask for help, although this can be difficult for a number of reasons:

- You have to admit both to yourself, and to other people, that something is wrong, and that you are not in the best of health.
- By asking friends and family members for help, you may feel it changes your relationship with them and makes you feel dependent.
- You may feel reluctant to burden family and friends who are already very busy.
- Asking for help means showing appreciation and gratitude and having to be perpetually grateful to others is hard.
- You may feel that by asking for professional help you will lose control over your private life.

What can be positive about asking for help?

- People may have to ask for help on many occasions and for a number of reasons. Learning to do this can be a challenge, particularly if you are not used to it. However, there are benefits:
- You no longer have to try to disguise your difficulties.
- By sharing your private feelings and fears you are showing that you trust others.
- You no longer feel isolated in your fight against Parkinson's.
- It often strengthens the bond between you and the people who help you: other people like to be able to help. They no longer have to stand by and do nothing.
- It means that you have more time for other things.

How do you deal with the help that you ask for and receive?

- Asking for help is not a sign of weakness. It does not mean that you have failed. In fact it is an achievement rather than a failure because you have faced up to your situation honestly and that takes courage. Neither does the fact that you are being helped by others mean that you are relinquishing control: you are the one who will make the decisions.
- Be absolutely clear about what you are asking for and what you want. Seek help in a 'businesslike' manner. Make your agreements clear and set your limits carefully. You could say "I need this and I don't want that". Then you will each know what to expect from one another.
- If problems arise due to misunderstanding about roles and expectations, it is much better to discuss this openly and honestly, rather than let it lead to irritation or distrust.
- A great deal of professional help is available, depending on your particular needs and circumstances. For further information on whom you can talk to, see Chapter 16 'Outline of Professional Help'.
- Try to remember that talking about your illness and your feelings can help you come to terms and cope with the difficulties you are facing, can strengthen and develop important relationships, and can ensure you receive the help and support you need.
- The social worker will be able to advise you about the kind of help that Social Services are able to provide. They may not be able to meet all your needs, but your social worker will tell you about other services that can offer appropriate help.

- If problems arise with professional helpers - or with friends and family - this may lead to irritation, anger and distrust if you do not say anything. If you can remain honest and open, you will find that you can prevent or rectify these problems. You may perhaps be able to discuss some of your concerns with your social worker, or use him as an advocate in getting the improvements in service that you require. In any case, talking about these problems may not only result in an improved quality of assistance, but better relationships as well.

43

authors: - Mrs B. McCall, Parkinson's Disease
Society, UK
- E.H. Coene, M.D., September Foundation,
the Netherlands
advisor: - E. Falvey, Care Services Manager,
Parkinson's Disease Society, UK

6

Information for partner, families and friends

Summary
It is sometimes said that you're never sick alone. After all others too will be involved in the consequences of Parkinson's. This is true in the first place for the people closest to you, such as your partner, your family and your friends.

This chapter has been written for the people who are helping you. It describes how to go about the care, so that problems are avoided. A number of tips:

- Be clear as to the help being provided, so that misunderstandings do not arise.
- Don't take over everything, but allow him or her to do as much as possible. It's important for people to retain their independence.
- Take good care of yourself. Many carers have a tendency to neglect themselves, for example by eating badly or getting too little sleep. After a time this can result in the care becoming too arduous.
- Allow time for yourself. You too have a life. Make sure that you regularly get a little fun.
- Get help on time. Looking after someone with Parkinson's can be demanding. It's advisable to seek help well before you reach the stage when you cannot manage alone.
- Don't let the Parkinson's dominate everything. Life is a lot more than Parkinson's!

Introduction

Parkinson's Disease does not affect just the person with the condition. If you are a partner, relative or friend you will live with Parkinson's too. How much your life is affected by Parkinson's will depend on your individual circumstances. These may include the symptoms, the specific help that the person with Parkinson's needs, and your relationship with that person.

This chapter considers the role of partners, relatives and friends and provides information to help you cope with caring for someone with Parkinson's.

The following subjects are dealt with in this chapter:
- What is a carer?
- Coping with caring
- Make it clear what you would like to do
- Encourage independence
- Divide tasks up
- Accept your feelings and talk about what you are doing
- Look after yourself
- Keep time for yourself
- Seek help before the problems reach crisis point
- Plan treats together
- Keep your sense of humour
- Further help

> *"Going to the hospital for the consultations together with my partner who has Parkinson's helps me also. It gives me an insight into what's going on and how the disease is progressing and how the medication needs to be altered. I think doing that makes life easier for me, because I'm not on the outside looking in. I'm there being a partner and being part of it."*

Remember, however, that as each person with Parkinson's is different, so too is the experience of people caring for them. Therefore you may never experience some of the situations described in this chapter.

What is a carer?

The term 'carer' is used to describe anyone who is looking after or providing support to someone who is ill, elderly or disabled. A carer works voluntarily and without payment. You may not think of yourself as a carer. You may not like the term as you see yourself more as a parent, child, partner or friend. However, the term can help some people. It recognises the job that many carers do is one that can sometimes be demanding and difficult. It also recognises the fact that carers have needs. The term carer can also help you separate the job of caring from your relationship with the person you care for.[1]

Carers can be anyone of any age - partners, relatives or friends.

Caring can mean different things to different people and the form the caring takes will be very individual. When someone is in the early stages of Parkinson's, caring may mainly involve providing moral support and encouragement. As the disease progresses, you may find that you also have to provide personal and practical care.

Coping with caring

From discussions with carers connected with the Parkinson's Disease Society, the following have been highlighted as important considerations for anyone caring for a person with Parkinson's.

Make it clear what you would like to do

If you offer to help someone, make it clear what you are and are not willing to do. This will prevent unrealistic expectations and the feeling that you have been landed with all the work. If you don't want to do certain things, then do not do them. For instance, you may not want to wash someone because that is too intimate. If you end up doing things you don't want to do, resentment will build up. Consider what alternative solutions can be found. Do not feel ashamed about drawing the line - it does not mean that you do not care about the person you have been helping. You should also agree on when you would like to help. You should also allow time to do things for yourself without feeling guilty.

> *"Once a week I spend an afternoon out with a friend of mine. We go into town or visit the hairdresser's. However, first we go and drink coffee somewhere. She lets me vent my feelings for the first half-hour and then we have fun. Those afternoons are really important to me."*

Encourage independence

If you look after someone, this can change the original relationship you had. The person may become more dependent on you, and this can sometimes cause problems. You may feel that your relationship used to be an equal one, but that now you have to make most of the decisions. You may feel these changes threaten the bond that exists between the two of you. It is a good idea to discuss these matters with each other - this allows you to air your feelings about the new situation and how you adapt to the changes in your lives. This is discussed further in Chapter 12 'Relationships'.

Some people may find it difficult to accept help and may find it humiliating. This is discussed in Chapter 5 'Talking about your illness'. Always treat someone with respect. Supporting a person often means stimulating him to solve problems himself. If he is still active, encourage his independence rather than attempting to take over. Do not just talk about what that person is unable to do, but discuss the things that remain stable or are even improving.

Do not treat him as if he is a child by shielding or protecting him unnecessarily from anything unpleasant. This is patronising and discourages him from dealing with his problems. It may also encourage dependency. For instance, if you try to hide family problems from him, this means that you are also isolating the person from the rest of the family at a time when he needs to be involved.

It is also possible to inundate someone with good advice. People with Parkinson's are adults and are capable of making their own decisions. Avoid the temptation to take the person over by providing help that they have not asked for or unnecessarily taking over various tasks. This also encourages dependency.

Divide tasks up

If you and the person with Parkinson's live in the same house you can, for instance, agree that you will take on the physically demanding tasks such as

vacuum cleaning and gardening. In return, the other person can take responsibility for organising the finances and other administration. Sometimes this may mean a change in traditional roles, but it can work very effectively. Take pride in any achievements you make, either separately or together.

Accept your feelings and talk about what you are doing

If you are helping someone it is advisable to talk about what you are doing. Ask the person if it is a good moment to help him. This allows them to keep in touch with what is going on, and gives them choice.

Acknowledge and accept your own feelings

Not everyone with Parkinson's requires a lot of looking after but sometimes they do. You may sometimes feel that you do not get the praise that you deserve. Although you may love the person you are caring for, you may also sometimes feel angry, guilty, or resentful. Do not let these feelings fester. Accept them as entirely natural. The practical daily reality can often be completely at odds with many people's romanticised view. A common complaint is that visitors always ask after the person with Parkinson's and not after you.

You may also feel that you are bearing the brunt of any anger and resentment felt by the person with Parkinson's. Because you are close at hand you are first in the firing line. This can be extremely hurtful, but it is worth remembering that usually this rage is not aimed at you personally, but is the result of all the difficulties associated with Parkinson's.

Make sure that you express your true feelings. You can make the person aware that although you understand the reasons why they are being difficult, he or she has no right to take it out on you. If you feel unappreciated, or you feel the demands on you are unreasonable, do not just put up with it, say something.

> *"What I sometimes find hard is, that Dad gets all the attention. I suppose it is only natural, because people want to know how he is. But they often forget to ask how I am, as if nothing has changed for me. Usually I do not let it worry me too much. I'm not after compliments or anything. But sometimes I get annoyed and feel as if I've been ëforgotten'. Everyone needs some kind of attention and support ñ and that includes me, even if I am not sick myself. The good thing is, that Dad realises it. I sometimes notice that he turns the attention towards me. And it is not that I demand it, but it's nice of him when he does so."*

Talking about how you feel will make things easier. Do not be afraid to talk to someone if you think it might help. Many carers find contact with others in a similar position invaluable. The Parkinson's Disease Society and specific carers' organisations can put you in touch with other carers.

Look after yourself

Your own health is very important, do not neglect it. Set realistic goals for yourself and your partner. Try to maintain a rewarding life and do not try to do too much. Many carers find relaxation techniques such as yoga, meditation and reflexology helpful. Chapter 23 '*Complementary therapy for Parkinson's?*' and Chapter 32 '*Coping with stress*' contain useful information.

Accept help from other people and make sure that you have time for yourself away from caring. If you find that caring is becoming a burden, contact your Social Services Department and ask them to assess your needs as a carer. In 1996, The Carers Recognition and Services Act 1995 came into force. This Act gives carers, on request, the right to an assessment of their needs, when the local authority has made an assessment of the person they are caring for in respect of Community Care services or services for children under the Children Act. The carer must be providing or intending to provide regular and substantial care. The results of the carer's assessment will be taken into account when the local authority is making decisions about services to be provided.

Sometimes respite care can be arranged to give you a break. This means that alternative care is provided either in the home or elsewhere.

Keep time for yourself

Keep time for yourself for hobbies, visits to friends or anything else you enjoy. Try to keep your social life as normal as possible: you have a life to live outside your role as carer. This may not be easy to arrange but you and the person for whom you are caring will experience benefits.

Seek help before the problems reach crisis point

There are all sorts of professionals who can help you cope with caring. Occupational therapists, social workers, Parkinson's Disease Nurse Specialists or District Nurses, for example, can make a lot of difference. Even if you feel that you do not need help at the moment, you had better make plans for the future and make enquiries about the resources available. Don't wait until you are completely exhausted before asking for help. Some procedures such as social security benefits, and home modifications can take some time to arrange.

Many people hesitate about involving professional help. They feel as though they have failed or are abandoning the person they are caring for. This is not the case. By seeking help, you are actually increasing the chance that you will be able to cope in the long term. You may also prevent yourself from feeling trapped. Some people find it difficult to let a stranger into their home. Although it may take a bit of getting used to, remember that this person can give you the chance to catch your breath and gain new strength.

Professionals can also answer questions, will take a dispassionate view and have previous experience of situations that you are facing. They are there to help you. Many people with Parkinson's and their partners say that, with hindsight, they wish they had been quicker to seek outside help (see Chapter 16 '*Outline of professional help*' for more information).

"I can honestly say that without the nurse I couldn't have coped. She never made me feel I was inadequate. She always had time for me and made a point of seeing me on my own."

It is also highly advisable to consider arrangements for emergency care should you take ill. Carers Emergency Cards, which can be kept in a purse or wallet, are available from the Parkinson's Disease Society and the Carers' National Association. On these you can list your details, who you care for and who to contact in an emergency.

49

Plan treats together

Have fun together, and make sure that Parkinson's does not dominate everything.

Keep your sense of humour

So many carers say that keeping their sense of humour has helped enormously with caring. Do not let little things throw you. Learn to laugh at and with each other.[2]

Further help

The Parkinson's Disease Society can offer you support and advice to help you understand more about Parkinson's and to help you with the practical and emotional aspects of caring. A carers' video and carers' handbook are currently in production. If you are a young carer (i.e. under 21 years), the Parkinson's Disease Society has produced information specifically for you, based on interviews with other young people who are caring for someone with Parkinson's. Many carers also find involvement with the local branch helpful. (More information on the services provided by the Society is contained in Chapter 15).

There are also a number of specific carers' organisations that can offer you help and support. These include the *Carers' National Association*, which represents the interests of carers and offers practical advice and information. They also have carers' groups where carers can meet one another for self-help and mutual support. *The Princess Royal Trust for Carers*, has set up a number of carers' centres in the United Kingdom, where carers can obtain information and advice. They also have carers' groups. *The Association of Crossroads Care Attendant Schemes* provides respite care services in the home to give carers a break. They have also developed specific projects, most notably for young carers.
Further information is available from:

The Parkinson's Disease Society of the United Kingdom
215 Vauxhall Bridge Road
London SW1V 1EJ
Telephone: 020 7931 8080
Helpline: free phone 0808 800 0303 - Monday to Friday 09.30 to 17.30 hrs.

50

Carers' National Association
20/25 Glasshouse Yard
London EC1A 4JT
Telephone: 020 7490 8818
Helpline: free phone 0808 808 7777
e-mail: info@ukcarers.org

The Princess Royal Trust for Carers
142 Ninorief
London EC3N 1LB
Telephone: 020 7480 7788
e-mail: info@carers.org

The Association of Crossroads Care Attendant Schemes
10 Regent Place
Rugby
Warwickshire CV21 2PN
Telephone: 01788 573 653

Notes

Notes

author: - Mrs L. Huysmans, occupational therapist,
Gaasperdam Nursing Home,
the Netherlands

advisors: - Mrs L. Hoyle, physiotherapist,
Penrith Hospital, UK

- Mrs E.M. Zoetemeijer, rehabilitation
specialist at the Groot Klimmendaal
Rehabilitation Centre, the Netherlands

7

Tips for everyday living

Summary

The complaints affecting movements can make all kinds of daily routines more burdensome. For example: washing, shaving, dressing, house-keeping and cooking.

This chapter will be provide tips on how to carry out daily routines. These tips are designed to make these routines easier, so that you can continue to do them independently.

- Some tips have to do with the *approach* to certain routines. You can for example modify your daily schedule to make sufficient time for certain activities and to have sufficient time to rest between the various activities. Or: when you write, use block letters because you will probably then write more clearly.
- Other tips are directed towards *safety*. One example of this is to ensure that the bathroom is warm before using it. If you move slowly, you may cool off too rapidly in a chilly bathroom. Another example is the installation around the house of handgrips on the walls, so that you will have more support in potentially hazardous areas (at the top of the stairs, toilet, and shower).
- Lastly many tips concern *aid appliances*. You shouldn't think in this connection immediately of large and complicated equipment, many appliances being in fact small and 'quite ordinary'. You can for example dress and undress a good deal more easily with a dressing stick. Other examples of everyday appliances are modified cutlery, an electric toothbrush, elastic shoelaces, etc.

Help with everyday living

This chapter offers information on how you can try to remain active and to continue with those activities that are important to you. Try to maintain your independence, even if it involves extra time and effort. For instance, if you are too tired to do everything you would like to do, discuss with your family or the occupational therapist how to prioritise tasks in such a way that you still have the time and energy to do the things that you want to.

Discuss with the occupational therapist any of the pieces of advice offered in this chapter if you have questions about them. Ask for further ideas if you need to.

When planning activities, consider when you are due to take your medication and whether this will affect the timing of what you want to do.

This chapter covers:

1 Tips for organising your day
2 Eating
3 Grooming
4 Washing, showering and taking a bath
5 Using the toilet
6 Getting dressed
7 Using the kitchen
8 Additional domestic activities
9 Communication
10 Walking
11 Chairs
12 Beds
13 Driving

1 Tips for organising your day

- Begin each day by making a list of all the things you must do and the things you want to do. Intersperse the easy and the difficult tasks throughout the day.
- Let other people do the heavy household duties.
- Think about when you might like other people to help you.
- Allow adequate time for everything.
- Maintain a routine in your life - but do not feel you have to be a slave to it.

2 Eating

- While eating or drinking, tuck your elbows in to your sides or use your elbow as a support (see drawing).
- Make the distance between your hand and your mouth as short as possible by, for instance, raising the level of your plate.
- If you are slow at eating, use a keep-warm plate, so that your meal does not get cold.
- Use a mug with two handles. A firm grip often reduces tremor.
- Use heavier cutlery if you suffer from tremor.

- If necessary, you can use curved cutlery so that you do not need to turn your wrist (see drawing).
- Use a plate guard that clips onto a plate rim to prevent food spillage. Alternatively use Steel-lite plates.[3]
- Use a drinking straw with a one-way valve to prevent liquid going back down the straw.[4]

3 Grooming
- Make sure that the light is good.

- If you have a tremor in your arm, you may find that your upper arm will shake less if you tuck your elbow in to your side before cleaning your teeth, shaving or putting on lipstick.
- Use an electric, preferably cordless, razor.
- Use an electric toothbrush.
- Long handled brushes/combs may help with hair care.[5]
- Use a large working surface where you can reach everything easily

"In the beginning my husband wasn't at all interested in devices that could help him function. He was too proud to think about it, too macho actually. I may be sick, he used to say, but I'm not a nerd... It was hopeless. But one day he fell over when he was taking a shower. Broken hip. It didn't just mean a load of problems for him ñ I had to deal with it as well. It meant I had to do more for him... it was at that point that I said to him: once you're better, if you don't rush off and get some devices to help you I'm going to stop looking after you and you can go into a home. There's no way I'm going to be the victim of your macho ideas!... I didn't mean it, of course, but it shook him up. A few days later he made an appointment with the occupational therapist."

4 Washing, showering and taking a bath
Safety in the bathroom should be seen to.
- Do not lock the bathroom door if you are likely to need help.
- Make sure that the bathroom is warm; you must not risk getting cold if you are slow.
- Shower or wash yourself sitting down, for instance, on a plastic garden chair. There are also special shower seats available.
- Place rubber or other non-slip bathmats in front of and in the bathtub in order to prevent slipping (check whether it is suitable for the bath finish).
- Have grab rails fitted beside the bath and/or toilet. Do not try to hang onto soap dishes, taps or towel rails.
- There are special rails available that can be attached to the side of, or across, the bath to make it easier to step in and out .
- Use a bath board and/or seat if you are no longer able to sit down in the bath or stand up to get out of it.
- Make sure that everything you need is within easy reach. You can buy soap on a rope which can be hung from a tap, soap dish or shower to be safer and more accessible.
- Empty the bath before you step out of it.
- If you use a wheelchair, consult your occupational therapist for advice on grooming and on organising your bathroom.

5 Using the toilet
- Use a stable raised toilet seat or have a high pedestal fitted.
- Have grab rails fitted, so that you can pull yourself up.
- Do not use the wash basin to pull yourself up.
- Do not lock the door if you are likely to need assistance.
- Use a urinal or a commode if the toilet is not close enough to your bedroom.

> *"Sometimes I really get a kick when I find a simple solution for one of my problems. When I go to the toilet, for example, I have to leave the door unlocked because I can't turn the lock. But I wasn't exactly happy with the situation, because there's no way of stopping someone from just walking in. Then I thought of hanging a notice on the door with "ENGAGED" and "FREE" on it. I felt really proud of the idea!"*

6 Getting dressed
- Choose clothes that are easy to put on and take off, such as loose clothing made of stretchy materials and has a front fastening and no (or few) buttons.
- Use simple fastenings such as large buttons, zips with a tab pull or a keyring, and Velcro. (A tip for Velcro: wash with both sides pressed against each other, otherwise it picks up fluff and loses its grip.[6] Never wash Velcro at a high temperature, i.e. 90 degrees).
- Do not combine rough textures such as a woollen jumper over a cotton blouse or a towelling dressing gown over flannel pyjamas.
- Slip-on or elastic-sided shoes or zip-fastened shoes are easiest to put on.[7]
- You can use a long handled shoe horn to help you to put on shoes. Ordinary laces can be replaced by elastic ones.

56

- Use a sock/stocking aid to help with putting on socks and tights.
- If you experience problems with pulling your coat onto your shoulder, you can sew a loop, made of tape/bias binding, to the inside of the armhole that is difficult to reach. An occupational therapist can explain how you should do this.
- You can use a dressing stick (see drawing) which can be bought from shops selling equipment for the disabled.

This stick has a rubber thimble (available from office suppliers) on one end and a hook on the other. It enables you to pull your trousers up with the hook, or to push your blouse or jacket over your shoulder with the rubber end.

- Experiment with dressing in different positions, e.g., putting on clothes such as underwear and trousers while lying down. Other useful suggestions are included in 'Dressing for Disabled People' which is published by *The Disabled Living Foundation*[8] and a leaflet on clothing for people with Parkinson's which is available free of charge from the Parkinson's Disease Society.

N.B.
People in wheelchairs should wear clothes made of materials that 'breathe' such as cotton and towelling. Thick materials will make you perspire. This in turn leads to a damp skin which is more easily damaged. People in wheelchairs should sit on smooth material. Pleats can create areas of pressure that increase the risk of sores.

Adapted clothes for people inwheelchairs

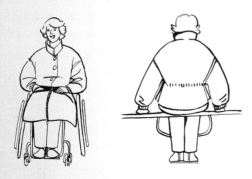

- A wheelchair cape that is extra long at the front (see drawing).
- A jacket that is shorter at the back (see drawing). This means that the person in the wheelchair does not have to stand up to put it on or take it off.

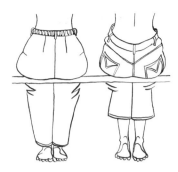

- Wheelchair trousers. These trousers are higher at the back. The legs are extra long and the zip extends to the crotch (see drawing).
- Mail order suppliers. There are specialist suppliers of items such as open back clothing and adapted trousers. These include Berbette and Elderwise.[9]
- 'Special Collection', a catalogue for easy dressing, is also available. Further information and advice about clothing problems can be provided by The Disabled Living Foundation.[10]

7 Using the kitchen

- Keep things together that are for the same purpose, e.g. put all the coffee gear in the same cupboard.
- Arrange things so that they can be picked up easily with two hands.
- Avoid piling things on top of each other.
- Clear away all the things that you never or almost never use in the kitchen, so that they do not get in your way.
- Try to do as many things as possible while seated. You might find a perching stool helpful, so ask your occupational therapist.
- Gather together everything you need before you start cooking.
- Use electrical appliances, e.g. can openers and mixers.[11]
- Begin to prepare meals well in advance, e.g. while the children are at school.
- Keep some instant meals in stock for periods when you are less able to cope.
- Choose strong and unbreakable crockery.
- Think about investing in labour-saving equipment such as a dish washer and a food processor.
- Avoid carrying things: slide things across the draining board and put the saucepan down before filling it with water from a jug.

- Use a wire basket inside a saucepan when cooking vegetables. Lifting the basket avoids the need to pick up a heavy saucepan to strain the vegetables after cooking.[12]

- Arrange the fridge in such a way that everything is within easy reach. Have it raised if necessary.
- Place a newspaper on a surface where you are peeling or chopping. This allows you to clear the waste away easily.

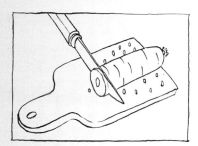

- Use a special chopping board (see drawing).
- If you are not able to prepare meals yourself, there are firms who supply pre-prepared meals. These can also be bought in many supermarkets.

8 Additional domestic activities

- Do your ironing while sitting down, even at a table.
- Sit down when removing articles from the washing machine, or have the machine raised.
- Do not fill buckets right up to the brim.
- Make sure that there is a stock of cleaning products both downstairs and on the upper floor to avoid having to carry things up and down.
- Use a mop to clean the floor. Be careful not to leave it slippery.
- Think about using a shopping trolley.
- You can apply for regular domestic help through the local authority (see Chapter 26 'Patients' and carers' rights').
- People in wheelchairs may need to adapt their kitchens and change their methods of working. You can obtain advice from your occupational therapist.

9 Communication

- Practice writing with felt pens. Use capital letters and say the letters out loud as you write.

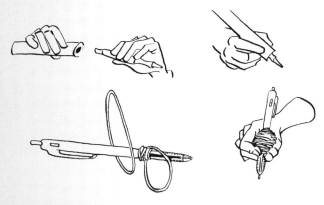

- Some people find it easier to grip a pen covered with elastic bands or the insulation material used for gas pipes (see drawing).

- Printing and lifting the pen after each letter will make the writing clearer and more normal in size
- Learn to type if writing becomes impossible. You might think about doing this anyway.
- A personal computer (a PC) will offer opportunities especially if you use a modem. This will enable you to communicate with other PC users via a telephone line.
- A wide range of communication aids can help people with speech problems. These range from simple communication boards and lightwriters to 'high tech' equipment. For example, you can type a text into a keyboard which appears on a display. This device includes a speech amplifier which amplifies a soft voice and can also be used in combination with a phone. There is also a model that speaks the text out loud. Further advice can be obtained from a speech and language therapist see Chapter 19 '*Speech and language therapy*') or your local Communication Aids Centre.

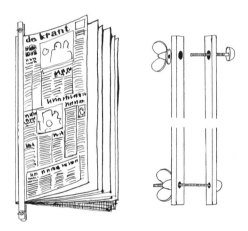

- Use things that make reading easier: a magnifying glass, large print books, 'talking' books or a newspaper holder may prove helpful.
- It is better to have telephone sockets in several rooms. A push-button phone is easier to use than one with a dial.
- Special telephones are available such as 'handsfree' phones, phones with extra large buttons and telephone stands.
  Try this equipment out at a Communication Aids Centre.[13]
- Purchase a cordless or mobile phone and make sure that you have more than one connection in your home.
- Some phones have a memory to store the numbers that you use most frequently, others can remember the last number you dialled.

10 Walking

- Talk to your physiotherapist about which walking appliance is most suitable for you.
- Make sure that you are well supported. Remove unnecessary obstacles, door sills and loose rugs so that you do not trip or need to alter your walking rhythm. See Chapter 8 '*Help with movement*'.

11 Chairs

- Make sure that you have a chair that offers good support and has arm rests. Also make sure that it is the correct height. Do not use loose cushions. Specially designed chairs are available with high backs and seats so ask your occupational therapist for advice.
- Some people with Parkinson's need a wheelchair. An occupational therapist or physiotherapist will advise you on the most suitable type. Wheelchairs may be ordered from the hospital therapist or from your GP.
- There are electric wheelchairs and scooters for outdoor use. These will have to be bought privately or financed through grants from charitable sources. For further information please contact The Disabled Living Foundation.[14]
  Your occupational therapist can provide advice on how to maintain the right posture in a wheelchair.

12 Beds

- Have your bed raised on blocks. This will help with getting in and out.

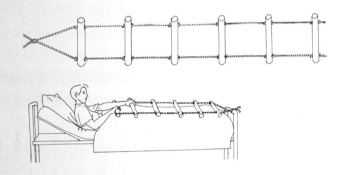

- Use a rope ladder (see drawing)
- Attach a special rail to the side of your bed.

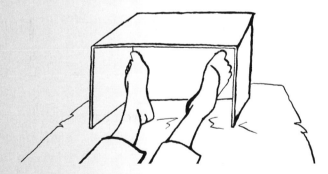

- The weight of a duvet or blankets can be relieved by placing them over a sturdy cardboard box at the foot of your bed (see drawing).
- Alternatively use a blanket frame.
- If you are having difficulty with sitting up in bed and/or getting in and out of bed you may benefit from a bed that raises and lowers itself electrically.
- If you experience pain or develop sensitive areas from lying in bed, you should consult your GP or district nurse about the possibility of borrowing/hiring a special mattress. The nurse will also advise you on the prevention of pressure sores.

- For hints on getting into and out of bed, see Chapter 8 'Help with movement'.

13   Driving

Parkinson's can affect driving. It will not necessarily lead to your losing your licence, but you are legally obliged to disclose to the DVLC any disability that you know you have. Failure to inform the DVLC will result in your insurance being null and void. The Parkinson's Disease Society has a leaflet about driving and licences and will also offer advice on these matters and on insurance. A car with automatic gears is easier to drive and you may find power steering beneficial. You can ask your occupational therapist for advice.[15]

authors: - Mrs E.A. Kooij, physiotherapist, Nieuw
Unicum Nursing Home, the Netherlands
- H. Koelmans, physiotherapist, Nieuw
Unicum Nursing Home, the Netherlands
- E.H. Coene, M.D., September
Foundation, the Netherlands

advisors: - Dr. J. van Manen, neurologist, advisor to
the Dutch Parkinson's Disease Society,
the Netherlands
- Mrs L. Hoyle, physiotherapist, Penrith
Hospital, UK

8

Help with movement

Summary

Parkinson's Disease can have an adverse effect on movement, and therefore on all sorts of every day activities, such as walking, getting in and out of bed, getting up and sitting down in a chair, turning over in bed, etc.

Other general problems include keeping your balance, turning around and 'freezing' becoming rooted to the spot and being unable to continue. This is annoying, and it can make your day-to-day life that much more difficult.

The medication prescribed for Parkinson's can help to relieve the problems but there are also many tips for each problem that patients can use to help them cope. The tips are listed in this chapter. But as far as all problems associated with bodily movement are concerned, the following is always true: when you have Parkinson's you can no longer move automatically. So before you make a movement, think about and spread complicated movements out over a series of steps. And what's more: don't hurry, and don't try to do more than one thing at a time.

Introduction

Parkinson's Disease can have an adverse effect on all sorts of things that you do every day, such as walking and getting in and out of bed. This can be a nuisance, but there are ways to limit the consequences. In this chapter we give you tips for coping with a number of possible problems.

We suggest that you also read Chapter 7 *'Tips for everyday living'*, which covers other everyday tasks such as dressing, washing, eating and cooking. Chapter 13 *'Care at home'* gives a number of hints for lifting someone who is ill. The Parkinson's Disease Society's booklet called 'Living with Parkinson's Disease' also provides useful information.

The following are dealt with in this chapter:

1 Walking
2 Turning round
3 Freezing: remaining rooted to the spot in one position
4 Keeping your balance and falling
5 Getting up off the ground
6 Sitting down in a chair
7 Getting up from a chair
8 Turning over in bed
9 Turning over in bed with help
10 Getting into bed
11 Getting out of bed
12 Getting out of bed with help

"At first sight you'd think my wife was as light as a feather. But it's no joke if you have to lift her up – say, from the chair to the bed. After a couple of weeks I started having back trouble. It's not so surprising because she can hardly help at all. Ever tried to lift a four and a half-stone child? No problem. But try and lift a bag of potatoes weighing four and a half stone – you'll rupture yourself. The physiotherapist taught me a few lifting techniques. Simple things, really, such as keeping your feet apart, bending your knees, keeping your back straight – that kind of thing. It's also much better for my wife, because in the beginning I was lugging her about more than lifting her."

General hints

- If you have Parkinson's, movement may no longer be automatic; you must think consciously about it. The following hints will help you to do this.
- It is often difficult to do more than one thing at a time if you have Parkinson's. Do not, for example, talk when you are going to sit down in a chair and do not look at your wristwatch while you are walking. Concentrate on one thing.
- If you do something in a hurry, it often does not work and there is a greater chance of an ccident. Some things seem to go quicker in the end if you just take time.
- It's a good idea to divide a complicated manoeuvre (for example getting up out of a chair) into little movements and do these little movements consciously and in order.
- Stop if something does not work. Try it again after a break.

1 Walking

"Just imagine. At my age I've had a walkman from my grandchildren. And very useful it is too! I've discovered especially that if I listen to music while I'm walking along the street I keep up a better rhythm. I've even come to appreciate the music my grandson listens to!"

Many people with Parkinson's take small shuffling steps and are in danger of falling over because they are bent forward. They then try to overcome this by taking even quicker steps. This means that they cannot stop once they get going and, in the end, may fall over or bump into something. In addition, they often put their toes down first and then their heel, and do not swing their arms.

Before you start walking
- Try to relax. The more tense you are, the more difficulty you will have in walking.
- Make sure that your feet are firmly on the ground so that your heels touch the ground.
- Set your feet at least 8 inches (20 cm) apart. Do not take a step if your feet are close together because that can disturb your balance.
- Stand up as straight as possible and try not to lean forward. It can help to hold your arms behind your back.
- The following exercise can help you to stand up straight. Stand with your back as flat as possible against a wall. The back of your head, shoulder blades, buttocks, calves and the back of your heels should touch the wall. Stand like that for at least a minute, and in your mind trace the line from the crown of your head to the back of your heels. Try to get a clear idea of how you are standing. Then walk around, go back, stand up against the wall again and look at how far you are bent forward. Do this about five times, morning and evening. This will help you to know how it feels to stand upright.
- If you find it difficult to walk, you can use a walking stick. This can give you support especially if you have a tendency to fall forward. It also makes other people aware that you have difficulty walking. A stick is not a help for everyone, for some people it can be a nuisance. There are other special resources available to help with walking, ask your physiotherapist.

The steps
- The first step is important, because if that goes well, usually the rest will too.
- Concentrate and try to take a big a step.
- When you take a step, put your heel on the ground first and then your toes.
- Pick your feet well up when walking. If you have difficulty lifting your foot off the ground imagine that you have to step over an obstacle.
- The size of the steps you take is also important. When walking, put your feet down at least a foot's length apart. This will help with your balance.
- If when walking you notice that you are making ever quicker and smaller steps, just stand still (perhaps even say, "Stand still" out loud). Then stand up straight and walk calmly on, picking your feet well up.

Further tips
- If you walk on paving slabs on the pavement, try to make your steps one slab long. This can make walking easier.
- Counting out loud can improve your rhythm and also make walking easier. Walking to the rhythm of music can help too. You could sing a song, hum or listen to a walkman with music or a metronome beat (but do not turn it up so loud that you cannot hear the traffic).
- If you have problems picking up your feet, the following exercise can be helpful. Put a row of books on the floor, about a step apart. By walking over the books

you are forced to pick up your feet.

- If you have problems keeping your balance, do these exercises with someone else around.[1]
- If walking is very difficult, it is good to have a rest for a while. Think beforehand where you are going to walk, where your supports are, where you can hold on to something and where you can get your breath back.
- It is worth checking that you are wearing suitable shoes. You may prefer leather or resin soled shoes, especially if you feel as if your feet tend to stick to the floor when you walk. If you have a tendency to lean forward, flat shoes are recommended. If you have a tendency to lean backwards, broad and higher heels will usually help.[2]

"At one stage my husband found it so difficult to walk that he couldn't even go out on his own. At the time I wanted to cancel my Wednesday afternoon tennis lesson because I didn't like leaving him alone. He said that I should go on with the lessons. Looking back on it I'm really happy about it because I still love to play tennis. And he enjoys himself too, an afternoon at home on his own."

2 Turning round

- When you want to turn around, do not try to pivot on the spot on one leg, or cross one leg over in front of the other, because you are likely to fall.
- Always keep your feet a foot apart.
- Never turn around in one go. Change direction by turning in a wide circle using small steps (see diagram below).
- You will find under 'Freezing' below, tips that may help you if you find you freeze to the spot whilst turning around.

3 Freezing: remaining rooted to the spot in one position

- People with Parkinson's may have difficulty performing a series of movements or sequences, and they may 'freeze', i.e. become rooted to the spot, unable to continue. This can happen in the middle of walking, when negotiating a doorway or an obstacle on the floor, or when adjusting their steps to avoid bumping into people in a busy street. Freezing usually only lasts several seconds but people may feel helpless or frightened. Fortunately there are ways of coping and you may be able to develop your own tricks to help.

Ways of preventing freezing

- Freezing occurs more often if someone is under pressure, worried, or is trying to do several things at once. If you are relaxed, freezing happens less often. Don't be afraid of freezing. In an emergency such as a fire or traffic accident, people with Parkinson's are suddenly able to do remarkable things.
- As freezing often occurs in particular situations, such as when you are going towards a doorway, crossing a road or turning round, you can prepare yourself for it. Try the following tips. Many people find it helpful to put signs on the floor in the home. You can put white sticky tape on the floor, for example, between the living room and the kitchen. It seems that this prevents freezing although it is not clear why it works. Imagining a line on the floor can also help

and distractions such as whistling, talking to another person or counting out loud seem to help too.

- If may also help if something is put down in front of your feet, such as a sheet of white paper or someone puts their foot in front of yours and you are able to step over the obstacle and walk on.
- If you notice, while walking, that you are going to freeze then stand still and put your heels firmly on the ground. Stand up as straight as possible, so that your knees are straight. Be careful that you do not lean over backwards.
- Walking to the rhythm of music can help avoid freezing. A walkman can be useful for out of doors but do not turn it up so loud that you cannot hear the traffic.
- Freezing can often be improved by adjustments to medication, so ask your doctor to review the dose and timing of your drug therapy.

Getting started again

- If you panic or get angry with yourself it will only make things worse. The best thing to do is to relax, although that is easier said than done. Try to sit down or to lean against something. Breathe evenly. Just think to yourself that in a short while it will all be over and you can get on with whatever you were doing. Relaxation exercises can help when freezing occurs. For more details, see Chapter 32 'Coping with stress'.
- It is often sufficient to stand up straight with your head up. Stand relaxed on your heels with your toes turned up a little and then walk on.
- If this is not sufficient, then, if possible, hold tightly onto something. Rock to and fro, left to right. Then try to take steps on the spot while you are still swaying with the same rhythm. Count out loud, "One, two, three". After a short time it is usually possible to carry on walking. If doing it this way does not work, then stop and think of something new and start again.
- Other people can help you with this. They can stand behind you holding you firmly by the shoulders, then moving you slowly back and forth by the shoulders, first from left to right and then forward and back. Try counting out loud at the same time. If you get into the rhythm they can give you a *gentle* push and you can then usually go on by yourself. It is advisable to perform these movements as calmly as possible.
- Sometimes, when freezing is severe, it is not possible to move the whole body. In such a case, start with any part of the body (arm, head, etc.).
- If these tricks do not help and it is still important that you move on as quickly as possible, you can do a couple of other things. If you are on your own, it can help to sink down to your knees and creep forward. Another trick that sometimes helps is to shut your eyes and walk on. Hold on to something firm so that you cannot fall.
- If freezing is severe, and none of the above tricks help, you may need to just wait until the episode passes or sit down and wait until the medication works again. Speak to your doctor about reviewing drug therapy.

4 Keeping your balance and falling

As a consequence of Parkinson's it can be more difficult to keep your balance and there is a greater chance of falling. There are a number of reasons for this. Some people lose their balance more quickly because of their bent posture. Although reflexes usually ensure that balance is restored so that the person does not fall, these reflexes work less well in someone with Parkinson's. Parkinson's can also cause dizziness and eye problems, which may result in problems with balance. Medication can also affect balance. Parlodel and levodopa, for example, can cause people to see 'black before the eyes' if they stand up too quickly (orthostatic hypotension).

Prevention

- Look ahead while you are walking; if you look at the ground you are more likely to adopt a bent posture, and that can invite a fall. A walking stick can give useful support, although for some people, it may hinder rather than help. It sometimes helps to carry something heavy while walking such as a briefcase, a heavy walking stick or handbag.
- For eye problems: see Chapter 27 *'Particular symptoms'*. You can also consult your GP or an eye specialist.
- If you feel dizzy when you get out of bed it may help to sit up first and just wait. Stand up slowly from the sitting position while holding on to something. Wait for a few seconds before you start to walk.
- Adjusting medication can sometimes be helpful. Speak to your doctor about this.
- It seems that problems with balance get worse if you do not walk very much. So, although it sounds contradictory, go on walking as much as possible, visiting people, doing housework etc.
- Take sufficient rest. If you are tired you will trip and fall more often. Rest at regular intervals when you are busy doing something such as going for a walk or hoovering.
- When you are on a bus, hold on tight before you sit down or you could fall when the bus sets off.
- Ask someone to help you if you have to walk down a slope.
- Choose shoes that are neither too rough (that can cause problems if you shuffle along) nor too smooth (because of the danger of slipping). If you have a tendency to fall backwards, wear shoes with a high heel, or shoes that are built up inside. If you tend to fall over forwards, choose low-heeled shoes.
- If your balance is badly affected do not be ashamed to use a wheelchair when, for instance, visiting a museum. This may be a nuisance, but is better than falling down or staying at home.

Making the home safer

A number of things can be changed in the home to minimise the chance of a fall. See Chapter 7 *'Tips for everyday living'* for further information.

- Put handgrips on the wall where you often get up from a sitting position or where you can slip e.g., beside the toilet, in the shower, on a slippery floor and by the bed. Rubber mats in the bathroom and a chair under the shower can increase safety. Make sure that the lighting is good, then you will trip less often. Have extra light switches put in and keep torches in a few places in case the electricity goes off.
- The WC can be raised with a special seat or a raised lavatory pan.
- Put fixed floor covering or rubber edges on the stair treads.
- Mats can be a hazard as you can trip over them (particularly if you shuffle along) or slip on them if the floor underneath is slippery. Remove them or fix them down with tacks or adhesive.
- Be careful with kitchen steps.

- Keep the floor clear and remove as many things as possible that you could trip over, such as electric cables, loose edges of carpet or holes in the floor covering.
- Don't use wax polish because it makes the floor too slippery.
- Make sure that there is not too much furniture in the room and that you have enough room to walk, for instance from your chair to the door. Don't use furniture to lean on if it is on castors.
- Remove or put pads on pieces of furniture with sharp edges and corners such as tables. Don't have tables with glass tops. Never put anything at the bottom of the stairs in case you fall on it.

Falls

- If you do fall, try to be as relaxed as possible. Do not fight against it. Try to go down slowly on to your knees or roll gently and keep your arms close to your body. This is easier said than done, but it does reduce the chance of injury.
- If you often fall, then walk round with someone else who is strong enough to catch you.
- Alarms for people at risk of falling can be carried or worn as a bracelet or necklace. When activated they connect with a control switchboard and relay a message to the appropriate agency.[4]

5 Getting up off the ground

- Should you fall, do not get up immediately but stay on the floor for a moment or so in order to get over the shock and check if you are bruised or have injured yourself.

- When you want to start getting up, lie on your back, pull up your knees and put both feet flat on the ground.
- Clasp your hands together and hold them up with your elbows straight. Then in one movement roll on to your side.

- Lift yourself with your lower arm and turn over onto your hands and knees.

- Look for firm support such as a bed or chair and crawl to it. Put your hands on it, move your stronger leg forward and stand with the support of the chair. Take care if it is on castors.
- If you are unsuccessful, call for help and try to keep as calm as possible. Once on the floor you are in no danger of falling again, so it is better to keep warm and stay on the ground. If someone is there, he can help to make you comfortable by putting a duvet or a blanket over you and giving you pillows to rest on before they call for help.
- If someone is going to help you, do not let him try to pull you up, because this is usually too heavy a job and can be dangerous. Get up in the way described above, letting the other person help you.

6 Sitting down in a chair

- For a comfortable position, a stable upright chair with arms is the best. You can raise the seat of a low chair with an extra cushion.

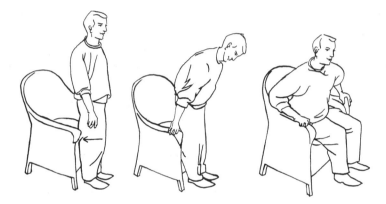

- Stand with your back to the seat of the chair and the back of your knees touching it. Do not try to sit down while you are too far away from the chair.
- Hold the arms or the seat of the chair firmly. Bend forward and sit down as you slowly bend at your hips and knees.
- If you find it difficult to walk as far as the chair imagine that there is something behind the chair that you want to reach.

7 Getting up from a chair

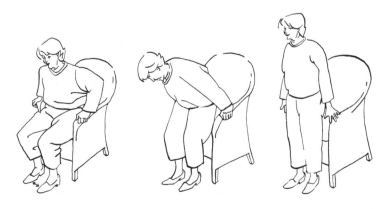

- Wriggle your bottom forward to the edge of the chair
- Firmly put your feet flat on the ground about 9 inches (25 cm) away from each other. Your heels must touch the ground. Put your feet slightly under the chair.
- Put your hands on the arms or the seat of the chair.
- Lean forwards as far as possible. Do this from the hips, so that your back remains as straight as possible.
- Push yourself forward with your arms and stand up in one movement.
- When you are standing up, move your feet a little wider apart, so that you are standing firmly before you start walking.
- If the chair is by a table you can use this to steady yourself once you are standing up. Make sure the table is sturdy and has stable legs so that it will not over-balance or shift if you need to lean on it. Put your forearm and the palm of your hand flat on the table.
- It sometimes helps to count while you are standing up. It can also sometimes be necessary to rock backwards and forwards a few times beforehand in order to summon enough energy.
- A low chair is sometimes hard to get out of. You can solve this problem by putting an extra firm cushion on the seat or even by raising the whole chair on wooden blocks or on a platform. However, the best solution may be to buy a higher chair or to ask your local Social Services department to supply you with one, or to advise you further.
- It can sometimes help to raise just the back legs of the chair a couple of inches (5 cm) by putting something under them. The chair then slopes forward a little, which makes standing up easier. Make sure that the chair is steady.
- Getting out of a car is easier if you are sitting on something slippery such as a plastic bag or a piece of silk or satin. You can then turn round easily.
- If you need help, it may be enough just to hold someone's hand firmly. This can give you the lead and the confidence you need. A lot of force is not necessary.

8 Turning over in bed
- It is easier to turn over on a firm mattress.
- If the mattress is very soft you can perhaps put a board underneath it.
- Turning over is easier on smooth sheets such as nylon or satin ones. The sheet should be kept stretched taut, which can be done by putting braces on the four corners. Wearing knitted socks also gives you more grip on the sheets.

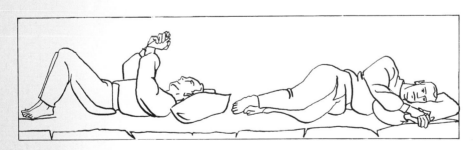

- To turn from lying on your back to your side, bend your knees and put your feet flat on the mattress.
- Clasp your hands, stretch out your arms and lift them up towards the ceiling until they are right in front of you.

71

- Turn your legs/knees to the side
- Turn at the same time your head and arms to the side.

- You can turn over further by gripping the mattress.
- If you are on one side and want to turn to the other, you have to do this manoeuvre twice, first to turn onto your back and then again to turn onto the other side.

9 Turning over in bed with help

To turn to the left:

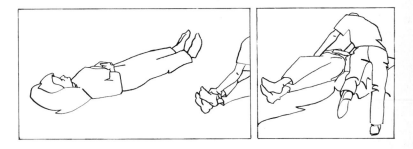

- You, or your helper, should cross your legs, right over left.
- The helper should stand on your left by the side of the bed, with one knee on the edge of the bed. The knee of their other leg should be slightly bent.

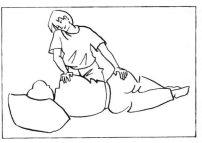

- The helper should put his right hand round your right shoulder and his left hand round your right hip.
- The helper then rolls you onto your left side, pushing with his knee against the bed. He should keep his back straight to avoid back problems.
- The helper should not push or pull you, but try to work with the movements that you make yourself.

To turn to the right:

- To turn to the right, you and your helper should follow the same procedure the other way round.

10 Getting into bed

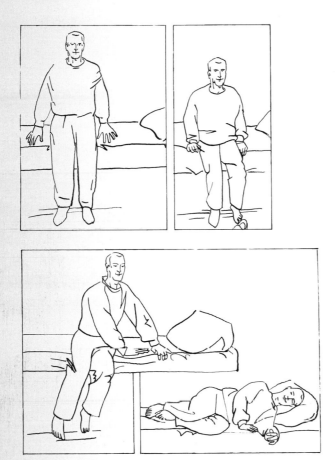

- Stand with your back to the bed.
- Sit on the edge of the bed with your bottom at the place it will be when you are lying down. If you sit too close to the pillow you will have to wriggle down the bed. If you sit too close to the foot of the bed you will have to wriggle up the bed.
- Put your head on the pillow and lift your legs into bed.
- A special frame fitted alongside of your bed may be useful. An occupational therapist should be able to advise if this would be suitable for you (see Chapter 18 '*Occupational therapy*').

11 Getting out of bed

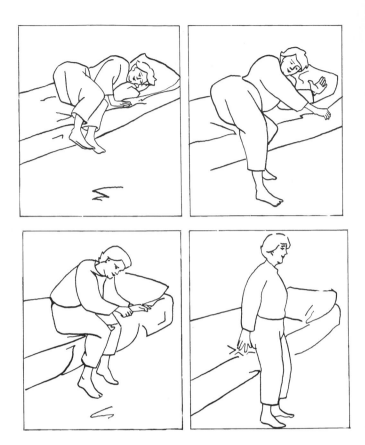

- Turn onto your side (see above) and swing your legs over the edge of the bed. You are now lying on one arm.
- Put the hand of your free arm flat in front of you on the mattress.
- Bend your head so that your chin is on your chest and lift it up.
- Push yourself up with your hand and forearm until you are sitting on the edge of the bed.
- If your main problem is getting into a seated position, you could consider an electrically operated bed, mattress or mattress section.
  You can contact your local Social Services department or ask your doctor to refer you to an occupational therapist.

"The physiotherapist taught me a few lifting techniques. Simple things, really, such as keeping your feet apart, bending your knees, keeping your back straight – that kind of thing. It's also much better for my wife because in the beginning I was lugging her about more than lifting her."

12 Getting out of bed with help

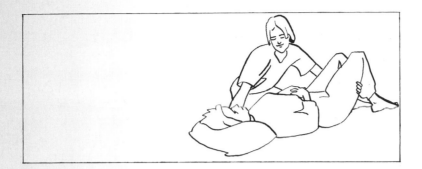

- Lie on your back. Pull your knees up and put your feet flat on the mattress.
- Your helper should then take firm hold of you under your head and under your knees and should pull your feet out of bed.

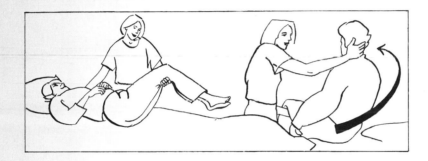

- You can then sit upright in one movement. Your lower hip will act as a pivot to support you while you are sitting up.

authors: - Mrs E.A. Kooij, physiotherapist, Nieuw
Unicum Nursing Home, the Netherlands
- H. Koelmans, physiotherapist, Nieuw
Unicum Nursing Home, the Netherlands

advisors: - Dr. E.M. Zoetemeijer, rehabilitation
specialist at the Groot Klimmendaal
Rehabilitation Centre, the Netherlands
- Mrs L. Hoyle, physiotherapist, Penrith
Hospital, UK

9

Exercises

Summary

Parkinson's Disease makes it more difficult to move. But people with Parkinson's are still advised to move as much as possible. That's because it keeps the muscles strong, it's good for the heart and lungs and because people feel better when they are more active.

Doing exercises is one way of keeping on the move. The exercises that any particular person is able to do will depend on their general physical fitness but also on the Parkinson's symptoms. Because the symptoms of the disease differ from person to person and can increase and diminish over a period of time, patients are advised to draw up a programme of exercises jointly with the doctor and the physiotherapist.

This chapter offers a range of exercises.

When you start doing exercises, don't forget one thing: build them up gradually. Do your best, but make sure that you don't get over-tired or start to feel pain.

Keeping up a programme of exercises is easier if you pick exercises that appeal to you, or if you make the exercises part of your daily routine and the people around you encourage you to do them.

Introduction

This chapter offers information on Parkinson's and exercises, and covers:
- General advice
- Basic exercises
  - lying on your back
  - sitting in a chair
  - sitting in bed
  - lying on your stomach
- Supplementary exercises
  - standing behind a chair
  - sitting on a stool

Exercises

Physical exercises cannot prevent the development of Parkinson's Disease but they can limit its consequences. Doing daily exercises will help to maintain your muscle strength. Your heart, blood vessels and bronchial tubes will also be affected by the amount of exercise you take. Many people, of course, simply feel better if they are fit.

This chapter includes some general suggestions concerning exercise. It describes a number of basic and supplementary exercises that you can do at home while walking, standing, sitting and lying down. Start with the basic exercises, then once you have mastered these you can try the supplementary exercises, which are more difficult.

Please note that the exercises in this chapter are a general guide and do not cater for individual needs. If you have any doubts about whether the exercises are suitable for you or if you have difficulties with the activities, ask your doctor to refer you to a state-registered physiotherapist who will be able to assess and guide you further.

"During the day I use my bedroom as a gym. I try to do my daily exercises there. If things aren't going well, I spread the exercises out throughout the day. Or even over two days. It's important that I just keep going."

Parkinson's and movement

People with Parkinson's often experience difficulties with movement. This can be caused by:
- stiff muscles and stiff joints
- the fact that some movements, such as sitting down or standing up, no longer occur without conscious thought
- difficulties with beginning or ending a movement, particularly when walking
- balance problems, which frequently cause falls.

All this can mean that people with Parkinson's can become nervous about moving and as a result move around less and less. This is why exercise needs to be part of a daily routine.

"Before I got Parkinson's I was a sports fanatic. Running, football, sailing – I thought it was all great. Now I can't do it any more, but I refuse to sit on my backside. Sport is a tough proposition if you've got Parkinson's because you mustn't do too much or too little. Now I make a sport of just doing enough. And that means that I really do benefit from the sports I used to do, because they taught me how to keep a close eye on my body."

77

GENERAL ADVICE

- Try to remain fit and active for as long as possible. Try to maintain your normal daily routine and do as much as you can yourself, even if it takes more time.
- Try to relax as much as possible both before and during the exercises. Allow enough time for each exercise.
- At first, do each exercise two or three times a day and gradually build up to ten times per exercise. Don't exhaust yourself, however.
- Stop if you experience pain while exercising, or opt for less strenuous exercises.
- Parkinson's affects automatic movements, so concentrate on these so that you can perform them as well as possible.
- The aim of all these exercises is to make your muscles and joints more flexible. They also help to maintain your automatic movements and improve your general physical condition.
- If you find it difficult to find time to do these exercises on your own, it might help to do them with someone else. You might consider joining a keep fit class. You are advised to consult your doctor or physiotherapist before taking up a new form of exercise.

These exercises are not specifically intended to build up muscular strength, because that is often unnecessary in the case of Parkinson's Disease. The main aim is to maintain posture and joint flexibility.

At first you may find it difficult to perform these exercises because it is complicated to read and exercise at the same time. You may find it useful to ask someone to read out the instructions as you do the exercises. Alternatively you could record the exercises on an audio cassette which you could play as you exercise.

BASIC EXERCISES

Lying on your back

These exercises can be performed lying on your back, on a mat or a thin mattress.

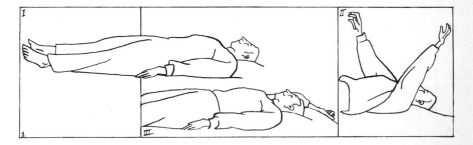

1. Stretch one arm out above your head, next to your ear. Keep the other arm alongside your body. Switch their positions simultaneously by swinging your arms.

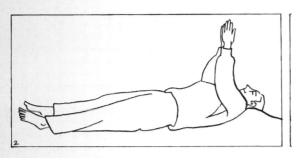

2. Put your hands together, stretch your arms and move them upwards so that they are straight above you. Twist your arms as far as they will go to the right and then to left, while keeping your hands together. Your shoulder will also turn, but keep your hips firmly on the floor.

3. Raise one leg with the knee bent. Grab your knee with both hands and try to touch it with your nose. Try to keep the knee of your other leg straight on the ground. Repeat this exercise with the other leg.

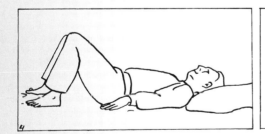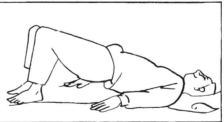

4. Bend both knees and place your feet flat and parallel to each other on the ground. Lift your bottom off the ground. As your bottom lifts, your knees should move in a forward direction over your heels. Do not push back through your shoulders.

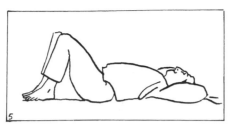

80

5. Bend both knees and place your feet parallel to each other flat on the ground. Take both knees over as far as they can go to the left, and then over to the right. During this exercise, the shoulders should not turn; keep them firmly on the floor.

6. Raise one leg with the knee bent towards your chest. Grab your knee with both hands. Now straighten the bent knee. This will increase the flexibility of the muscles along the back of your leg. Hold the stretch for a few seconds, but take care not to overstretch. Repeat this with the other leg.

Sitting in a chair (or in bed with your back supported)

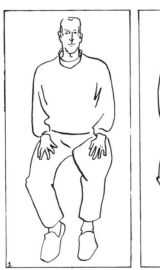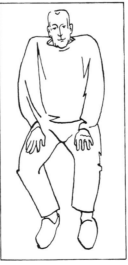

Raise your shoulders to your ears and hold them there while you count to ten.

Sitting in bed

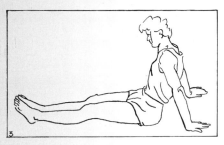 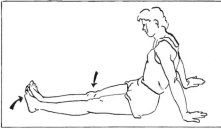

1. Stretch your legs and curl your toes as far as they will go towards you. Press your knees down onto the mattress.

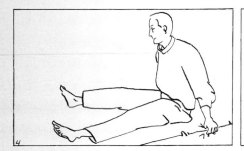 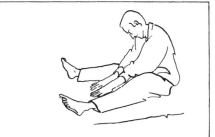

2. Spread your legs as far as they will go and try to slide down the mattress with your hands as far in front of you as possible.

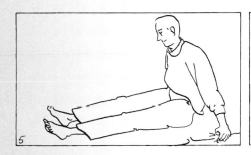 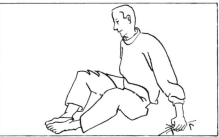

3. First stretch your legs, then bend your knees and place the soles of your feet against eachother. Your legs will then fall open much in the way that they do when you sit cross-legged.

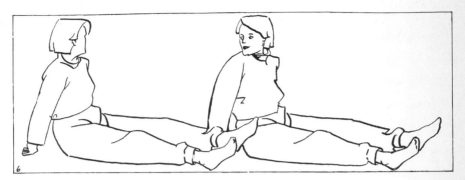

4. Turn your head first to the left and then to the right. Your shoulders must remain facing forwards.

Lying on your stomach

Try to spend about 15 minutes each day lying on your stomach, preferably without a pillow beneath your head. This allows you to stretch a number of muscles in your body so that you can use them more effectively.

"I've got one of those home trainers – it's a bike. Just the thing for me, because I was a postman for a long time and I used to cycle around twenty-five miles every day. No, honestly, it was twenty-five miles, because I used to make deliveries in a couple of villages. I thought it was great, always being in the open air. You could see all the seasons change. Now I try to make sure that I do some cycling on the home trainer every day, even if it's only for a short time. Usually I watch TV when I'm doing it.
Yesterday I was watching one of the stages of the Tour de France. Crazy, but I automatically started pedalling harder than usual..."

SUPPLEMENTARY EXERCISES

Standing behind a chair

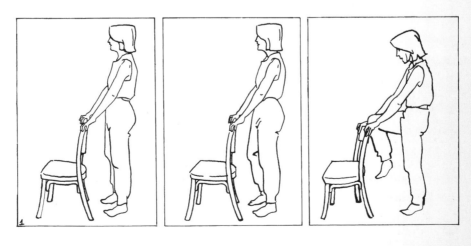

1. Stand facing the back of the chair. Take hold of the back but lean on it as little as possible. Bend one leg while raising your upper leg. Repeat this exercise with the other leg.

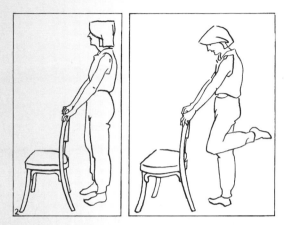

2. This is the same exercise, but this time you raise your leg behind you. The leg may be either straight or bent. Repeat this exercise with the other leg.

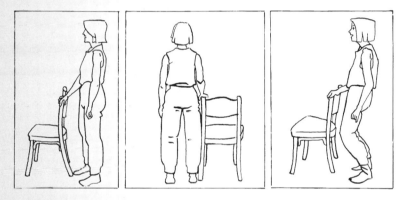

3. While standing alongside the chair hold onto the back of the chair with one hand. Place your legs slightly apart. Bend your knees and make sure that your heels do not leave the ground. While keeping your back straight, stretch your knees once more..

4. Hold onto the back of the chair. Place one foot at some distance straight in front of the other. Both feet should point straight ahead. Bend your front knee while keeping your back straight. Make sure that the heel of your back foot remains firmly on the ground.

Sitting on a stool or a firm bench without a back support

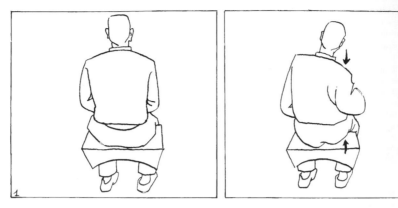

1. Raise one buttock as high as possible and bend the shoulder on that side down towards your buttock. Keep your feet on the ground. Repeat on both sides.

2. Cross your arms in front of your chest and turn your shoulders as far as they will go to the left and to the right.

3. Swing your left and right arms up in opposite directions past your body.

84

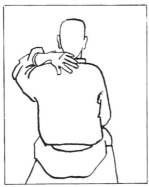 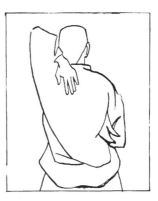

4. Place one hand behind your neck and try to push it as far as it will go down towards your buttocks. Repeat with your other hand.

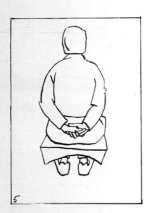 

5. Clasp your hands behind your back and raise them as far as they will go. Your upper body must remain straight; do not bend forwards.

Further information

'Living with Parkinson's Disease' is a booklet published by *The Parkinson's Disease Society*. It contains exercises that you can practise at home as well as hints on how to overcome the most common difficulties.

A leaflet 'Physiotherapy and Neurology' is available from *The Chartered Society for Physiotherapy*, 14 Bedford Row, London WCIR 4ED.

authors: - Mrs A. Dral, dietician, Academic Medical
Centre, University of Amsterdam,
the Netherlands
- Mrs C. Jonkers, dietician, Academic
Medical Centre, University of Amsterdam,
the Netherlands
- Mrs G. Pasqua, dietician, Academic
Medical Centre, University of Amsterdam,
the Netherlands
advisors: - Mrs M. Bhinda, Senior Dietician,
The National Hospital for Neurology &
Neurosurgery, London, UK
- Mrs N. Haakman-van Thiel, dietician,
Dutch Parkinson's Disease Society,
the Netherlands

10

Diet

Summary

Some complaints can result in difficulties in eating and drinking. Including problems with chewing and swallowing. You can address this by taking food in a different form. For example: mashed foods, thick soups and fruit purée. You can also adapt your manner of eating, for example by taking smaller mouthfuls and chewing them more slowly.

Other complaints too can cause problems with eating and drinking:
• Tremor can make it difficult to prepare food.
• You may develop pain in your mouth from very sharp, salty or sour foods.
• Your tiredness may prevent you from cooking fresh food every day.
• You may no longer be able to use ordinary cutlery effectively.

This chapter explains how you can do something to address these problems.

Some unusual problems with eating and drinking will also be addressed:
• If you are using medication that contains levodopa, you must be careful to avoid too much protein in your diet.
• People with Parkinson's can become underweight (because their complaints result in them eating too little) or overweight (because their complaints lead to too little mobility).
• People with Parkinson's are sometimes constipated. This may be in part due to the medication or to a change in eating habits.

Tips will be given for this too.

At the end of the chapter a few rules of thumb for a healthy diet are provided: eat three meals a day, eat a varied diet, drink sufficient fluids, observe the rules of hygiene when preparing and storing food and be moderate in your consumption of fat, sugar and salt.

Introduction
This chapter provides information on how to cope with the influence that Parkinson's can have on eating, on your medication and on your body weight.

This chapter covers:
1 Problems with chewing and swallowing
2 Problems with tremor
3 Sore mouth
4 Tiredness
5 Mechanical problems
6 Combining protein and medicines that contain levodopa
7 Problems with body weight
8 Constipation
9 General advice for a healthy diet
10 Alternative diets

1 Problems with chewing and swallowing
If Parkinson's has caused you problems with chewing and swallowing, you may need to adapt the form in which you take your food. In this way, you will still be able to eat a full range of foods and get the nutrition you need. You should find the following ideas helpful. If your symptoms are more serious, ask to see a speech and language therapist, who can advise on chewing and swallowing problems.

General
- Try firm foods such as mashed foods, thick soups and fruit purée (without skins and pips). They are easier to swallow than thin liquids or dry, crumbly solids.
- Avoid dry foodstuffs such as biscuits, dry bread, etc. They may make you choke. Try moist biscuits such as sponge fingers or mini rolls instead.
- Avoid 'lumpy' solids in liquid, such as mince in gravy, or thin soups with chunks of vegetables or meat.
- Try to sit upright during a meal. Eat slowly and chew well. Take small mouthfuls if chewing is difficult.
- Do not eat too much at one sitting. It is better to eat small helpings more frequently, i.e., 4-5 small meals a day rather than 3.
- Allow yourself the time to eat. You can prevent your food from becoming cold by using a plate warmer and taking smaller portions. You can also re-heat your food in an oven or in a microwave. It may help to present your meals in an attractive way.
- Sips of cold water before a meal will help to improve your swallow. Yawning before a meal may help to relax the throat.
- If you find food or tablets difficult to swallow, you should consult your GP, consultant, speech and language therapist or pharmacist for further advice. Some tablets are available in a soluble form, or can be crushed and mixed with mousse or yoghurt. You may find it easier if people encourage you, by saying "swallow" calmly and firmly. Take your time.
- Please see Chapter 19 'Speech and language therapy'.

> *"I was never a great eater, but since I've had Parkinson's mealtimes have turned into minor disasters. I find it hard to chew and swallow. And I began to dislike the very idea of eating. And all that mashed up food! Lying there in a little sad heap on my plate... In the beginning I used to miss a meal now and then. I'll keep my figure, I used to say. But you can't keep that up for long: I really got too thin. Now I make a point of eating enough. If I'm not too tired I try to lay the table nicely with a tablecloth, serviettes and a vase of flowers. And then you automatically feel more like eating.*
> *I guess I'll never really love eating."*

Semi-solids

If you are experiencing difficulties with swallowing, you may need to opt for semi-solid or liquidised foods, and thickened liquids. Most thickeners need to be cooked before they're effective. These include flour, cornflour, instant potato mix, rice flour, corn meal, milk powder and custard powder. Some commercially available thickeners do not require cooking. You can use them in soups, custards, porridge, mixed meals and, in some cases, cold drinks such as fruit juices, milk, custard, mousses and yoghurt.[4]

Cold meals

- If you eat bread, remove the crusts and use soft fillings such as processed cheese and smooth meat pastes, pâté, sandwich spread and cream cheese.
- Wholemeal bread is usually easier to swallow than white bread, which tends to form a solid mass in the throat.[8]
- Instead of eating bread you could try porridge (which you can make yourself or buy ready-made) or custard, yoghurt, or curd cheese with fruit purée.

Hot meals

You can use a mixer or blender to purée foods such as meat, fish, chicken, vegetables and potatoes. You can then incorporate extra gravy, sauces and juices. This will make them easier to eat and add to their nutritional content.

- For a mixed meal, you can prepare all parts of the meal in the normal way until they are cooked; then mash or mix them thoroughly and evenly with additional stock, gravy, soup, sauces or the water drained from the vegetables.
- Stew can be put through a blender and then strained to make a thick soup.
- Do not use baby foods, because although they may be the right texture, they are nutritionally inadequate.

Fruit

- You can blend fruit using a liquidiser or mixer and, if necessary, dilute it with fruit juice, milk ice-cream, cream or a very little water.
- You can use fruit juice from a packet or a bottle enhanced with extra vitamin C but fresh is best. Orange and grapefruit juices contain the most vitamin C; other juices contain smaller amounts. Drink at least one glass a day.

2 Problems with tremor

Tremors can make it difficult to prepare food. It may be useful to use:[5]

- a wire basket to hold vegetables inside a saucepan when cooking. Lifting the basket avoids the need to pick up a heavy saucepan to strain the vegetables after cooking.
- electrical appliances: can openers, mixers, etc.
- plates, cups and cutlery that have been designed to reduce the problems of tremor and muscle rigidity. For instance: a two-handled cup or a drinking straw with a one-way valve that prevents the liquid from reversing down the straw.

3 Sore mouth

Extremely sour, sweet or salty foods or spicy herbs may irritate the mucous membranes of the mouth and can cause pain while eating. The following tips may help alleviate that pain.

- Add a little cream to sour foods.
- Add sour cream or unwhipped cream to sweet foods.
- Replace hot herbs and spices with green herbs and vegetables such as parsley, celery, chives or dill.
- Hot foods can make your mucous membranes feel particularly painful. Cold meals such as ice-cream, sorbet and cold milk pudding act as an anaesthetic. Ice cubes also have the same effect.
- Take good care of your mouth, despite the pain. Brush your teeth three times a day with a soft toothbrush and using only a small amount of toothpaste. Rinse well. Occasional rinsing with salty water (one teaspoon in a glass of water) also helps to remove food particles. If your symptoms persist, ask to be referred to a dental hygienist.

Some people experience problems with their teeth or dentures (which can be ill-fitting or difficult to keep in place) and these problems can affect their eating. Going to the dentist, however, can be difficult for some people, and many dentists' surgeries are inaccessible to disabled people. The British Society of Dentistry can advise people with disabilities or dentistry problems.[10]

4 Tiredness

If you are no longer able to cook yourself a meal and there is no one to help, there is still a range of
possibilities to explore. You could discuss the following ideas with a dietician so that you eat a diet
that is both nourishing and enjoyable:

- Pre-cooked meals (deep frozen and fresh) for heating in a conventional oven or microwave. These are good replacementas for freshly prepared meals although they are often more expensive.
- Meals from food that does not need cooking, such as bread, cheeses, cold meats, fruit and yoghurt for example.
- Services such as 'meals on wheels'. A dietician or social worker will advise you on how to arrange these.

5 Mechanical problems

If eating has become difficult because you find it hard to use normal cutlery and crockery, you should ask to be referred to an occupational therapist. They can arrange for simple adaptations so that you can feed yourself. (See Chapter 7 'Tips for everyday living').

6 Combining protein and medicines that contain levodopa

Some combinations of medicines and food can lead to adverse reactions. Some medications (e.g. Madopar and Sinemet) contain levodopa. Levodopa's active ingredient (L-dopa) is a protein. Eating a high protein food at the same time or shortly after taking these medications can block the absorption of levodopa and decrease its effect (for more information on these drugs see Chapter 29 'Medication that contains levodopa'). Nevertheless, protein is important as:

- A diet with insufficient protein is nutritionally incomplete and therefore unable to maintain the body's general condition.
- It is extremely difficult to exclude protein from your diet and is impractical when you are eating with other people and perhaps cooking for them too.

However, it is advisable not to consume too much protein in one meal, but to spread the foods out evenly throughout the day. Meat, fish, chicken, eggs, meat products, cheese, milk and milk products, soya products (soya milk, tofu and quorn) all contain higher amounts of protein. Therefore you should not eat more than the quantities mentioned in the list on the previous page at each meal.

Some people are recommended to take nutritional supplements in order to gain weight and should be aware that some of these may contain high levels of protein. If you experience any problems with the working of the levodopa as a result, then you should ask to see a dietician for further advice and alternatives.

Take care with the timing of your medication and mealtimes. You should take any medication containing levodopa not less than half an hour to 45 minutes before any meal or large snack. This way your protein intake from food is less likely to interfere with the levodopa.

Do not take any medication for at least 90 minutes after eating. Take it with a low protein drink such as water, tea, black coffee, lemonade, a soft drink, fruit juice, vegetable juice or herbal tea. The exact timings of the medications will need to be discussed with your doctor, consultant or nurse.

7 Problems with body weight

Many people find it difficult to maintain their correct weight. People with Parkinson's may have problems with their weight either through not eating enough or through eating too much. Lack of appetite, side effects of medication or problems with chewing or swallowing may cause you to lose weight. However, you may become heavier because you're less active than you used to be or because you are eating more out of boredom.

The following list includes everything a healthy adult requires each day. Be aware that only basic foodstuffs have been included. If you cannot eat one of the foodstuffs mentioned here, you should replace it with something comparable. Variation is important and easy to achieve.

Recommended daily quantities of foodstuffs for an adult

Dairy products (milk, yoghurt, cheese)	2 portions
Meat, fish, chicken, tofu, soya, egg (cooked weight)	2-3 portions
Starchy foods (e.g. bread, cereals, potato)	5-6 portions
Vegetables	3-4 portions
Fruit	2-3 portions
Fatty and sugary foods (e.g. butter, margarine,oils, biscuits, cakes and sweets)	Small amounts occasionally

(Taken from: Eight Guidelines for a Healthy Diet, HEA, 1997)

How to lose weight
By using the above list, you can check whether you are eating more than you need each day. Stick to the recommended amounts but if you continue to gain weight, consider the following suggestions:
- Reduce sugar or replace with sweeteners in coffee and tea
- Replace lemonade, ordinary soft drinks and fruit juice with mineral water and sugar-free (diet) soft drinks
- Reduce the fat content in your diet by using low-fat products such as skimmed milk and low fat spreads. Switch to low-fat cheeses and lean meat products
- Reduce your intake of snacks such as sweets, cakes, biscuits, savouries and pieces of cheese. Replace these with raw vegetables, low-fat snacks, sugar-free chewing gum or drink an extra glass of water or a cup of tea/coffee (with no sugar), diet yoghurt or fromage frais.
- Cut down on alcohol or substitute with low alcohol drinks.

How to gain weight
Check the list above to see whether you are eating enough. If you are eating less than the suggested amounts, try to increase your intake by eating little and often during the day. You might choose to eat extra snacks of high-calorie products between meals or eat 4-5 small meals a day. Other suggestions are:
- Substitute low calorie drinks with fruit juices and ordinary fizzy drinks.
- Replace low-fat and skimmed milk products with ordinary milk products.
- Use margarine and butter on bread instead of low-fat margarine.
- Replace low-fat cheese with full-cream cheese and hard cheese.

91

- Increase or even double your sandwich filling.
- Add unwhipped cream or use full-cream milk in your coffee/tea, yoghurt, custard, milk pudding, milkshakes and malted milk drinks.
- Add a full cream milk to custard, porridge, mashed potatoes and sauces.
- Add grated cheese to sauces, vegetables, mashed potatoes and casseroles.
- Add a little butter or margarine to sauces, thick soups and mashed potatoes.
- Add sugar and honey to food and drinks such as porridge, custard, yoghurt, milk pudding, milkshakes, tea and coffee. Because the taste of sugar can be cloying, you could use instead some of the sweeteners on the market such as Fantomal, Dextro M, Nutrical. These taste less sweet, so you will be able to add more of them to your food.
- Extra nutritional supplements may be recommended by a dietician or your doctor.

> *"I've lost yet another pound, so that my weight is now 55 kilos (about 8 stone) for a height of 1 metre 70 (5 ft 7 inches). On the one hand, it's great to be slim; my clothes suit me better and I feel younger but I don't want to be too slim or skinny. Why's this happening? I'm eating enough. Of course, meals do take longer and are more difficult to prepare now and sometimes I'm simply too tired to make myself a hot meal or to do the shopping. But is that really the reason why I'm losing all this weight? I've decided to ask my neurologist to refer me to a dietician. He will be able to advise me about a more suitable diet."*

8. Constipation

Constipation may result from Parkinson's and its medications but it can also be due to a change of diet, lack of mobility and exercise and/or drinking too little. The following suggestions may help:

- *Sufficient fluid.* Drink at least one and a half to two litres (8 to 10 cups) a day. Alternate between the following drinks: water, tea, coffee, vegetable juice, fruit juice, herbal drinks, (diet) soft drinks, lemonade and mineral water.
- A glass of lukewarm water on an empty stomach.
- *Sufficient fibre.* Fibre is the somewhat indigestible vegetable nutrient that promotes bowel movements partly by absorbing fluid in the lower intestine. This makes the movement softer and gives it greater bulk. Fibre can be found in grain products such as wholemeal bread, rye bread, whole-wheat cereals, pasta, brown rice, oatmeal and muesli, vegetables, fruit (also dried fruits) and nuts.
- *A good breakfast.* For instance: two slices of whole-meal bread, a large bowl of porridge or a portion of yoghurt with four spoons of muesli or a wholemeal cereal e.g. Weetabix, Branflakes, Shredded Wheat etc. (See also Chapter 27 'Particular Symptoms').

9. General advice for a healthy diet

Everyone needs to eat a balanced, healthy diet each day. People with Parkinson's Disease are no exception to this. A balanced diet is one that contains all the essential nutrients. These nutrients are not available in one single food and so it is the combination of a variety of foods that produces a balanced and therefore a healthy diet. During an illness the body needs nutrients in greater amounts so it is even more important to maintain a balanced diet. This also applies if you have difficulties with eating (chewing or swallowing) or a poor appetite.

A healthy diet will enable the body to store certain nutrients. These reserves allow the body to function well at times when your appetite is poor, such as when you are ill or have an infection. The following suggestions will help you to eat healthily:

- *Eat three regular meals a day* with the occasional snack and drink between meals. This will ensure your body gets a gradual and adequate amount of nutrition.
- *Eat a varied diet.* This will allow your body to acquire all the nutrients it needs. It can also stimulate your appetite.
- *Make sure that you drink enough.* Our bodies are two-thirds liquid. We must drink at least a minimum of 8-10 cups of fluid each day to prevent dehydration and constipation. This can be in the form of milk, coffee, tea, mineral/tap water, fruit juices and soft drinks. Alcohol is not considered as part of your fluid intake and too much can damage your health. Moderate amounts are fine, i.e., 1-2 glasses a day.
- *Be hygienic.* Bacteria flourish on food, so make sure that you prepare and store food in a hygienic manner. Avoid contact between raw and cooked foods, especially through the use of kitchen utensils. Make sure that everything is clean when you are preparing food. Follow the 'use by' dates and storage advice on packets.
- *Be aware of your total fat, sugar and salt intake* to prevent long-term health problems. A diet that contains a high level of fat and sugar can lead to obesity, and an increased risk of heart and vascular disease while too much salt can lead to high blood pressure and can increase the risk of strokes. Your doctor or a dietician can advise you on healthy levels of intake.

If you are eating a healthy and varied diet, vitamin supplements will not be necessary. However, if you are in doubt, ask your doctor or consultant for further advice on the appropriate choice and whether, for example, Vitamin B6 (pyridoxine) can interfere with your medication.

10. Alternative diets

Some alternative or complementary therapies recommend particular diets. If you decide to switch to one of these diets, we suggest that you first consult your doctor or a state registered dietician. With their help, you can ensure that your diet is balanced so your nutritional intake and condition do not suffer.

Addresses

Some useful addresses for special utensils/stay-warm plates, etc.

Smith & Nephew Homecraft Ltd.
Shelley Close
Lowmoor Road Business Parc
Kirkby in Ashfield
Nottinghamshire NG17 7JZ
Tel: 01623 754 047

Nottingham Rehab
Excelsior Road Ashby Parc
Ashby
Leicestershire LE65 1NG
Tel: 01159 452 345

author: - E.H. Coene, M.D., September
Foundation, the Netherlands
advisors:- Mrs A. Beattie, occupational therapist,
Independent Occupational Therapy
Services, , Glasgow, UK
- Dr. E.M. Zoetemeijer, rehabilitation
specialist at the Groot Klimmendaal
Rehabilitation Centre, the Netherlands

11

Sports, hobbies and holidays

Summary

Many people take part in sports and hobbies and almost everyone takes the occasional holiday. These activities may be harder for people with Parkinson's, but that's not the same as saying that they are impossible.

In this chapter, tips are given on practising sports and hobbies and on holidays.

- Sport often remains a worthwhile possibility (and is strongly recommended!). Some concessions may be necessary, for example to the tempo you adopt. If you have great difficulties with your complaints, you might be able to turn to a club specially addressed to people with a handicap.
- Adjustments are possible with many kinds of hobbies. For example: gardening with specially adapted garden tools, writing with an (adapted) computer, 'reading' audio books, etc.
- Holidays are still a practical possibility, either alone or with a group. Adjustments may be necessary, depending on your complaints. The PDS organises holidays for people with Parkinson's.

Introduction

Sports, hobbies and holidays are at least as important for someone with Parkinson's Disease as they are for anyone else. They are relaxing; they can contribute to your physical condition, may lead to social contacts and are a source of self-confidence and pleasure. However, your symptoms may make it more difficult to participate as other people do or as you yourself have done in the past. This chapter includes information about what is available for people with Parkinson's. It is only a starting point however; depending on your interests, you could expand on it in many ways.

This chapter looks at:
- Sports
- Hobbies
- Holidays

> *"I play the trumpet in a brass band. A lot of practice is required to keep everything supple. For the last three years I've been playing with my left hand, because the fingers of my right hand are no longer fast enough. It took me months to learn. Luckily the people in the brass band are very understanding. They're making me a left-handed trumpet, so that I can continue to play for many years to come".*

Sports

- You could join a sports club. Choose a sport where you will not be hampered by your symptoms. However, if this does happen you should discuss with your GP, neurologist and sports instructor ways of adapting and adjusting so that you can still participate in sessions and competitions.
- You could join a sports organisation with a section for disabled sportsmen and women. This makes it possible for people with particular symptoms to participate in sporting activities. The choice is wider than you may think and includes angling, golf, riding, sailing and swimming. Local Authority swimming pools sometimes have special sessions for disabled people. There are usually hoists and a variety of buoyancy aids available.[1]
- Some groups have been set up specifically for the disabled and so are intended to include people with Parkinson's. Information is available from the British Sports Association for the Disabled.
- We recommend that you first consult your doctor about whether you are suited to the sport of your choice.

Hobbies

Because of the wide range of hobbies available, we have decided to include just a few possibilities. All these activities are widely enjoyed and many would provide the opportunity to learn new skills.

Drawing/Painting [2]

'Conquest' is the Society for Art for the Physically Disabled. It encourages groups to form and to exhibit their work. 'Conquest' publishes newsletters and information sheets; it also organises classes in some areas. Some local branches of the Parkinson's Disease Society run art classes for people with Parkinson's and their carers.

Games [3]

The home computer is a good source of games. It can provide you with crosswords, chess, bridge and many other traditional games as well as a vast array of modern computer games. The Disabled Living Foundation and the Disabled Living Centres also have games that are specially designed and easy to handle.

Writing

The home computer can also be an important aid for writers or people who would like to start to write. Anybody can learn to use one - there are often introductory classes run by local libraries or colleges. There should be writing groups available in your area, which will also probably be advertised through the library or in guides to local further education courses.

"A short time ago I discovered a new hobby: the Internet. And I'm sixty six… My son suggested it one day, he's a real computer whizz-kid. I was really amazed how much information you can get hold of, it's really unbelievable. And it wasn't even hard to do: just practised a couple of times and then I had it. Now I do a lot with it. Recently I was sitting there 'talking' to an American on the computer, like talking with the keyboard. They call it 'chatting'. He has Parkinson's as well and we sat and talked about that. I thought it was great, it was dead easy. Now I spend an hour a day on the Internet to chat with people. I've even managed to make a few new friends."

Music

You can follow your interests in music in many ways. As well as the radio, TV and the CDs and tapes that are available in local music shops, you can get access to an enormously wide range of music through your local library. If you enjoy live performance, check with your local or regional concert halls to find out what access facilities there are for disabled people. Local music making groups - jazz, light opera, chamber music, choirs - will advertise in libraries and local press. Churches and colleges can also be a good source of live music.

Spoken word

Do not forget that novels and plays are increasingly available on tape. For many people, hearing a favourite actor read, adds another dimension to the book. Again, check out your local library.

Gardening

Gardening is an activity for people of all ages and abilities. You can bring colour and interest into your life with window boxes as well as flowerbeds. If you are no longer able to garden in the way you used to - perhaps because you find bending a problem - you could tackle this in a number of ways. You could talk to your occupational therapist about aids to make you more mobile or stable; you could think about how you might introduce a raised flowerbed into your garden; you could re-plan other parts of your garden to make them easier to manage.

Even if you can no longer garden as actively as you used to, it is possible to get a great deal of pleasure from visits to gardens. National Trust properties often have wonderful gardens attached. Many local NT groups organise bus trips to these. Addresses from your local library.

Holidays [4]

You can make your own holiday arrangements or you can go with a group. Group holidays have a number of advantages: you don't have to organise so much yourself and it's a good way of meeting people. The disadvantage is that you have less privacy. We recommend that you contact your travel agent or travel organisation to check that what's offered in the brochure will in fact be provided. Do this before making reservations or finalising anything. You can also discuss the nature of your problems and state clearly the help or facilities you will need. Have the travel organisation put in writing what has been agreed so that, if necessary, you have something to refer to later.

The Parkinson's Disease Society organises holidays and provides information on travel organisations and places that are suitable for people with Parkinson's. The Society runs special holidays for individuals and couples each year at various locations around the country and their holiday brochure is available f.o.c. One of the organisations used by the Society is the Winged Fellowship Trust - a charity committed to providing real holidays for people with disabilities. It has purpose-built or specially adapted holiday homes, which can cater for people with severe mobility problems. It also recruits young volunteers who help to look after the holiday-makers.

Holidays abroad

You should remember to arrange adequate insurance cover when going abroad. Medical assistance is free in all European Union countries although you should make sure to complete form number E111 (from the Post Office) before you go.

"At first I wasn't keen on going on a group holiday. Not my style, I thought. But after a couple of typical English summers I began to get a real hankering to go abroad. A different language, different food, a different environment. So I went on a group holiday. And, to be honest, I had a really great time. There are a few disadvantages being abroad, but on the other hand you're always a bit more flexible when you're on holiday. It's easier to think to yourself: what are you getting all worked up about...?"

Further information

Tripscope is an organisation that specialises in helping to plan journeys for people with disabilities. RADAR (The Royal Association for Disability and Rehabilitation) produces very informative guides on holidays both in the British Isles and abroad. If you are travelling by rail, the various rail companies have a unit for disabled passengers and you can telephone their switchboard for help. If you need an escort the St. John Ambulance or The British Red Cross will generally be able to assist you. Sometimes help can also be obtained from local charitable organisations such as Rotary, Round Table, Lions or Soroptimists.

There are several other organisations that can help with arranging holidays, such as the Leonard Cheshire Foundation, the Holiday Care Service/Holiday Helpers and the John Grooms Association for Disabled People.

Useful books

'Door to Door' - a guide to transport for people with disabilities. (The Department of Transport).
'Flying High' - a practical guide to air travel for elderly people and people with disabilities. (The Disabled Living Foundation).

'Accessible Holidays in the British Isles' - a guide for disabled people. (British Tourist Authority (020 8846 9000) in association with RADAR and Holiday Care Service - 01293-774 535. Cost : £7.00).

Financial Help

Trade unions, professional organisations, services benevolent funds and churches may be willing to provide funding for your holiday. More information is available in a book called 'The Charities Digest', listing many of these organisations. 'A Guide to Grants for Individuals in Need' also provides useful information.. The Holiday Care Service can put inquirers in touch with possible sources of financial help. The Parkinson's Disease Society tries to ensure that no one goes without a holiday because of a shortage of funds, and they have a member of staff who is expert in identifying sources of help.

Addresses

British Sports Association for the Disabled
Solecast House
13-27 Brunswick Place
London N1 6DX

British Red Cross
9 Grosvenor Crescent
London SW1X 7EJ

Conquest
3 Beverley Close
East Ewell
Epsom
Surrey KT17 3HB

Disabled Living Centres Council
1st Floor, Winchester House
11 Cramer Road
Kennington
London SW9 6EJ

Disabled Living Foundation
380-384 Harrow Road
London W9 2HU

Holiday Care Centre
2nd Floor Imperial Buildings
Victoria Road
Horley
Surrey RH6 7PZ

John Grooms Association for Disabled People
10 Gloucester Drive
Finsbury Park
London N4 2LP

Leonard Cheshire Foundation
26/29 Maunsel Street
London SW1P 2QW

The Parkinson's Disease Society
215 Vauxhall Bridge Road
London SW1V 1EJ

RADAR
12 City Forum
250 City Rd
London EC1V 8AF

Tripscope
The Courtyard
Evelyn Road
London W4 5JL

The Winged Fellowship Trust
Angel House
20-32 Pentonville Road
London N1 9XD

author: - Mrs P. Smith, (former) Director of Operations, Parkinsonís Disease Society, PD Expert/Project Consultant Overbridge Training, UK

advisor: - E. Falvey, Care Services Manager, Parkinson's Disease Society, UK

12

Relationships and communication

Summary

Parkinson's can change many aspects of your life. This applies to your relationships too. This chapter will explain what can happen.

It transpires that changes in communication - speech, body language and touch - have the greatest impact on any relationship. For example they can result in a conversation being unsuccessful. This can be frustrating, particularly when the fact that Parkinson's is the cause of the problem is not understood.

Parkinson's will also affect your sexual relations. Many people with Parkinson's experience sexual difficulties. These may involve sexual interest, desire, arousal and orgasm. These may however be addressed successfully:

Discussing matters openly with your partner can forestall many problems.

Changing your routine (when and how you make love) can bring new interest to any sexual relationship.

Professional help is available for sexual difficulties.

It is moreover certainly not the case that Parkinson's will cause your relationships with others to deteriorate. This will depend on how you and the others deal with the changes. Experience teaches that relationships can even be strengthened because people begin to feel more affinity for one another.

Introduction

This chapter looks at the importance of private and public relationships in our lives, how relationships change over time because of changing circumstances, and how people living with Parkinson's can come to terms with these changes and take an active role in making and maintaining enriching relationships.

It covers:

- Communication
- Changes in relationships
- Changes and Parkinson's
- Changing relationships and Parkinson's
- Sexuality
- Parkinson's and good relationships

Communication

The most enriching and sustainable relationships are those where we connect with people who have shared interests and values; where we have a clear understanding about each other's roles, boundaries and expectations; and where we have respect for one another's and respond to one another's needs. Good *communication* is essential if relationships are to be developed and nurtured. Through communication we discover and maintain our shared interests and by communicating we can redefine our roles, boundaries and expectations of one another as relationships change.

Communication is about imparting or exchanging information, ideas and feelings, and we do this through speech, writing or non-verbal communication such as posture, gesture and touch. Both the quantity and the quality of the information we are comfortable in sharing, and the method of communication we use, will vary from one relationship to another. It will depend whether the relationship exists in the private or public arena and on the roles, boundaries and expectations we have developed.

For example:

- we exchange factual information during meetings, through letters or over the telephone with business colleagues or our bank manager
- we discuss shared experiences, feelings and mutual acquaintances with our children and close friends, and re-affirm our relationship with them through touch, or a hug
- we use personal endearments, touch, and sexual intimacy to communicate our love and feelings for a partner

Non-verbal communication is learned long before we learn to use language, so posture, the tilt of the head, the raising of an eyebrow, a frown or a smile, can communicate many words, especially between people who know each other well.

Changes in relationships

Relationships are dynamic - they change over time. If shared interests or agreed behaviour and roles change, if there is a loss of self worth or mutual respect, and if communication breaks down, then relationships will be at risk.

"He's not the man I married, things have changed, but then they do, don't they. I've changed too. In lots of ways, despite the difficulties, we're closer now than we ever were."

Some relationships do not survive - one or more persons may choose to break the connection and go their separate ways. Sometimes people stay together, trapped in a negative and destructive relationship because of social constraints or family pressures.

But many relationships grow stronger over time and survive major change. Good communications will enable the exchange of information, honest feelings and a desire to explore new opportunities. With appropriate support, personal space and time, interests and values can be re-established; roles, behaviour and boundaries can be re-drawn.

Changes and Parkinson's

Being diagnosed with an illness such as Parkinson's has been likened to ' .... an assault on one's identity'. So coming to terms with a major change like the diagnosis of Parkinson's will take time, during which there may be a number of pressures on the relationships of those who 'connect' with you.

You will probably go through a number of changes which are characterized by certain emotions (denial, resistance etc.).

It will take time to pass through the different stages and the amount of time will vary from one individual to another. It can take up to two or three years for someone diagnosed with a condition like Parkinson's to pass from the denial to the commitment stage, and they could respond in the following way as they gradually come to terms with this major change in their lives:

Denial: "You're not to mention this to the children or any of our friends. I'm sure the doctor has got it wrong. So I don't see any point starting these tablets or telling anyone."

Resistance: "I might have Parkinson's, and OK physiotherapy and speech therapy might help some people, but I'm not going to need that sort of thing"

Exploration: "I've asked the doctor to let me have some information on Parkinson's and he gave me a leaflet from the Parkinson's Disease Society. I might contact them. I'd like to know a bit more about it."

103

Commitment: "I met some people outside Tesco's - they were handing out leaflets on Parkinson's. I told them I'd got it and they invited us to one of their meetings. Do you fancy going?"

Partners and family members also go through these stages. It is quite likely that the different people who connect with the person with Parkinson's will be at different stages of the curve, and as a result their needs, values and expectations will no longer be in harmony. For example:

Husband   *"You're not to mention this to the children or any of our friends. I'm sure the doctor has got it wrong. So I don't see any point starting these tablets or telling anyone." (Denial)*

Wife   *"I was numb at first but now I need to talk to someone. I need to find out more about it. What does it mean and what will happen in the future? Perhaps I could talk to someone else whose husband has got it." (Exploration).*

Son   *"Apparently Dad's been diagnosed with Parkinson's - but we're not to mention it. I've read a bit about it and of course it's a shock, but nothing is going to change for a long time, and then only slowly. At least now they know what it is they can get him on the right tablets which will help. We really need to sit down and talk about it - they may need a bit of help in the future." (Commitment)*

Daughter   *"Mum rang about next weekend. They've been to the doctor and he says Dad's got Parkinson's. We're not supposed to know. I can hardly believe it - he just seemed a bit slower than normal. I don't think I can face him at the moment. I'm afraid I said that something had cropped up and we wouldn't be able to make it. I need a bit of time to think about this." (Resistance).*

The symptoms of Parkinson's which are described in Chapter 2 and Chapter 27 progress very slowly, but can affect the activities of daily and nightly living, e.g. walking, talking, eating, smiling, driving, turning over in bed; and leisure activities such as playing a musical instrument, dancing and sport. Stress can make activities more difficult to perform and depression and anxiety can be common.

To a greater or lesser extent therefore the process of change may have to be negotiated a number of times if, for example, you have to give up driving or take early retirement from work, or if you can no longer do the things you used to do and others have to help you or do them for you.

Everyone experiences change in their lives, not just people who live with Parkinson's. Change means that things will be different in the future - it doesn't mean that they will be worse. Many changes lead to new and better opportunities, but we need information and time to adapt and respond positively to change.

105

Changing relationships and Parkinson's

The changes experienced because of Parkinson's may affect the important factors in developing and maintaining relationships which have already been mentioned, namely:

- shared values, interests and activities,
- agreed roles and boundaries
- feelings of self worth
- communication

Some people have found that long-standing relationships have broken down: either because they can no longer participate in the social activities or roles which formed the basis of the relationship; or because they, their family, friends or colleagues have found it difficult to adjust to the changes caused by Parkinson's. Probably changes in communication - speech, body language and touch - will have the greatest impact on any relationship. If conversation is difficult, or body language misunderstood, there is the risk that other people may gradually withdraw or talk to your partner instead. This will leave you feeling frustrated and excluded and them feeling embarrassed and guilty. Even a cuddle or a hug which doesn't need words but does so much to reaffirm special relationships and mutual feelings of self worth, may be a problem at certain times of the day:

"When the simplest movement appears slow, clumsy and uncontrollable it seems more dignified not to try. ...An attempted hug can end up looking like some kind of feeble assault - or even slapstick comedy, when leaning forward to bestow an affectionate kiss, one ends up spread-eagled in a heap as a result of shaky balance." [1]

Being able to laugh with others about the situations caused by Parkinson's, can be a great help in relieving tension and anxiety, and re-defining expectations. However this is only possible if you feel secure in your relationship and both parties understand the reason for the changing behaviour.

> *"My wife has had Parkinson's Disease for over 10 years. We have had a wonderful marriage and I still love her dearly, but I don't think she feels the same about me any more. For as long as I can remember, when we went out walking or were just sitting together, we always held hands. I would squeeze her hand and she would squeeze my hand back and I knew we were all right. But now, when I squeeze her hand she doesn't squeeze mine back, she doesn't really respond to me in the same way at all."* [2]

106

It is important to remember that the loss of body language and difficulty in initiating a response, are symptoms of Parkinson's - they are not symptoms of a failing relationship. With the appropriate information and understanding established relationships can adjust and thrive, and new friendships can develop.

Over time private relationships may be forced into the public domain as they gradually have to open up to admit involvement, advice, and regulations from public or outside agencies. Personal and private difficulties might have to be talked about with total strangers; assessments and referrals might need to be made; and other strangers might have to be called in to help or to take over roles. It may be necessary for a person with Parkinson's to move into residential or nursing home care, because they can no longer manage at home or because their partner needs a break. Professional carers should be aware that they need to support their clients through such periods of change. They should provide information, time and personal space to ensure that important private relationships are not threatened and to enable new public relationships to develop. Good communication and the re-defining of roles, expectations and boundaries is essential.

Sexuality

We all have physical needs for closeness with the people we love and care for. We need to be touched and held to be reassured that we are both loved and loveable. Sex is an important part of a loving relationship with a partner. Feeling 'good' about yourself is an important factor in expressing your sexuality or responding positively to others.

A small study on Parkinson's and sexual function in 1982 showed that a high proportion of people with Parkinson's and their partners reported having sexual problems. These related to sexual interest, desire, arousal and orgasm. However, this did not apply to all couples - so having Parkinson's does not mean that sexual problems are inevitable, and where problems existed they could not simply be explained by the physical symptoms of Parkinson's or side effects of medication. Stress, depression and anxiety were highlighted in the report as being more important factors. In fact the sexual problems mentioned and the influencing factors which were identified, are similar to those reported in other studies by couples where neither partner has Parkinson's.

In the study, Dr. Richard Brown looked at ways couples could help themselves to respond positively to avoid the stress and anxiety which caused sexual problems:

- Talking things over with your partner is essential to avoid a vicious circle of stress and worry which cause sexual problems, which cause more worry .... and so on. If there are things you like or don't like about sex, tell your partner, rather than hoping that they will guess.

- Changing your routine (when and how you make love) will bring new interest into any sexual relationship. This is particularly important where one partner has Parkinson's. For example, having sex last thing at night may be the worst time if the person with Parkinson's' medication is wearing off and both partners are tired. The 'man on top' position may not be ideal if the man is the one with Parkinson's, so try other positions - it can be fun to experiment.

- Don't be afraid to ask for help. Talking through problems with an independent third party - such as your GP or a Marriage Guidance Counsellor - can be helpful. Or you could ask to be referred to a sex therapist. Sex therapy is not a quick solution to sexual problems - it takes time and commitment from both partners. But it can be fun!

- Remember that no two couples are alike. If you are both happy just to be close to one another and to cuddle, or only need sex once a month, then you do not have a sexual problem. If a full and frequent sex life is an important part of your relationship and you are able to respond positively to change by adapting your routines, Parkinson's need not prevent this.

> *"They say that sex is something you can learn. But when I got Parkinson's I had to unlearn some things and learn new things. But the thing that stays the same is love - especially love."*

Parkinson's and good relationships

There are a number of things you can do to sustain and develop important relationships with others:

- remember - you are a very special person!
- make every effort to communicate. Let people know how you feel and do not be afraid to express your emotions
- keep up with your hobbies, leisure and social activities for as long as possible - try to find ways of adapting them if things become difficult
- ask for information about any important changes that you are experiencing and share this with relatives and friends. It will help you all to understand about Parkinson's, the help that is available and the choices you can make

- find out about the Parkinson's Disease Society local Branches and young people's groups, so if you choose to you can meet other people who understand the challenges you are facing and who can share with you in new opportunities
- ask for regular assessments of your drug therapy and early referral to the physical therapies (speech, physio and occupational therapy). These will ensure optimum control of your Parkinson's symptoms and help you maintain your communication, mobility, independence and leisure activities
- insist on time to discuss with relatives and close friends the implications of any major decision you are asked to make
- encourage your partner to take "time out"- to pursue their own interests and identities
- ask about counselling which can help individuals and couples come to terms and manage better the changes in relationships caused by emotional stress, sexual difficulties and feelings of loss of self worth. Counselling can also help people to work through the loss and bereavement if a relationship ends
- if you need help from external agencies, ask for a designated key worker to limit the number of strangers you have to share your private life with, and to enable important professional relationships to develop
- try to maintain your sense of humour (even though it may be difficult at times). Laughter is a powerful antidote against tension and stress. It will enable the important people in your life to laugh with you.

Despite the many internal and external pressures upon them, private and public connections can thrive within re-defined boundaries. Living with Parkinson's does not exclude people from making and maintaining enriching and sustainable relationships, through which they can regain their place in society and feel valued, safe and secure within it.

> *"When we're out people say 'How is your wife?', and I say 'She's right here, ask her!' They mustn't leave her out".*

authors: - Mrs S. Thomas, Nursing Policy and
Practice Advisor, The Royal College
of Nursing, London , UK
- E.H. Coene, M.D., September
Foundation, the Netherlands
advisor: - Mrs C. Grijns, visiting nurse,
Amsterdam, the Netherlands

13

Care at home from partner, family and friends

Summary

The Parkinson's complaints may become so serious that the person requires home care. This doesn't immediately mean professional care. Partners, family and friends can often do a great deal.

This chapter will provide practical information on home care. This information is useful for people who are being cared for at home and for their carers.

- Home care requires careful planning. Care has to be taken for example, that various types of help provided by the different carers complement each other.
- Help from the district nurse, who can often see that other professional help is arranged, for example the loan of aid appliances.
- The fitting out of the room used by the person with Parkinson's requires some modifications. An intercom may be useful.
- You may need some assistance with your personal grooming. This chapter provides several tips on this, for example how you can be washed in bed and how you can be assisted with dressing and undressing.
- Good dental hygiene is of extra importance to people with Parkinson's, either because the mouth is very dry, or because too much mucus is being produced.
- This chapter provides practical tips on small items of care: the care of teeth, nails and hair. Tips are also provided on assistance with shaving.
- Some medical complaints are discussed that may arise with people who are being cared for at home, such as incontinence and bedsores. Measures to address these are also described.

Introduction

At a certain point a person with Parkinson's Disease may have so many symptoms, that they require nursing at home. Caring for someone at home has the advantage that the person with Parkinson's can continue to live as part of the family. However, caring for someone is not an easy task and can mean that care has to be provided for many hours a day, often over many years.

This chapter covers:
1   Home nursing: advantages and pressures
2   Co-ordinating home care
3   What the district nurse does
4   Practical points to consider when caring at home
5   Washing
6   Dental hygiene
7   Dentures
8   Nail care
9   Shaving
10   Hair care
11   Dressing
12   Bladder and bowel problems
13   Bedsores (pressure sores)
14   How to make up a bed with someone in it

To help with caring, the district nurse can provide professional advice and practical information about how to care. They can help the person being cared for to maintin his independence and also provide emotional support and advice on financial help to the whole family. Additionally there are Parkinson's Disease Nurse Specialists who have extensive knowledge of the disease and the drugs used in its treatment.

This chapter includes advice on how to care for someone at home. How much care is required will be determined by the extent of the illness, the home environment and other people's response. This chapter deals with general aspects of home nursing. For more specific information, other chapters may also be helpful including:

- Chapter 6 'Information for partner, families and friends'
- Chapter 7 'Tips for everyday living', which includes advice on how to make a few simple adaptations to the home and daily life
- Chapter 9' Exercises', which includes exercises for someone in bed
- Chapter 16 'Outline of Professional Help', which includes information on people who can provide additional help with home nursing
- Chapter 17 'Physiotherapy', which includes information on how a physiotherapist can help to keep muscles and joints supple.

1 Home nursing: advantages and pressures
Care at home for the person with Parkinson's often involves help from family, friends and professionals. Care at home has many advantages: people can stay in their own environment, retain control over their life and stay in contact with familiar people. This arrangement, however, can sometimes be hard on carers or those who provide help with care. Chapter 6, 'Information for partner, families and friends', looks at ideas that will help carers meet their responsibilities to the person who is ill and take care of themselves as well.

2 Co-ordinating home care
The care required by people with Parkinson's is multidisciplinary. This means that many people may be involved in home nursing: the district nurse,

Parkinson's Disease Nurse Specialist, occupational therapist, dietician etc. To ensure there is no overlap or omission in care, it may be useful to make one person responsible for ensuring that all the care given is properly co-ordinated. It does not matter who that person is; it can be the person with Parkinson's, their carer, a friend, the GP or one of the other members of the professional team. This person can function as the contact person between all members of the care team.

Help needs to be provided at the right time by the right person, so it's a good idea if all the carers involved meet regularly in order to discuss the care given. Professionals usually keep a care plan in which care details are recorded. This is normally drawn up by the district nurse in consultation with the person needing care and/or their carer.

> *"I've come to realise that you have to keep control over your own life. Lots of people have a tendency to believe and do everything that a professional carer tells them. It's not surprising, because it's the carers who understand the problem. But on the other hand, I'm the only one who knows how I feel and what I want from life. And I'm not going to have anyone else make decisions for me on that score.*
>
> *No, I don't think my carers find me annoying. On the contrary, I think they are actually glad about it. My GP once said that he sometimes finds it hard to deal with people who do absolutely everything he tells them. 'After all', he said, 'it's their life'."*

111

3 What the district nurse does

District nurses specialise in caring for people in their own homes. They can help with the practical tasks of caring by undertaking an assessment of the needs of the person who is ill and teaching carers how to manage. They are also "gatekeepers" for other nursing and support services that may be needed:

- equipment loan services
- chiropody
- continence services
- night-sitting services
- respite care

A local district nurse will also be generally well informed about all the possible care options locally.

4 Practical points to consider when caring at home

When looking after someone at home, a carer needs to ensure that the house or flat is organised in such a way as to make it free from potential hazards. Furniture should be arranged to give maximum ease of movement about the house. Hazards can be avoided by careful planning. For example, floors should not be highly polished, there should not be loose rugs or trailing cables, which increase the risk of falls and lighting should be adequate. It may be useful to consider installing additional handrails on stairs and in hallways for safety. An occupational therapist will be able to advise on this. (See Chapter 7 'Tips for everyday living').

It is recommended that the room in which the person with Parkinson's spends most of his time is comfortable, warm and well ventilated. The bathroom and toilet should be easily accessible. Independence should be encouraged at all times and it is advisable that the person does not spend too much time in bed. If he has to spend a great deal of time in one room, perhaps his bedroom, bear the following points in mind:

- The room should be as bright and cheerful as possible
- The bed should be accessible from three sides and at an appropriate height for moving and handling. Low double beds are the worst for back strain.
- A comfortable chair in the room will allow the person to leave his bed. There should also be additional chairs for visitors.
- Central heating may make the air dry; good ventilation will ensure ample fresh air and allow odours to escape. Make sure that a window is left open for at least half an hour a day.
- There must be a way for the person to contact a carer when they are out of earshot. A bell, baby intercom or buzzer are ideal.
- Other handy items to include in the room are a bedside table, radio or television and books and magazines for reading.

> "In fact I qualify for a nursing home, but that's the last thing I want. I want to be nursed at home, even though it's quite difficult. You have to organise a lot, often ask for help, have a great deal of patience and so on. But it usually works quite well. The hardest thing, actually, is that it's such a burden for my husband. I'm sometimes afraid that he feels 'obliged'. And in fact he is, because he can hardly say: see to it yourself... We talk about it regularly. I ask him how _he_ is. Then he says – very quickly – 'I'm OK'. 'No', I say, 'I want to know how you really are.' He doesn't like that because he's not one to talk about himself much. But I know he's like that so I just go on asking. I simply want to know what he really thinks and whether he can still cope with the caring..."

Developing a routine

We all have a routine in our lives: when we get up, eat and go to bed. When caring for someone with Parkinson's, it's a good idea to try and maintain their routine for them. It is in everyone's best interests for them to retain as much independence as possible and a routine with which they are familiar may help with this. Independence maintains purpose in life, is psychologically better than dependency and also helps maintain manual dexterity and a sense of achievement.

5 Washing

An all over wash, bath or shower is essential each day to maintain cleanliness and prevent odours which can quickly develop when people are immobile. Before a person attempts to bathe, a carer should make sure they can accomplish the task and that help is at hand if needed. The district nurse may be able to suggest pieces of equipment that can help with bathing. Alternatively, a bed bath is just as refreshing when a bath or shower is difficult.

Washing someone in bed
Washing can be tiresome and painful for someone who is ill and frail. The following advice is for carers.

Talk to the person with Parkinson's and decide between you when he or she feels up to it. Also find out what he or she wants to do alone. For someone who has to spend long periods of time in bed, washing the face and hands regularly is very refreshing.
To wash someone in bed you need:

- A bowl of warm water
- Towels and flannels
- Soap and non-irritating bath oils

Make sure that you will not be disturbed and that the room is warm and draught-free. Place a towel beneath the person you're washing. Help with undressing and leave them covered with a top sheet for warmth. Wash and dry every part of the body in turn (first the face, then the chest etc.). Keep to the following routine:

- Face, chest, arms, back. Dress the upper part of the body
- Legs (change water)
- Lower body.

Do not use soap if the skin is irritated or switch to non-irritating soap. Change the water whenever necessary (also if it cools down). Wear gloves when you wash an incontinent person because of risks from intestinal bacteria. Dry the skin well, especially in the 'folds': crotch, armpits, between the buttocks and between the toes. This will prevent irritation and chafed areas.

6 Dental hygiene
Dental hygiene is particularly important for people with Parkinson's. They may be suffering from a dry mouth or from excessive saliva and may therefore easily choke on food residues.

Daily, after meals:
- Brush teeth with an electric toothbrush and a brand of toothpaste that protects the gums. Don't stop brushing teeth if gums are bleeding. Gums can be massaged with a soft toothbrush or a children's toothbrush.
- Food particles can be removed with dental floss or by using toothpicks. Special flossing equipment with handles is available and, if necessary, it's possible to adapt the handle.
- Rinsing the mouth: first spit out/lean forward/ if necessary take a sip of water through a straw/then fill up the left cheek/spit out/take a sip of water/fill up the right cheek/spit out/and repeat once more.

- Be especially aware of posture during rinsing because of the risk of choking. The Parkinson's Disease Society produces a useful booklet on dental care for people with Parkinson's.

7 Dentures

You are strongly advised to take care of dentures, because if they do not fit properly, eating and speaking can become difficult. Dentures should not be cleaned with toothpaste as this may scratch them. Denture pastes are available or cleaning with soap and water is just as effective. While dentures are out being cleaned, the mouth can be rinsed and gums gently massaged with a soft toothbrush to remove any debris. Food particles trapped under dentures can cause ulceration and discomfort. Check regularly with a dentist to ensure that dentures fit well, as any weight loss can cause loose dentures, friction and mouth ulceration.

8 Nail care

Toe and finger nails should be kept short to prevent any skin damage from scratching. Toe mails should be cut straight across and finger nails rounded with the rough edges smoothed away. See a doctor or chiropodist about ingrown toe nails. If nails are too hard to cut safely, see a State Registered Chiropodist.

114

9 Shaving

Shaving can be difficult for someone with Parkinson's. An electric razor is an alternative to wet shaving for someone who wants to remain independent.

10 Hair care

If hair washing is difficult at the sink, a carer can balance a bowl on the person's knees and get them to bend forwards for their hair to be washed. Alternatively a hair washing bowl can be bought to wash the person's hair in bed. Visiting hairdressers are also very useful. It can be a good morale boost for ladies to have their hair done by a hairdresser.

11 Dressing

Try to retain both normality and independence for as long as possible. Getting dressed each day can help with this. Do not rush dressing. Clothing can be adapted to make dressing and undressing as easy as possible. See Chapter 7 *'Tips for everyday living'* for some tips on getting dressed. Zips and Velcro are much easier for people with limited co-ordination or manual dexterity to manage. Socks should fit well and not bunch up under the toes where they could cause pressure. Tights may be difficult to get on and off, so ladies may prefer stockings or socks instead. Avoid ones with elasticated tops, which can restrict the circulation and make the feet swell. Properly fitting footwear is important. Try and avoid keeping slippers on all day, as these are hazardous for walking and allow the feet to swell.

12 Bladder and bowel problems

Bladder and bowel problems are common at all ages in both men and women, but embarrassing to talk about. Sometimes the person being cared for may become incontinent but this should not be accepted as inevitable with

Parkinson's. Sometimes incontinence can be cured and in almost every case there are ways of managing the symptoms.

For problems with incontinence one should get professional help. Speak to the district nurse or ring the *Continence Foundation*, helpline 020 7831 9831. There are many different products that can help with incontinence and these people can suggest a suitable one for you. A useful publication about bladder and bowel problems in Parkinson's is obtainable from the Parkinson's Disease Society. It is called "Looking after your bladder and bowels in Parkinson's" and is available free of charge.

13 Bedsores (pressure sores)

Bedsores are a serious problem that can occur to anyone who has to stay even for short periods in bed, chair or wheelchair. They are most likely to appear in bony areas such as heels, hips and elbows. Sores can take many weeks or months to heal, so prevention is better than cure. Carers can take care of the skin and protect it from injury by paying attention to the following:

- Inspect skin carefully twice a day and pay particular attention to reddened areas that have remained red after the position has been changed
- Change any wet bedding immediately and clean the skin if soiled. A soft cloth will reduce the chance of injury to the skin
- Beware of damaging the skin with hot water and use only mild soap
- Relieve pressure by regular movement. The position should be changed at least every 2 hours in a chair or bed
- Make sure bedding is free from creases or crumbs that could cause friction
- Do not use hot water bottles as these could burn the skin
- Bony areas may need a pillow or sheepskin positioned to prevent friction
- Beware of tight clothing and buttons on skirts and trousers
- If skin appears reddened or if the skin breaks, contact your nurse or doctor immediately.

Your district nurse can advise you on suitable pressure relieving aids and may be able to arrange for the loan of some of these items.

14 How to make up a bed with someone in it

Carers can ask their district nurse to help them make up a bed with someone in it. It might be a good idea to practise this procedure, so that you know how to do it properly. If the person in the bed is weak or suffers from a lot of pain, it is much better to make up the bed with someone else's help.

Method: Take off the blanket. Leave the top sheet and one pillow. Roll the person to one side of the bed. Roll the sheet that needs changing to the middle. If a drawsheet is used (a removable piece of sheeting or towelling placed across the middle of the bed over the bottom sheet) then move this too. Place the clean sheet (plus the drawsheet) halfway onto the bed and tuck it in. The person is then rolled back over the bump in the middle and onto the clean half. Remove the half that still needs to be changed. Stretch the clean sheet(s) into place and tuck it in. Make sure there are no creases in the bottom sheets as these could cause friction on the skin.

authors: - Mrs S. Thomas, Nursing Policy and
Practice Advisor, The Royal College of
Nursing, London, UK
- E.H. Coene, M.D., September
Foundation, the Netherlands
advisor: - Mrs C. Grijns, visiting nurse, Amsterdam,
the Netherlands

14

Lifting techniques

Summary
This chapter is intended for those people who are caring for someone with Parkinson's at home. It addresses specially-adapted-methods of lifting; such as is needed to help someone from bed into a chair. Inappropriate lifting techniques can very easily result in the carer developing back complaints. By employing specific lifting techniques, this can usually be avoided.

This chapter will provide some rules of thumbs that you can apply in all cases. For example: be careful, tell the person being assisted what is going to happen, remove pillows and the like. And: try as much as possible to avoid lifting altogether, trying rather to roll, to slide or to turn.

Lifting itself also has special rules: always stand as close as possible to the person to be lifted spread your feet, keep your back as straight as possible, bend your knees (not your back) when you stoop or lift, and tense your stomach muscles firmly.

In addition to these general rules, this chapter will provide step-by-step information for lifting in particular situations. These are situations where you as carer will be frequently involved, such as for example helping someone from a chair into bed (and vice versa) and turning someone who is lying in bed or helping him or her to sit up.

Introduction

If you are a carer for someone with Parkinsonís, you may often have to help them move around. It is advisable to do this the right way, because moving someone who is unsteady or frail can be potentially dangerous for both of you. You could both fall down, slip or damage your back. Your district nurse or physiotherapist should be able to advise you about the best ways for moving and handling. It might be a good idea to use moving and handling equipment for safety. There is a variety of equipment available that includes hoists, slings and transfer boards.

This chapter covers:
1 General rules
2 Important points
3 Lifting someone from a chair to a bed
4 Lifting someone out of bed and onto a chair
5 Turning a person in bed
6 Sitting someone up in bed

The safest method for moving and handling is to let the person you care for do as much as possible for himself. Try not to lift him at all. If you want more comprehensive information about safer moving and handling, many local areas give such courses for carers. Contact your disability information service for details of local courses. Its number is in the Yellow Pages.

1 General rules
Moving someone always requires care so that the person being moved is safe and comfortable while the helper does not strain his back. Ask the district nurse to demonstrate moving and handling techniques and to practice them with you.
- Moving someone always involves the risk of an accident, so first practice on someone who is not ill.
- Tell the person you are helping what you are doing.
- Explain how he can help you.
- Remove cushions and other possible obstacles.
- Lift as little as possible; rolling, tilting or turning are usually sufficient.
- The height at which you work should be right for you. Place blocks or trestles under a normal bed or use a bed with an adjustable height.

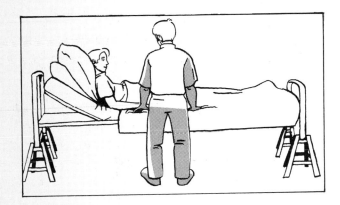 

2 Important Points
- Position yourself close to the person you are helping so that if necessary you can use your body to help him.
- Decide on the correct position to help move the person you're caring for. This might be:
  - on his least painful side
  - on the side where you can best exercise control over him.
  - on the side where you can look him straight in the face
- Make sure that your posture is correct for lifting: slightly spread your legs to make yourself more stable. Make use of the possible support provided by the bed.

117

- When you bend or lift, bend your knees and not your back. Many strains are caused by faulty lifting. Let your legs take the strain.
- Always keep your back straight. Bend at the knees and/or hips instead. This way you can keep your back straight even when bending over a bed.
- Make stomach and thigh muscles work. Tightening stomach muscles when moving from a bed or a chair is important in avoiding back strain.
- If someone is suffering from muscular rigidity, then it is advisable to move the affected limbs first before attempting to move the person. This is particularly important when he has been lying or sitting in the same position for a considerable period of time.

  The most important direction for movement is the one opposite to the position in which he has been sitting or lying. After a person has been lying flat, therefore, the legs should be flexed several times; after sitting in a chair, the knees should first be stretched.

In Chapter 8 '*Help with movement*' you will find further useful information. See in particular: standing up from a chair; getting into and out of bed; turning over in bed. The following techniques should also be useful in helping you care at home for someone with Parkinson's and for helping you take care of yourself.

118

3 Lifting someone from a chair to a bed

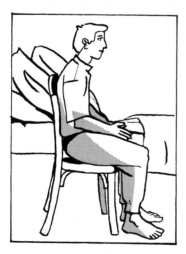

- Make sure that the chair or wheelchair is placed parallel to the bed.
- Put the wheelchair's brakes on.
- If possible, remove the wheelchair's armrest next to the bed together with both the footrests.
- Stand in front of the person and position his feet and knees.
- Get him to put his arms round your neck.
- Bend your knees and put your hands round his back at the level of his shoulder blades.
- Straighten your knees so that you stand up together.

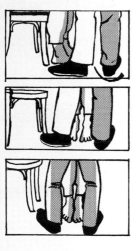  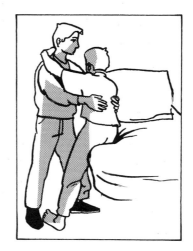

- As soon as you are both firmly upright, turn the person towards the bed.
- Make a quarter turn so that the person's right hip rests against the mattress.
- Now gently lower him onto the bed.

"I had to get used to it at first, having a stranger around all the time. For instance, I had real problems about being helped to get out of bed. You're standing there in a sort of hug with a complete stranger! Things got better after a couple of weeks, I got more used to it. Later on I was even able to joke about it - you know, things like 'I've never got so intimate with someone so quick as I have with you!"

4 Lifting someone out of bed and onto a chair

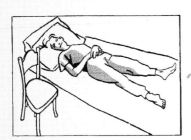  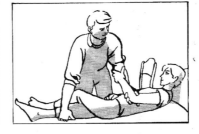

- Make sure that the chair is placed parallel to the bed.
- Cross the person's legs and tilt them over the edge.
- Stand between the person's head and his legs.
- Take his left arm and pull/lift him into an upright position.

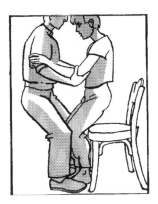 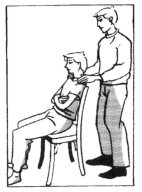  

- Bend your knees.
- Take the person's elbows and ask him to hold onto your upper arms.
- The position of your feet and knees will stop the person from slipping or his knees giving way.

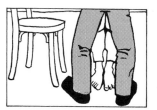 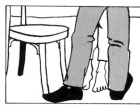 

120

- Once you have assumed a firm position, turn your left leg towards the chair.
- The person can now move towards the chair, taking small steps.
- Move your right leg so that your foot is now next to his.

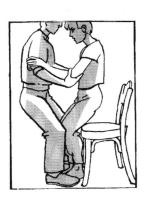 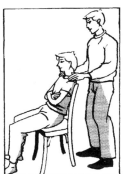  

- When you are once again in a firm position, bend your knees and lower the person into the chair.
- To settle him comfortably, stand behind him and ask him to cross his arms.
- Put your arms under his armpits and hold him by his forearm.
- Lift the person slightly to let him settle comfortably.

A rotating device placed beneath the person's feet may help in turning them. This is often useful for heavy people with very stiff legs.

5 Turning a person in bed

When turning someone in bed, it is advisable to have him hunch up so that he becomes as narrow as possible. A narrow body is easier to move than one that is spread out.

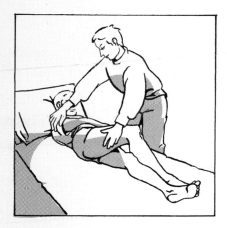
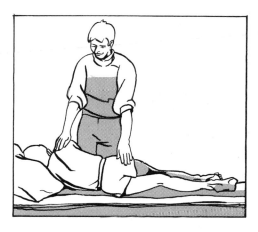

- Place the person's legs together and ask him to cross his arms over his stomach.
- Cross his legs: the right leg uppermost when tilting him onto his left side and the left leg uppermost when tilting him onto his right.
- Turn the person over.

6 Sitting someone up in bed

There are various ways of helping someone to sit up in bed, which are illustrated below. The person should co-operate as much as possible.

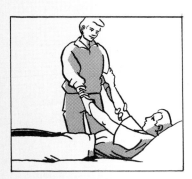

- Take the person's wrist and lower arm and move to the foot of the bed. Gently pull him into a sitting position. Arrange pillows for support.

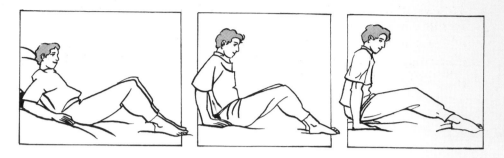

- The person draws his knees up and presses down with his hands on the mattress. By pushing with his feet, he can move to the head of the bed.
- Whenever a person cannot co-operate fully, two people will usually be needed to sit him upright in bed. Do not struggle on your own. Ask for help from a family member, neighbour or the District Nurse.
- There are two ways of lifting and you can see which one suits you best and causes you less strain.

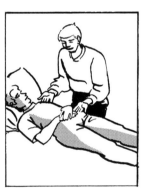 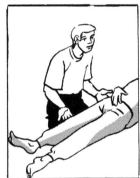 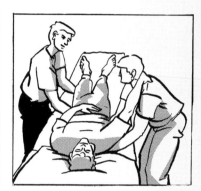

- One person puts an arm under the person's thighs and his other arm under the lower back. The second person places one hand low down the back and the other under the shoulder blades.
- Both people flex their knees and hips slightly. At a given signal, they both straighten their knees and hips and move to the head of the bed.

 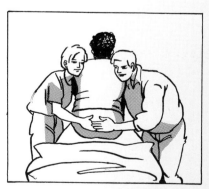

Another technique

- Two carers stand on either side of the bed, facing the head end.
- The shoulder closest to the person in bed is positioned under his armpit.
- The carers clasp hands under the person's knees and place their other hand on his lower back.
- The person places his arms across the carers' backs.
- At a given signal, the carers straighten their hips and knees and move the person in the direction required.

authors: - Mrs B. McCall, Information Manager
Parkinson's Disease Society , UK
- Mrs E. Bennion, Chairman of YAPP&Rs,
the young-onset special interest group of
the Parkinson's Disease Society and
Trustee of the Society, UK

15

Help from The Parkinson's Disease Society (PDS) of the United Kingdom

Summary

The PDS is an organisation of and for people with Parkinson's. There are nation-wide approximately 230 local sections offering extensive help and support. A review of their work is given in this chapter.

In the first place the PDS organises a number of welfare services. You can for example contact the confidential Helpline service, where you will find a sympathetic ear. The staff of the Welfare Department will be able to answer your questions, for example questions on practical issues, aid appliances, benefits, insurance, financial problems, employment and driving. You can also raise questions about holidays, including the holidays that the PDS itself organises.

The PDS also provides information and awareness activities. You can address all your questions on Parkinson's to the PDS. There is extensive information material available: a wide range of publications, cassette tapes, video's and a CD-ROM.

The PDS is also engaged in research. More than one million pounds per annum is devoted to research, distributed over approximately forty projects. To finance this and other projects fundraising activities are organised throughout the UK.

The PDS organises special activities for a number of groups, such as young people with Parkinson's (the YAPP&RS) and black and minority ethnic communities.

Anyone can become a member of the PDS. Membership costs approximately 4 pounds per year. You will then receive the newsletter quarterly.

Introduction

This chapter offers information on the PDS and covers:

- You are not alone
- The Parkinson's Disease Society of the United Kingdom
- Welfare services: the Care Services Department
- Information and awareness activities
- Research
- Fundraising
- Local help and special interest groups
- PDS Branches
- YAPP&RS (Young Alert Parkinsonians, Partners and Relatives)
- Ethnic groups
- International initiatives
- Joining the PDS

"I found it's been a great help to share my experiences with other people with Parkinson's. This is something that's a bit of a surprise. When you think about it, large numbers of people must go through Parkinson's, at least in the early stages, in sheer isolation, because they are scared and ashamed to go out and admit it to other people. They don't know anyone who has it perhaps. .... I found joining the Parkinson's Disease Society brought me into contact with people."

125

You are not alone

If you have recently been diagnosed with Parkinson's Disease, you may be feeling unsettled and afraid of what the future holds for you. Most newly diagnosed people will find that the period immediately following diagnosis is a very difficult time. You may find you have to deal with moments of uncertainty, lack of understanding and fear while you come to terms with the diagnosis and how it will affect your life

If this is how you feel at the moment, be assured that most people find that this initial period of depression and uncertainty does eventually ease and they start coping with Parkinson's and finding ways to overcome problems that occur. Because Parkinson's is such an individual condition, the length of time it may take you to start accepting your diagnosis will depend on many factors. These include what type of person you are, your particular circumstances and the availability of information, advice and support.

Please do not feel that you have to cope with Parkinson's alone. The PDS can help you. We have a great deal of knowledge and expertise that you can use to help find answers to the questions you have. However, we don't simply help the newly diagnosed; we can be a continual help to you and your family.

We can, for example, put you in touch with other people who have Parkinson's and their families through our local branch network and YAPP&RS groups for younger people with Parkinson's. Many people find it helpful to talk with people who are dealing with the same or similar situations, who will understand what you are going through. Your partner, relatives or friends may also enjoy meeting other people with Parkinson's and their relatives and friends. This contact and the other services that the PDS offers can make a big difference to your ability to cope with Parkinson's. It will also help you maintain a good quality of life and make informed decisions about any aspects of your life that are of concern to you.

The following information provides an overview of the services that the Society can offer you. Don't be afraid to contact us: the PDS are here to help.

The Parkinson's Disease Society of the United Kingdom

The PDS of the United Kingdom was founded in 1969 by Mali Jenkins, a carer whose sister, Sarah, had Parkinson's. When Mali's sister was diagnosed, they were surprised to find that no Society existed to help them with the many questions they had. They therefore decided to found one. The initial purpose was to provide information and support to people like themselves who were coping with Parkinson's. Over the years the services provided have greatly increased and the Society is now a major medical charity helping all people with Parkinson's, their relatives, friends, and the professionals who look after them.

> *"I'm not the group type, but I became a member of the PDS straight away. It's a question of practicalities. You can get all sorts of information from them for instance. Very useful, because if you have to find it all out for yourself it takes ages. At the moment it's more a question of a kind of solidarity. We've got to help one another, I believe, because there's still tons of things that need to be better organised."*

The aims of the Society are the same now as they were when the Society was formed. They are:

- To help patients and their relatives with the problems arising from Parkinson's.
- To collect and disseminate information on Parkinson's.
- To encourage and provide funds for research into Parkinson's.

Welfare services

The PDS runs a confidential helpline service which you can call Mondays to Fridays from 09.30 – 17.30. The helpline is staffed by two nurses with considerable experience of Parkinson's Disease. They can offer you a listening ear to help you talk about how you feel and discuss any questions you have about Parkinson's and its treatment. The helpline is available on a freephone number: 080 8800 0303.

The Care Services: the Care Services Department employs other staff who can help you with information and advice on practical issues, including getting help with equipment, benefits, insurance, financial problems, employment and driving. (For example, see Chapter 24 'Work' and Chapter 25 'Welfare benefits').

The PDS can also help you with information on holidays. PDS organises a special holidays programme at locations throughout the United Kingdom. These holidays are designed for people with Parkinson's and their families and cater for any special needs. PDS can also provide you with information on other types of holidays that may be suitable. (See Chapter 11 'Sports, hobbies and holidays').

As Parkinson's progresses, respite care and residential and nursing home care can become very important. PDS is involved in developing high standards of practice in all these areas and can refer you to appropriate schemes in your area. (See Chapter 22 'Care in a residential or nursing home').

Information and awareness activities

The Information Department responds to queries from people with Parkinson's, their families and friends, and the professionals who care for them. These queries may include questions about Parkinson's, its treatment, therapy, complementary medicine and diet. If necessary, you may be referred to another organisation or agency to help you get the information you need.

A wide range of publications, cassette tapes, videos and a CD-Rom is available in order to provide you with information about all aspects of Parkinson's. These include information and videos specifically for the newly diagnosed as well as for people who have had Parkinson's for some time. If you become a member of the Society you will also receive a quarterly newsletter, "The Parkinson", which includes information about the latest advances in Parkinson's research, news, and tips and advice from other people with Parkinson's and carers.

The PDS is recognised as the national voice for people with Parkinson's, and as such campaigns on your behalf. Using the media, advertising, and information materials, the PDS is determined to improve understanding of Parkinson's amongst the general public.

Research

The PDS funds over 40 research projects in the United Kingdom and spends more than £ 1.2 million a year on research. Medical research is dedicated to finding the cause, cure and prevention of Parkinson's and developing improved and new treatments. The PDS's internationally acclaimed Brain Research Centre in London uses donor tissue from people with and without Parkinson's to research the processes in the brain related to Parkinsonism.

The PDS also has a special interest group for medical research called the Special Parkinson's Research Interest Group (SPRING). Members of SPRING help the PDS to increase the profile of medical research and raise funds to support projects throughout the United Kingdom.

Further details can be obtained from: SPRING, P.O. Box 440, Horsham RH13 7YE, Telephone: 01483 281 307.

127

The PDS also funds welfare research. These projects aim to develop models of good practice in the management of Parkinson's and improvement of services. Many projects have also focused on rehabilitation and the needs of carers.

Fundraising

The PDS could not function without money of course and the Society raises money to fund its services and projects. Events and activities are held throughout the United Kingdom. If you are interested in fundraising, there are many ways that you can help. Contact the Society for more information on fundraising events.

Local Help and Special Interest Groups

Local help and support is very important.

The PDS has field staff based throughout the United Kingdom. They develop local branches in their area and liaise with local health and social care providers, promoting the PDS's welfare, education, research, and fundraising work. In 1995 the Scottish Resource, a regional office based in Glasgow, was opened. Another office in Wales has just been opened.

PDS Branches

There are 250 PDS Branches throughout the United Kingdom, all run entirely by volunteers. Branches offer you help, advice and mutual support as well as opportunities to participate in social activities and help with fundraising initiatives. They usually meet on a monthly basis and can provide you with advice on facilities in your local area. Many of them also have welfare visitors, who can visit you in your home to discuss your situation and advise you on help that is available. If you would like to make contact with your local branch, contact the PDS and you will be put in touch with your local area officer who can give you details..

YAPP&RS (Young Alert Parkinsonians, Partners and Relatives)

This is the young onset special interest group of the PDS and its main aim is to foster mutual support for younger people of working age who are affected by Parkinson's. They offer opportunities to:

- share information
- communicate with each other and offer support
- meet on a regular basis
- establish a network for young people with Parkinson's throughout the UK.

YAPP&RS encourage professionals to be aware of the individual needs of younger people living with Parkinson's.

The group does significant work and focuses on the particular problems of younger people: the problems of work, financial pressures, relationships and the strains of bringing up a family.

There are 15 regional sub-groups around the country that arrange informal meetings. National meetings are held every two years, usually over a weekend. A magazine called YAPmag is produced quarterly.

Further details can be obtained from:

YAPP&RS
c/o Ian Prest, Young Onset Development Manager
50 Reedly Road
Reedly
Burnley BB10 2NE
tel.: 01282 611 022
e-mail: iprest@parkinson's.org.uk

Ethnic Groups

The PDS is also looking at ways in which it can improve services to people who come from black and minority ethnic communities. The Outreach Service in Birmingham (West Midlands) employs two information officers who provide advice, information and support to people from these communities affected by Parkinson's. They have recently developed videos on Parkinson's for Afro-Caribbean and Asian people, with the help of a grant from the Department of Health.

Further information can be obtained from the Outreach Service for Black and Minority Ethnic Communities, Suite 312 Bradford Court, 131 Bradford Street, Birmingham B12 0NS. Tel: 0121 608 1661. Fax 0121 608 1667.

International Initiatives

PDS has also made contact over the last few years with sister organisations in other countries, particularly in Europe and America, and works closely with the European Parkinson's Disease Association (EPDA). The EPDA, formed in 1992, develops pan-European projects on Parkinson's which raise awareness of the condition at a European and global level.

These contacts are extremely important, because we can learn a lot from one another about coping and sharing information and initiatives on Parkinson's.

Joining the PDS

Please feel free to contact the PDS if you would like further information on any aspect of Parkinson's or wish to become a member. You do not have to be a member of the Society to receive help, but membership (£ 4.00 UK residents, £ 15.00 overseas residents) will ensure that you receive the most up to date information through our quarterly magazine.

Whether you have Parkinson's or are a partner, carer or family member, don't keep struggling by yourself. The PDS is there to help you find ways of helping yourself. Together we can improve the quality of your life.

Address

The Parkinson's Disease Society of the United Kingdom
215 Vauxhall Bridge Road
London SW1V 1EJ

Telephone: 020 7931 8080
Helpline: freephone 0808 800 0303
Fax: 020 7233 9908
e-mail: mailbox@pdsuk.demon.co.uk

"At first I thought it was all hopeless. I thought to myself: it doesn't matter any more, I'm never going to get better. But there came a time when things turned around. I started to think: do I really want to sit 'brooding' for the rest of my life? The answer was no. From then on I started to tackle my illness step by step. The thing that really helped was when I joined the PDS. They have meetings with other people with Parkinson's. 'Support groups' they call it. I learnt an enormous amount from those people. It turned out that I'd been stupid to think that nothing mattered any more. It's a simple fact that you can do a lot to cope well with the disease. Look, I know I'm never going to get better. I realise that quite well. And I can understand that that makes people depressed – I've been there myself. But believe you me, with a bit of patience, a bit of courage and a bit of support you can still do a lot. I might sound a bit overenthusiastic, but I really do mean it."

Notes

131

Notes

author: - Mrs P. Smith, (former) Director of
Operations, The Parkinson's Disease
Society, PD Expert/ Project Consultant,
Overbridge Training, UK

16

Outline of professional help

Summary
There is a great deal of professional help available to people with Parkinson's. This chapter will review this help, which can be split into two groups: the National Health Service and the Social Service Departments.

Within the *National Health Service* there are the community health services, which include the GP, the practice nurse and the Parkinson's Disease Nurse Specialists. Also in this group are the Hospital Services: the consultants, (specialised) nurses, a variety of therapists, social workers and dieticians.

In addition, all local authorities have *Social Services Departments* that are responsible for non-medical services for people with social and welfare needs. Their staffs include many social workers.

133

Introduction

This chapter gives an outline of the professionals in Health and Social Services who can help you, your partner, family and friends in the management of your Parkinson's. It gives a brief description of how they are organised, what they do and how you can contact them.

This chapter describes:
I   The National Health Service (NHS)
    A. Community Health Services
    B. Hospital services
II Social Services Departments

There is actually a great deal of professional help available, but it is sometimes difficult to know who does what, and where you can contact them.
Professionals working in the statutory services (the National Health Service and Social Services) provide the vast majority of help for people with health or social care needs. However, professionals working independently or through voluntary or charitable organisations can also provide valuable help.[1]

Major, welcome changes in the philosophy of care provision during the last few years, has meant that services have been set up to meet the different and diverse needs of individual 'users' (in our case people with Parkinson's) and their 'carers' (partners, family or friends). Ideally, users and carers should be 'centre stage' and should be able to access different professionals, according to their needs, and as their individual circumstances change. Professionals with different specialist skills should work closely with one another in teams to provide holistic and continuing care. Users and carers should have a 'key worker' (perhaps a Parkinson's Disease Nurse Specialist, a social worker or GP) with whom they can develop a special relationship and who they can turn to when help or advice is needed. The key worker can assess the situation and, with the user and carer, decide which healthcare professional or which service to bring in. In reality we know this does not always happen.

"You don't know who to ask or even what questions you should be asking. You end up feeling you're out there on your own."

I THE NATIONAL HEALTH SERVICE (NHS)

The NHS provides health care in both the community (in people's homes, or via health centres, clinics or practices) and through hospitals. Some healthcare professionals span both the community and the hospital setting.

A. COMMUNITY HEALTH SERVICES.

134

Primary Health Care Teams provide the 'front line' of health services within the community. They consist of general practitioners, practice nurses, district nurses, health visitors, a practice manager and receptionists. Sometimes they include other professionals, such as community-based physiotherapists or counsellors. Other professionals, such as dentists or chiropodists, work from surgeries or clinics within the community.

1. The Primary Health Care Team:

General Practitioner (GP)

GPs are doctors who head up the Primary Health Care Teams that are based in health centres or practices. GPs often know their patients and their families well and can therefore provide a holistic approach to their continuing care needs. However, because they treat patients with all types of conditions they cannot possibly know as much about Parkinson's as specialist neurologists and geriatricians. GPs act as gatekeepers to other health services, such as hospital consultants or physiotherapists, and many services are only available via a GP referral.

Under the Patient's Charter you have the right to be registered with a GP. GP practices must provide information about the range and times of their services so that if you are moving into an area or are thinking of changing your GP for any reason, you can visit surgeries to see the information they provide. Alternatively, you can contact the Health Authority or Community Health Council (see your local telephone directory) who can provide basic information on GPs in the area and advise you how to register.

See also Chapter 26 '*Patients' and carers' rights*'; '*Meeting Your Health Care Needs*' (1997), Parkinson's Disease Society; GP Guide '*Which?*' (September, 1996).

Practice nurse

Practice nurses work in GP surgeries and are a valuable source of information and advice about general health problems. They give injections, take blood and carry out regular health checks.

District or Community Nurse

District or community nurses visit people in their homes and provide a range of nursing care and advice including injections, treating pressure sores, lifting, bathing and incontinence. They can also arrange for equipment (eg. commodes), and services (eg. laundry services) and give nursing support and advice to carers. See also Chapter 13 '*Care at home*'.

Health Visitor

Health visitors work particularly with older people to prevent ill health and promote healthy living. They are a valuable source of information and advice.

"The help we get makes an enormous difference – we couldn't manage without it. It's not only the help itself, it's also the fact that you have to worry less, that you don't feel so abandoned anymore. It gives you the opportunity to think things like: well, the district nurse will think about that. I think it gives you a lot more peace and calm."

135

2. Other community based health services:

Parkinson's Disease Nurse Specialist (PDNS)

The Nurse Specialists are sometimes based in the community, working closely with GPs in a particular catchment area, or are based in the hospital setting working with consultant neurologists or geriatricians. See Hospital Services below.

Chiropodist (or Podiatrist).

People with Parkinson's can be particularly prone to problems with their feet because of the difficulties they may experience with walking, posture and foot cramps. They may also have difficulty bending over to take care of toenails. Chiropodists can provide regular footcare and treatment, including nail cutting, the treatment of bunions and ingrowing toenails. Treatment is available at the local clinic (see local telephone directory under Health Centres and Clinics) or can be arranged in your own home if you have a serious mobility problem. Some chiropodists work privately and you should ensure they are state registered with the letters SRCh after their names.

Continence Advisor

Continence advisors are nurses skilled in all aspects of the prevention and management of incontinence. They may be based in the community or work through your local Hospital Continence Advice Service. Incontinence is a common problem affecting 2 million people in the UK. Some people with Parkinson's may also experience difficulties controlling their bladder and bowels. If you are having problems speak to your GP who can refer you to a continence advisor, or contact the Continence Foundation Help Line who can give advice and the names of local continence advisors (see list of useful addresses at the end of the chapter). See also Chapter 27 *'Particular Symptoms'* and *"Looking after your Bladder and Bowels in Parkinsonism"* (1997), The Parkinson's Disease Society,

Community Psychiatric Nurse

Community psychiatric nurses can provide valuable help and advice to individuals and families where the person with Parkinson's is experiencing mental changes as a result of their Parkinson's symptoms or side effects of their medication. Referral is via the GP. See also Chapter 28 *'Mental changes'*.

Counsellor

Counsellors can help people to explore their feelings and any difficult aspects of their lives in non-judgemental and confidential counselling sessions. People with Parkinson's, their partners or carers, may have difficulty coming to terms with the diagnosis or living with the losses and changes that such a condition can cause. They may seek help, as individuals or couples, in coping with grief, anxiety, anger or fear, or with the stresses on their relationships. Counselling may be available free of charge on the NHS through GP surgeries or through the Clinical Psychology Services. Ask your GP about this. (Alternatively, there may be local voluntary organisations that offer counselling free or for a small charge. You can also contact a private counsellor whose charges will range between £ 15 - £ 40 per session. The British Association for Counselling has a list of accredited counsellors - see list of helpful contacts at the end of the chapter).

See also Chapter 4 *'Responding to the diagnosis'*, Chapter 5 *'Talking about your illness'*, Chapter 6 *'Information for partner, families and friends'*, Chapter 12 *'Relationships'*.

Dentist

Dental health is an essential part of general health care. Especially for people with Parkinson's who may experience problems cleaning their teeth or dentures, dribbling or drooling because of swallowing difficulties, or a dry mouth because of medication. Dentists usually work from surgeries in the community and have both NHS and private patients. If you have mobility problems and find getting to the dentist difficult you can ask your dentist, the Community Health Service or Community Health Council (see your local telephone directory) about the possibility of a home visit. The British Society of Dentistry for the Disabled (see list of helpful contacts at the end of the chapter) will have the names of dentists in your area who have an interest in treating people with Parkinson's. See also *"Parkinson's and Dental Health"* (1997), The Parkinson's Disease Society.

"All roads lead to Rome, so they say, and there are many roads that lead to professional help. Fine, but you do need a good map. At one stage I realised how it was, but before that I sometimes felt helpless. I had the impression that I was being sent from pillar to post. So usually I rang the GP to ask him if he could help. I think the poor man must have nearly gone crazy from all my phone calls, but you've got to do something. Yes, things are fine now. Actually, it's not all that difficult, but you have to know the route to take. Do I have any tips? Yes, and the best tip of all is: make sure you know what you want. What do you want help for? How often? That's half the job."

B. HOSPITAL SERVICES

Hospitals provide both in-patient and outpatient services under specialist consultants and departments. Services for people with Parkinson's may be organised in multidisciplinary teams, consisting of a consultant, nurse, physiotherapist, occupational therapist, speech and language therapist, dietician, social worker etc. Members of the team liaise closely with one another, with colleagues in other disciplines (if appropriate) and with colleagues in the community to provide holistic, continuing care. The hospital will also provide other specialist services such as urology, gynaecology or psychiatry which may also be relevant in helping people with particular problems, at particular times.

1. The multidisciplinary team:

Consultant

Neurologists and geriatricians (or physicians caring for the elderly), are the specialists most likely to be involved in the care of people with Parkinson's. Referral to a consultant is via your GP and under the Patient's Charter you have the right to be referred to a consultant, acceptable to you, when your GP thinks it necessary, and to be referred for a second opinion if you and your GP agree this is desirable. The Parkinson's Disease Society recommends that all people with Parkinson's should be referred to a consultant with a special interest in Parkinson's for confirmation of the diagnosis, specialist drug treatment and easier access to the multidisciplinary team. Some consultants have both NHS and private patients.

"I had a lot of trouble working well together with the specialist. To start off with I was in no mood to co-operate. Someone who just happens to know better and you can't contradict him. But things changed slowly and got better. Now I know that there are some things I'm prepared to accept, but some things I refuse. For instance: there is no way I want to be involved in tests of new types of medication. When he suggests that sort of thing to me, I just tell him I'm not interested. And now I feel that I'm much more on the same level as the specialist. We've never talked about it, but I think he sees me as an educated patient."

Nurse

Nurses work in outpatient clinics and provide the 'hands on' care for people who are admitted to hospital as in-patients. They work closely with consultants and their teams, undertaking a range of general nursing and highly skilled procedures to maintain health, dignity, independence and quality of life. They are also a valuable source of information and advice. Nurses may undertake further training to specialise in particular areas of nursing care, such as pain control or incontinence, or may focus on particular groups of patients, such as care of the elderly, neurology or Parkinson's. See Parkinson's Disease Nurse Specialists below. See also Chapter 21 'Care in a hospital'.

Parkinson's Disease Nurse Specialist (PDNS)

The Parkinson's Disease Nurse Specialists are not yet available in all areas, but their numbers are growing. They are sometimes based in the hospital setting working with consultant neurologists or geriatricians or in the community, working closely with GPs in a particular catchment area. They are experienced nurses who have undertaken special training on Parkinson's and therefore play a significant role in its treatment and management. They provide information, nursing care and support to individuals and families and liaise closely with other professionals to ensure ongoing assessment and continuity of care. Ask your hospital doctor, GP or your local branch of the Parkinson's Disease Society if there is a PDNS you can be referred to. See also Chapter 20 'The Parkinson's Disease Nurse Specialist'.

Occupational Therapist

These therapists play an important role in the management of Parkinson's and early referral is recommended. They help people with disabilities to achieve maximum function and independence by assessing their ability to carry out activities of daily living (such as eating and drinking, bathing and dressing) and advising on ways of making homes and workplaces safer and more manageable. They can also advise on appropriate adaptations, aids and equipment in the home and on leisure activities that will promote physical and mental well-being. Occupational therapists are based in both hospitals and the community (in local Social Services Departments - see below). Referral is through your GP or hospital consultant, or in some areas you can refer yourself. Occupational therapists work closely with other professionals to provide ongoing assessment and advice. See also Chapter 18 'Occupational Therapy'.

Physiotherapist

Physiotherapists use physical treatments and exercise to maintain loose joints and muscles; to improve co-ordination, dexterity, posture and breathing; and to teach techniques to improve walking, turning in bed etc. They therefore play a major role in the management of Parkinson's and early referral is recommended. Physiotherapists work closely with other professionals to provide ongoing assessment and advice. Some physiotherapists are community based and are attached to health clinics, but most work in hospitals. Referral is through your GP or consultant. See also Chapter 17 'Physiotherapy'.

Speech and Language Therapist

These therapists specialise in all aspects of communication, including speech, facial expression, body language and communication aids, and in swallowing problems. Early referral is recommended. Speech and language therapists work closely with other professionals in providing ongoing assessment, treatment and advice and play a major role in the management of Parkinson's. In most areas you can refer yourself by contacting the Speech and Language Therapy Department at the hospital, or referrals can be made through your GP or consultant. See Chapter 19 'Speech and Language Therapy'.

Social Worker

Social workers may be based in hospitals and provide important help and advice on non-medical issues, such as finances, transport, carer's support, discharge arrangements etc. (see Social Services below). If you are an in-patient or an outpatient and require social or welfare advice, simply ask to see the social worker. See also Chapter 21 'Care in hospital'.

Dietician

A healthy diet is essential to good health and advice from a dietician can be particularly important for people with Parkinson's who may have swallowing difficulties, problems with weight loss and constipation, or concerns about protein interfering with the absorption and effectiveness of levodopa. Referral to a dietician is usually through your GP or consultant, but in some cases you can refer yourself. Dieticians work closely with speech and language therapists when swallowing difficulties are involved, and can advise on food supplements, thickening agents etc., and with occupational therapists concerning useful cutlery and crockery. See also Chapter 10 'Diet', Chapter 19 'Speech and Language Therapy' and Chapter 18 'Occupational Therapy'.

139

2. Other hospital based professionals

Professionals specialising in other disciplines may be called in to assess, treat or advise people with Parkinson's from time to time, for example:

- *Gynaecologist.* Some younger women experience difficulties resulting from the interaction between their Parkinson's symptoms or medication, and menstruation, the menopause and the use of hormone replacement therapy.
- *Psychiatrist.* Mental changes may be experienced by some people, either as a result of their Parkinson's symptoms or from side effects of their medication.
- *Urologist.* Some people with Parkinson's experience particular difficulties with bladder control.

II SOCIAL SERVICES DEPARTMENTS

All local authorities have Social Services Departments (Social Work Departments in Scotland) which are responsible for non-medical services for people with social and welfare needs. They have the lead responsibility for Community Care - the provision of professional care and support to enable people who need help to live as independently as possible in their own homes or in a community setting. Each Social Services Department must produce detailed community care plans for their area, which will include information on assessment, eligibility and services. You can ask for a copy of your community care plans from your Social Services Department (see your local telephone directory).

Social Services staff who undertake assessments in order to provide flexible 'packages of care' to meet individual needs, are called care managers. These are usually social workers although sometimes community based occupational therapists also carry out assessments.

Social Worker

Social workers play an prominent role in the provision of community care and are also able to provide a wide range of information, advice and counselling support. They work closely with their Social Services colleagues, for example in care of the elderly or disability teams, and with health care professionals in multidisciplinary teams.

If you or your partner/carer need help you can ask for an assessment or re-assessment of your needs by contacting your Social Services Department direct. Your views, and the views of your partner/carer must be taken into account during the assessment. As a result of the assessment a 'package of care' will be planned which could include a number of services, for example, day centres and luncheon clubs, respite care, night-sitting services, home care, Meals-on-Wheels, adaptations to the home, special equipment, carer's support, advice on finances and benefits, residential homes (see below) etc. Assessments are free of charge although, depending on your financial circumstances, there may be some charge for services. If you believe your package of care does not meet your needs, you have the right to appeal. You also have the right to complain if you are not satisfied with the services or if services are withdrawn without a change in your circumstances . See also Chapter 26 *'Patients' and Carers' Rights'*; *"Meeting Your Social Care Needs"* (1998), The Parkinson's Disease Society.

Occupational Therapist

These therapists play an prominent role in the management of Parkinson's and early referral is recommended. They are based in hospitals (see Occupational Therapists under Hospital Services above, for a description of the role they play in the management of Parkinson's) and also in Social Services Departments where they may also undertake community care assessments. You can refer yourself to a Social Services occupational therapist. See also Chapter 18 'Occupational Therapy'.

Residential Care and Nursing Home Care

This care is available for people who require more help than can be provided in their own homes:

- Residential homes provide accommodation and care for people who need help with everyday activities
- Nursing homes provide accommodation and 24-hour nursing care

Social Services Departments publish a directory of homes which are registered in the area and some also provide leaflets giving useful questions to ask when visiting the homes prior to making a decision about moving. Costs of residential and nursing home care will vary from area to area, and unless you are able to afford the whole cost yourself, admission is arranged through Social Services following an assessment of your needs and of your financial situation. For further information and advice contact your local Social Services Department. See also Chapter 22 'Care in a Residential or Nursing Home'; "What to Look for in a Private or Voluntary Registered Home", Counsel and Care Fact Sheet Number 5.

Other Helpful Contacts for advice on professional help

Age Concern - Tel: 020 8679 8000
Association of Crossroads Care Attendant Schemes - Tel: 01788 573 653
British Association for Counselling - Tel: 01788 550 899
British Society of Dentistry for the Disabled - Tel: 01633 838 356
Carers National Association Helpline - 0345 573 369
Continence Foundation & Helpline - Tel: 020 7831 9831
Counsel and Care - Tel: 020 7485 1550
Parkinson's Disease Society Helpline - freephone 0808 800 0303
Relate (Counselling for individuals and couples) - Tel: 01788 573 241
SPOD (Association to aid the Sexual and Personal Relationships of People with a Disability) - Tel: 020 7607 8851

17

Physiotherapy

authors: - Mrs E.A. Kooij, physiotherapist at the
Nieuw Unicum Nursing Home,
the Netherlands
- H. Koelmans, physiotherapist at the
Nieuw Unicum Nursing Home,
the Netherlands

advisors: - Professor J.P.W.F. Lakke, chairperson of
the Medical Advisory Council of the
Dutch Parkinson's Disease Society,
the Netherlands
- Mrs L. Hoyle, physiotherapist, Penrith
Hospital, UK
- Dr. E.M. Zoetemeijer, rehabilitation
specialist at the Groot Klimmendaal
Rehabilitation Centre, the Netherlands

Summary

This chapter describes what a physiotherapist can do to help you and what you need to do to obtain that help.

People with Parkinson's can benefit greatly from physiotherapy. A physiotherapist can provide help with various problems and complaints, such as:
- problems with movement, for example when certain movements are no longer automatic
- making your muscles more supple; not only your physiotherapist can treat you actively for this, but can also teach you what you can do
- improve your muscle strength with specific exercises
- alleviate pain, with heat and other treatments
- improve your respiration by specific exercises
- improve your blood circulation when you are getting too little movement
- help you to retain your independence, by teaching you how to carry out daily routine procedures and how to use aid appliances.

You will find the physiotherapist via the Community Health Services. You will need a referral from the GP, practice nurse or hospital.

Introduction

People with Parkinson's Disease have movement problems, because the brain is no longer able to direct movement effectively. This leads to less movement or different movements, which can result in symptoms such as stiff joints, muscle pain and loss of muscle power. These indirect consequences can also affect movement. A physiotherapist can help people with Parkinson's by alleviating existing or preventing additional problems and by developing training for many different daily activities. We advise that you do not wait too long before calling on a physiotherapist's help. Early contact and advice may prevent problems developing in the future.

This chapter covers:
- What can the physiotherapist do?
- When should you go to a physiotherapist?
- Where can I find a Chartered Physiotherapist in Neurology?

"As a person with Parkinson's, I need occasional servicing just like my car. Physiotherapy is certainly a part of the process. When I first had Parkinson's, I even saw my physiotherapist once a week. The exercises made my muscles become more flexible. At the moment I go twice a year and that means that I resume my exercises and become less stiff."

Exercises that can be done at home are included in Chapter 9 *'Exercises'*.

What can the physiotherapist do?

Help if certain movements are no longer automatic
These are some movements you generally never think about that normally happen automatically such as walking, sitting down and standing up. Physiotherapy can help you to keep these movements supple or can make them supple once more.

Keep stiff muscles in motion
People with Parkinson's often experience stiff or rigid muscles. Physiotherapists try to alleviate this stiffness by carefully moving joints and by stretching muscles. They can also teach you to do this yourself.

Help to maintain muscle strength
If you use certain muscles less frequently, you will lose muscle strength. You can be given exercises to maintain muscle strength or to even improve it. The physiotherapist can help you with these exercises or can give you exercises to do at home.

Help to relieve pain
Depending on the cause, physiotherapists can help to relieve pain in a variety of ways including:
- the use of heat (paraffin packs, infrared light)
- cooling (ice packs or cold baths)
- physiotherapy equipment
- massage (classical, connective tissue and pressure point)

There are also physiotherapists who apply techniques such as acupuncture, meridian therapy and manual therapy.

Help you to maintain independence in your daily life
Parkinson's can make it difficult to continue performing certain actions in the way that you always used to. These include washing, dressing, eating, rolling over in bed and getting in or out of bed. Physiotherapists can teach you different ways of realising these actions by, for instance, employing different muscles or

by means of special equipment. An occupational therapist also works in this area. (See Chapter 7 'Tips for everyday living', Chapter 8 'Help with movement' and Chapter 18 'Occupational therapy').

> "Before I got Parkinson's I used to do a lot of jazz ballet. Now I join in the latest fashion – in my own way – and do some aerobics. I bought a video with exercises that I can do at home, at my own pace, and providing that my physiotherapist approves. I have to say that it's going quite well…And there's great music with the exercises, and as soon as my daughter hears a popular number played by a well known band she starts joining in."

Maintain or improve effective breathing

There are various methods a physiotherapist can prescribe to help you maintain or improve your breathing:

- Prescribe breathing exercises to prevent lung problems.
- Teach you certain positions to help any build-up of mucus in the lungs to move to the throat and be coughed up. Spending a lot of time in bed can make it more difficult to breathe deeply. If this leads to a build-up of mucus it can increase the risk of pneumonia.
- You can also learn certain breathing techniques to make the mucus pass into the throat from the lungs. These exercises and techniques can be facilitated by tapping on the chest, so that the fluid is loosened, or by applying vibrations to the chest with special equipment.

Help prevent circulatory problems

If your movement is severely restricted, insufficient blood will be circulated and muscles become weak or wasted. This can also increase the chance of bedsores and thrombosis (a vascular blood clot). To prevent this, the physiotherapist can regularly move the joints and stretch the muscles. This can involve physiotherapy equipment or massage.

Advise on equipment

For instance elbow crutches, four-legged canes, walking frames, a walking frame on wheels and a four-legged cane.

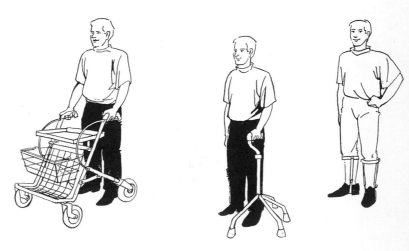

Advise and support for carers

- Your carer may need advice on how to assist you to move. A physiotherapist can advise carers on back care and the best way of helping you without damaging themselves. For example, many people find it difficult to get up from lying in bed to sitting on the edge. This is the type of problem with which a physiotherapist can help carers.
- Your carer may not understand why you are having difficulties moving, especially if sometimes you can do something and then another time you cannot. A physiotherapist can help by explaining how Parkinson's has affected your movement and give your carer tips on helping you in the best way.

When should you go to a physiotherapist?

We recommend that you contact a physiotherapist in all of the cases mentioned above. It is vital that people with Parkinson's don't wait too long before consulting a physiotherapist with their symptoms. Stiff or shortened muscles, loss of muscle power or stiff joints can often be prevented.

You will not need to be treated by a physiotherapist continually. Depending on your symptoms, you can also arrange for 'maintenance services'. In between physiotherapy sessions it is recommended that you take responsibility for yourself by following the advice given and by doing your recommended home exercises so that you gain the most from your treatment.

Where can I find a Chartered Physiotherapist in Neurology?

Physiotherapists are available through Community Health Services. You should be referred to a chartered physiotherapist (preferably one with a special interest in neurology) by your GP, practice nurse or hospital.

145

You may receive treatment in your home, at your local hospital or in a specialist neurological hospital. This will depend on the type of services available where you live. Most National Health Service physiotherapy departments have waiting lists. Some departments allow self-referrals, so you should contact your local hospital or health centre.

There are local branches of the Parkinson's Disease Society that arrange group physiotherapy services and there is also a growing number of private physiotherapists who run clinics and make home visits. If you opt for private treatment, you will have to pay for this yourself.

The Parkinson's Disease Society has published a useful booklet of exercises called "Living with Parkinson's Disease" along with a physiotherapy exercise tape.

A leaflet "Physiotherapy and Neurology" is available from The Chartered Society for Physiotherapy, 14 Bedford Row, London WC1R 4ED.

"I really do hate sport. When I was at school, gym lessons... yeah, well, I was the clumsy boy who was always chosen last for a team. So when the physio started talking about exercises he must have been able to read the message on my face. In the beginning the exercises were a failure. I was always on the lookout for an excuse not to do them.

But the physio was no fool. And then he discovered that for years I'd been taking walks. So he taught me to do various exercises while I was out walking. Half way along Wood Street I always stop to take a look in the bookshop window. I never miss. But now, at that stop, I turn a pen around a few times between the fingers of my right hand. It's a good exercise for the fingers. A bit further on, when I turn left into Pond Road, I do the same with my left hand. So I've got set places all the way along my walk where I do little exercises. It works much better because it's become a sort of ritual. The other day I forgot to do one of the exercises. So I went back to where I should have done it and did it... It's crazy, isn't it?"

author: - Mrs L. Huysmans, occupational
             therapist, Gaasperdam Nursing Home,
             the Netherlands
advisors:- Mrs A. Beattie, occupational therapist,
             Independent Occupational Therapy
             Services, Glasgow, UK
         - Dr. E.M. Zoetemeijer, rehabilitation
             specialist at the Groot Klimmendaal
             Rehabilitation Centre, the Netherlands

18

Occupational therapy

Summary
This chapter describes what an occupational therapist can do to help you,
and what you have to do to obtain that help.

If your complaints are making daily routine activities harder, it is highly
advisable to contact an occupational therapist. Don't put it off too long,
because an occupational therapist can also help you to avoid many
problems.

The occupational therapist can provide you with information about:
• self-care
• housekeeping
• mobility and transport
• leisure and hobbies
• work
• environment.

Besides information and advice on how to tackle certain activities, they
will teach you how to approach these activities in practice, advise on
adaptations to your home, supply special equipment and teach you how
to use it.

Occupational therapists are based in both hospitals and the community.
Referral is through your GP or hospital consultant, or in some areas you
may refer yourself.

Introduction

We strongly recommend that you contact an occupational therapist if you find
that Parkinson's Disease is interfering with your everyday life and if you can no
longer live, function or move around as you used to. Ideally, you should see one
much earlier, before any difficulties start because occupational therapy can be
useful even if your symptoms are not severe. Do not hesitate to seek help; a little
advice now may prevent a lot of problems later.

You will need to feel comfortable with the activities of daily living such as eating, washing, getting dressed and going to the toilet. The occupational therapist can teach you methods of adapting your environment in the best possible way. The primary aim is for you to keep doing as much as possible for as long as possible.

This chapter deals with:
- In which areas does occupational therapy help?
- Where can you find an occupational therapist?
- How does an occupational therapist work?
- Organising equipment or adaptations to the home

"I found that I quickly got used to all the alterations. I have problems with walking so I use one of those walkers with wheels. The raised thresholds in doorways have been removed from my house and the kitchen has been laid out so that everything's within easy reach. These are all things that you can work out for yourself but it was also handy to have someone else's advice."

In which areas does occupational therapy help?

The aim of occupational therapy is to help you maintain as high a level of independence as possible. Your occupational therapist (OT) will help you to plan a safe home environment and will advise you on how to do daily tasks in the best way. He can also advise on the provision of specialist equipment.

The occupational therapist can provide you with information regarding:
- Self care: eating, drinking, washing, toilet visits and bathing.
- Housekeeping: how to do it sensibly and how to avoid becoming exhausted.
- Mobility and transport: chairs, beds, adapted cars and wheelchairs.
- Leisure and hobbies.
- Work: methods of working and equipment.
- Environment: choosing the best layout, adapting your home, moving house.

For more information on these topics, see Chapter 7 '*Tips for everyday living*', and Chapter 8 '*Help with movement*'.

"I can't do everything myself any more, not like I used to, so the GP advised me to think about all sorts of devices that could help me. I was dead against the idea and kept putting it off. But one day my wife said to me: 'Hey, look at me. I wear glasses every day and that's a device that helps me, isn't it?' I'd actually never looked at it that way before."

Where can you find an occupational therapist?

Occupational therapists are employed in hospitals, Social Services Departments, day centres, residential homes, and some are in private practice. If you are attending a clinic or are a hospital in-patient it is usually the hospital doctor who will refer you for occupational therapy. However, in the community you can be referred by a social worker, district nurse, your GP, other health professional or you or your family can contact the occupational therapy department attached to your local Social Services Department.

How does an occupational therapist work?

The occupational therapist will discuss with you at any time the problems you are encountering. These may, for instance, include difficulty sleeping because of restlessness, not being able to turn over, pain and finding it difficult to get out of bed. They may also include problems with eating and dressing.

Those closest to you, the people you live with and those who care for you, will also be involved in this process. The course of Parkinson's varies with each person. This means that you and people closely involved with you can decide what is and is not a problem for you. The occupational therapist can:

- Provide advice
- Teach you to learn or relearn certain actions
- Teach you to perform certain actions in a different way
- Provide information and advice for your family and friends
- Advise on and supply special equipment and teach you how to use it.

Organising equipment or adaptations to the home

The occupational therapist takes a range of factors into account when considering what equipment or adaptations are necessary to help you live as independent a life as possible. These factors will include the creation of a safe environment for you, your feelings about the help you want and the feelings and welfare of your carer (if you have one) and your family.

The community occupational therapist, attached to your local Social Services Department, may be able to supply equipment or might suggest that you visit your local Disabled Living Centre to try out some equipment before deciding what you want to buy. Other sources of equipment are specialist firms such as Keep Able, which has showrooms and a mail order service.

Your occupational therapist may recommend that your home be adapted. Some adaptations are minor, some larger. Minor ones include raising electric sockets and fitting grab rails. Major alterations include installing a stair lift or building ramps or an extension to your home. If adaptations are required, the occupational therapist will make a recommendation to the local Social Services Department. Sometimes they will arrange for a tradesman to do the work, such as fitting grab rails. If a major adaptation is required, you will be given advice as to whether you are eligible for a grant. Sometimes you may have to contribute some of the finance yourself although the local authority may pay most of the cost.

If you need help or advice with the money side of things, you can also consult your local Citizens Advice Bureau or you could look at a copy of 'A Guide to Grants to Individuals in Need' published every year by the Directory of Social Change and available in your local library. The Parkinson's Disease Society may also be able to give advice on grants and funds available.

Useful Addresses:

College of Occupational Therapists
6-8 Marshalsea Road
Southwark
London SE1 1HL

Disabled Living Foundation
380-384 Harrow Road
London W9 2HU

Disabled Living Centres Council
1st Floor, Winchester House
11 Cranmer Road
Kennington
London SW9 6EJ

The Disabled Living Centre
260 Broad Street
Birmingham B1 2HF

Keep Able
(West Midlands Store & Mail Order)
Sterling Park
Pedmore Road
Brierley Hill
West Midlands DY5 1TB

authors: - Mrs S. Scott, Speech and Language Therapist, Scottish & Northern Regional Manager Parkinson's Disease Society, UK
- Mrs C. van Essen-Camper, Speech and Language Therapist, Dutch Parkinson's Disease Society, the Netherlands

19

Speech and language therapy

Summary

This chapter describes what a speech and language therapist can do to help you and what you have to do to obtain that help.

The speech and language therapist can help you when your complaints are impeding you with communication, or with eating and drinking.

When communicating with others speech, tone and expression and body language play a major role. Your complaints may restrict these features. For example: your facial muscles are stiff, making your expression less animated. A speech and language therapist can often provide significant help in this area.

You may be having difficulties with chewing and swallowing. This has made eating and drinking troublesome. Here too a speech and language therapist can do a great deal for you, for example by advising you on alternatives foods, your method of eating or specific aid appliances.

In most areas you can refer yourself by contacting the Speech and Language Therapy Department at the hospital, or referrals can be made through your GP or consultant.

151

Introduction

This chapter looks at the role of speech and language therapists in helping people with Parkinson's, their partners and family carers. Not surprisingly, speech and language therapists deal primarily with problems of speech and communication. However, they can also give important advice on swallowing difficulties.

Not everyone with Parkinson's will experience problems with communication or swallowing. But if you, or the people close to you, notice difficulties or changes, however small, then we strongly recommend that you seek advice from a speech and language therapist. The earlier you take action, the better the results.

This chapter covers:
- Assessment and advice from a speech and language therapist
- Communication
- Helpful hints for people with Parkinson's
- Helpful hints for partners, carers, family and friends
- Swallowing
- How Parkinson's can negatively affect communication

"Sometimes people found it difficult to understand me. I got very frustrated - especially when they just smiled, or nodded and pretended they knew what I was saying. In the end I just stopped trying - I wouldn't answer the phone and I stopped going out. That was before I started speech therapy. Now I've learned techniques to help me control my breathing and speak more clearly. I'm much more confident and last month I re-joined the local bowls club!"

Assessment and advice from a speech and language therapist

It is advisable to start speech and language therapy as soon as possible after your Parkinson's is diagnosed and before difficulties emerge. This will enable you, and those close to you, to maintain and improve your communication skills and be aware of changes as the condition slowly progresses. However, therapy is still very worthwhile if you have had Parkinson's and communication difficulties for a long time.

Referral

In many areas you can refer yourself to a speech and language therapist by contacting the speech therapy department at your local hospital. Make sure you ask for a therapist who treats adults with neurological problems.[2] In some areas referral is made through the GP or hospital doctor, so ask them to refer you if you are having difficulties. It might be a good idea to visit the speech and language therapist with your partner or carer and involve them in any future treatment. This will enable them to understand the difficulties and frustrations you may both be experiencing. Explain to the therapist that you have Parkinson's and that you want to avoid communication problems where possible, or describe any difficulties you are already experiencing. The information you provide, together with their assessment, will enable them to draw up an appropriate treatment plan and work with you, your partner or carer, to maintain and improve the quality of your communication skills.

What can the speech and language therapist do?

For example the speech and language therapist can advise:
- on exercises and techniques to help you control your breathing and the pace of your speech
- on helping you maintain and improve the volume, clarity and expression in your voice
- on facial expression and body language
- on posture and positioning
- on the best environment for speech and communication

- on portable amplification aids if your voice is quiet but clear, or on other communication aids, as appropriate.[3] (It is highly recommended that a speech and language therapist assesses you before you choose an amplification or other communication aid)
- partners and carers can be made aware of possible communication difficulties associated with Parkinson's and so avoid misunderstanding and frustration.

Communication

Communicating with others is a vital part of our lives. It enables us to express our thoughts, feelings and needs and to develop and maintain successful relationships (see Chapter 12 'Relationships and communication'). If something happens to interfere with our ability to communicate, then we will feel vulnerable and isolated. Researchers have found that communication can be broken down into speech (7%), tone and expression (38%) and body language (55%). This means that we can communicate with someone 'face to face' (by shrugging our shoulders or raising an eyebrow) without saying a single word! It also means that we can communicate with people in a different room or over the telephone, so long as our speech, and the tone and expression of our voice is clear.

Speaking clearly

To speak clearly, people need:
- good movement of the lips, tongue, soft palate and lower jaw
- good breath support and control
- good expression and flow of speech
- good speech rhythm

To understand what is being said, people need:
- good hearing
- a good command of the language and familiarity with dialect or accent

When all of the above are functioning normally people can speak and understand one another easily.

Parkinson's and communication

All of the components of communication - speech, tone and expression, and body language - can be affected by the symptoms of Parkinson's in the same way that they can affect other activities, such as walking or turning over in bed. For example: muscle rigidity of the lips.
More problems due to Parkinson's are described on page 209.

Helpful hints for people with Parkinson's.[4]
- face the person you are talking to
- do not try to talk to someone in another room
- if you have slipped down in your chair, people will find it harder to understand you; make sure you are well supported and sitting up
- avoid background noise (from a television, radio, washing machine etc.) when speaking
- do not talk when you are eating
- swallow your saliva before you speak

- think about *how much, how, and what* you are saying
- keep your sentences short
- take a little longer over each word or syllable, and put more emphasis on the important words
- do not repeat the same word or phrase if people have difficulty understanding you, use different words or pick a key word
- try to remember: breath-speak-breath-speak
- try to use facial expression to enhance and animate what you are saying
- make sure any dentures fit, and make an appointment to see your dentist if you have not done so recently
- get advice from a speech and language therapist

Helpful hints for partners, carers, family and friends [5].
- allow plenty of time to listen and for them to respond
- use your ears *and* your eyes
- listen carefully and talk normally
- avoid background noise
- have patience; do not interrupt or be tempted to finish a sentence for them
- if you do not understand, say so - do not pretend
- do not ask them to keep repeating something if you can't understand - ask them to say it in a different way
- communication is a two-way process, so keep communicating even if there is little response - holding a hand can help
- try to involve and include the person in conversations, where possible
- ask questions that can be answered with a simple 'yes' or 'no' if speaking becomes too difficult
- get advice from a speech and language therapist

154

Swallowing

It is not really surprising that the speech and language therapist can help with swallowing difficulties. Co-ordinating the muscles of the lips, tongue, palate and jaw with breathing - the activities involved in speaking - are also absolutely essential in eating, chewing and swallowing.

> *"I didn't even realise that Parkinson's was affecting his swallowing, or that the speech therapist could help us. But he got a really bad chest infection and the doctor said he probably hadn't been swallowing properly for a long time. Instead tiny bits of food and drink had gone down the wrong way into his lungs. He was given an antibiotic and then we were sent to the speech therapist. She gave him exercises, and me lots of tips about textures and temperature of food and how to sit him up properly. It's made such a difference. He seems to enjoy his food more and he's even put on a bit of weight."*

Not everyone with Parkinson's will have eating and swallowing difficulties, however if you do, early referral to a speech and language therapist is essential.

Following assessment the therapist can advise on:

- a safe swallow, to avoid food or liquid from 'going down the wrong way' and into the airways
- dribbling or drooling of saliva, food or liquid from the mouth
- the best posture and position whilst eating and drinking
- the most appropriate texture, consistency and temperature of food and liquids
- the rate of eating and drinking
- the most appropriate size of a mouthful of food
- special equipment
- special exercises and swallowing techniques
- tablets for difficulties with swallowing and the use of liquid medication

Speech and language therapists often work closely with doctors, dieticians, physiotherapists, occupational therapists and pharmacists, to maintain a safe, enjoyable and social environment for eating and drinking, and to provide useful information and support for partners and carers.

For more information see Chapter 10 'Diet', page 87.

How Parkinson's can negatively affect communication

Movement of the structures involved in speaking
- muscle rigidity of the lips, tongue, palate or lower jaw can cause speech to be less clear
- it may be difficult to initiate speech or respond promptly to a question, even though you know what you want to say and have heard and understood what others are saying to you
- you may stop, unintentionally, in the middle of a sentence, just like 'freezing' in the middle of walking

Breath control
- breathing may be weaker and more shallow, and you may not have sufficient breath to adequately support your speech, so sounds will be softer and hoarser
- speech may become more rapid and indistinct, with the words running into each other, if you try to get all the words out in one breath

Expression and flow of speech
- slowness of movement can affect the way speech sounds and some people describe their voice as being monotonous and lacking expression
- there may be an inability to emphasise important words
- if you need to take extra breaths this will interrupt the smooth flow of speech
- sometimes a repetition of syllables, words or phrases occurs, which will disrupt the flow of speech

Speech rhythm
- speech may sometimes be slow, or it may accelerate, with the words 'running away' from you, in the same way that steps can do in the middle of walking
- speech may be monotonous and lose its musicality

Facial expression and body language

- muscle rigidity and difficulty in initiating a movement can affect the muscles of the face and the body, reducing facial expression[1], gestures and body language. This apparent lack of response may be misunderstood and misinterpreted by others as apathy and disinterest
- poor posture and a stooped position may make eye contact difficult

Hearing

- hearing is not affected by Parkinson's but can be affected by age, and Parkinson's is more prevalent in the elderly population
- an older partner or carer may have difficulty hearing you if your speech is soft or quiet

A command of language

- command of language is not normally affected by Parkinson's
- however, some people experience a slowing down of their thought processes (bradyphrenia) in the same way that they may experience a slowness of movement (bradykinesia)
- research has shown that some people with Parkinson's have difficulty in interpreting the tone and expression in other people's speech. For example, sarcasm may be lost on them and the use of hesitation and emphasis may be confusing.

Side effects of medication

- abnormal, involuntary movements (dyskinesias) may result in the body, shoulders and head being turned away during speech and may make eye contact extremely difficult
- abnormal movements of the face and tongue can impair clarity of speech
- a severe 'off' period, which some people liken to a light switch suddenly being turned off, can make speech, facial expression and body language temporarily impossible

authors: - Mrs J. Hearne, Parkinson's Disease
Nurse Specialist, Department of
Neurology, Queen Elizabeth Hospital,
Birmingham, UK
- Mrs S. Preston, (former) Parkinson's
Disease Nurse Specialist, Ealing &
Hammersmith Health Authority, UK

20

Parkinson's Disease Nurse Specialists

Summary

This chapter describes what a Parkinson's Disease nurse specialist (PDNS) can do to help you, and what you have to do to obtain that help.

A Parkinson's Disease nurse specialist is a nurse who has specialised in the nursing of people with Parkinson's. The PDNS can help you with the following:

- the PDNS can assist you with your reconciliation with the diagnosis, for example with advice or with additional information on Parkinson's.
- the PDNS can help you to cope with Parkinson's and all its facets. For example: give you a great deal of information on the medication. This is called 'maintenance therapy'. It will enable you to control your complaints to the best of your ability.
- The PDNS is also able to anticipate actions needed should your complaints become more severe and can help you to prepare for this, for example by recommending that you consult particular specialists.

This chapter describes what a Parkinson's Disease nurse specialist (PDNS) can do to help you, and what you have to do to obtain that help.

A Parkinson's Disease nurse specialist is a nurse who has specialised in the nursing of people with Parkinson's. The PDNS can help you with the following:

- the PDNS can assist you with your reconciliation with the diagnosis, for example with advice or with additional information on Parkinson's.
- the PDNS can help you to cope with Parkinson's and all its facets. For example: give you a great deal of information on the medication. This is called 'maintenance therapy'. It will enable you to control your complaints to the best of your ability.
- The PDNS is also able to anticipate actions needed should your complaints become more severe and can help you to prepare for this, for example by recommending that you consult particular specialists.

Introduction

In the UK today there is a growing number of Parkinson's Disease Nurse Specialists (PDNS). They are highly qualified, well experienced and in a unique position of being able to concentrate on one disease in great depth. This means that if there is a PDNS in your area, they will be able to offer you, your carers, friends and family expert care and advice. PDNSs also act as a resource to other health or social care professionals.

The care and advice they provide is given in a logical, holistic manner which is sensitive to your needs. It can be divided into four main areas:

- Early advice after diagnosis
- Maintenance therapy
- Anticipatory care
- Palliative care
- other duties
- Referral to the PDNS

"The Parkinson's nurse now visits us regularly at home. She suggested a new tablet and some changes to the timing of the others. I now sleep through the night - something I haven't done for years - and this also means my wife gets a good night's sleep. She brought us hope and made a tremendous difference."

Early advice after diagnosis

The PDNS can give you, and those closest to you, the time you need to understand and accept the implications of the diagnosis. This takes the form of education and counselling at this difficult and sensitive stage when many of your values and hopes for the future are being challenged. The PDNS can help to guide you through this maze offering general advice on a healthy lifestyle as well as very specific advice on Parkinson's disease itself.

The PDNS will perform an in-depth assessment of your needs using sometimes quite complex questionnaires. This ensures that a specific baseline of information is recorded and will help in the future management of every aspect of the condition and your care.

Maintenance therapy

The PDNS will become a key player, with you, in the management of your Parkinson's, re-assessing or reviewing you as required and making timely referrals to the other members of the multidisciplinary team such as physiotherapists, speech and language therapists, etc. Information will be given on an individual basis to you, your carer or your friends and family as appropriate, to ensure that you maintain your independence. Confidentiality is respected at all times.

Advice can be given on every aspect of Parkinson's including the symptoms, treatment and the specific sources of advice, and information or facilities available in your own locality.

158

The PDNS is an expert on the practical manipulation of drug therapy, its complications and side effects, for example and can give advice on the timing of doses of medicine. Under locally agreed protocols the PDNS can titrate your medication to ensure that you are gaining the maximum benefit, using the minimum dose of the best medicines for you. The PDNS will monitor the effect of drug therapy and can be a source of advice for other health professionals regarding when to initiate or stop medication.

Anticipatory care

Over time the PDNS has become an expert in anticipating what pitfalls you may encounter or any problems you might have. It is his job to try to ensure these problems are minimised. For example if new medication is prescribed, the PDNS will confidently tell you if it is likely to make you feel dizzy, therefore requiring you to take time rising from a bed or chair to prevent you falling. Problems can be anticipated and measures can be taken to avoid difficulties wherever possible. Some PDNSs run, or help to co-ordinate, education sessions or classes where you can learn about the disease, the treatments, who can help you with specific problems and many more useful pieces of information.

Palliative care

The PDNS will continue with his individual assessment of your needs, which can become much more complex as Parkinson's progresses. He will advise you and other professionals involved in your care, on the most appropriate placement of services and care for you, at the same time ensuring that your own opinions are valued. Maintenance of independence and dignity are of the utmost importance.

Other duties

In your area the PDNSs may not only be involved in the direct care of patients, but may also have other duties. They often take part in clinical audit, and in the setting of standards of care. This ensures that you receive the best care available. Sometimes they teach formally at University or College courses. Local Health Authorities value expert opinions, meaning that the PDNSs can be involved in groups whose function is to collate your opinions and then pass this information on to people who are in a position to make changes to the way services are provided in your area. The PDNSs also have a professional obligation to ensure that they have up to the minute information on Parkinson's and its treatment. To do this they have to attend conferences, courses and study days.

159

"My father has Parkinson's, but the PDNS, each time she comes, also asks me whether I am all right. She has really helped me with my father. At first he was pretty unhelpful and seemed to regard everything I did as my duty. But the nurse used to make a point of telling him that he was very lucky to have me looking after him. Also, when we got the hoist and the other aids, the nurse told him it was for me as well as him, because I was just as important.

Another marvellous thing about the nurse and doctor is, that they always insist I know best about his condition. They always ask me for my opinion and often tell me that I am the expert and not them. It makes you feel you are doing a job which is worthwhile and that you count for something." [1]

Referral to the PDNS

Unfortunately, PDNSs are not yet available in every area, and where they are they may operate in different ways, according to local needs. Some are based in hospitals, some are in the community visiting people at home and some span both hospital and community. Others are involved in research projects connected with their role, the disease or drugs. You can sometimes access the PDNS via your GP, sometimes via the consultant or specialist you visit and some PDNSs can be contacted directly. Each area has a different system. Your local branch of the Parkinson's Disease Society may be able to help you access this service if you are having difficulty in your locality.

The PDNS is not a magic solution to all your problems. They can, however, offer you time to talk, listen and advise - a rare commodity these days! The PDNS can also offer continuity of care and be a link with other members of the multidisciplinary team. The PDNS provides a flexible, accessible, user-friendly service, that can offer you expert advice on your condition and treatment, and be a resource to you, your carer and your family.

author: - Mrs P. Smith, (former) Director of
Operations, The Parkinson's Disease
Society of the United Kingdom, UK
advisor: - Mrs R. Maguire, Clinical Nurse Specialist,
Cornwall Health Care Trust, UK

21

Care in a hospital

Summary

You may be admitted to hospital. This may be because of the Parkinson's, but it can also be for other reasons. In either case it's worth making a number of preparations.

It is for example advisable that you take all your medication, together with a list of the doses and times you take them, and any portable aids or equipment you use at home. When you are admitted, a nurse and then a doctor will take your full medical history. Tell them about your medication and any particular difficulties or help that you need.

You can obtain from the PDS a form on which you can list a number of important facts, such as a brief account of your medication and complaints.

You yourself can do much to contribute to your successful progress during your stay in hospital. Try not to 'just go with the flow', but try rather to exercise as much influence as possible on your treatment. If you remain active, more attention will be given to your complaints and wishes, and your recovery will probably be more rapid.

161

Introduction

This chapter looks at some of the concerns people have about going into hospital. It gives information about certain hospital procedures and offers some suggestions about ways you can help yourself, or help your partner or relative with Parkinson's.

The following subjects are introduced:
- Going into hospital
- Speech and communication difficulties
- Surgery and anaesthetics
- Drug trials
- Making a complaint
- Opportunities to access other professional help

- Discharge from hospital
- Patients and Professionals - a partnership

"It's either feast or famine. I had to wait weeks for an examination. Then suddenly the hospital rang to say that I could go in in two days."

Many people with Parkinson's are anxious about going into hospital where they will be away from their usual surroundings and routines. You may be particularly concerned that you will not be able to take your tablets at the times you need them, or that the staff will not understand your particular difficulties and that sometimes you can do things for yourself, while at other times you cannot.

If you are admitted to a ward which specialises in Parkinson's this usually means that the staff will have a good understanding of your condition and the need for accurate timing of your medication. However, if you are admitted for a medical or surgical condition that is not related to Parkinson's, or for respite care to give your partner a break from caring, then the ward staff may not be aware that Parkinson's is very complex and affects people very differently. They may also have an established procedure whereby they give out tablets every four hours on the drug round and this may not be at all appropriate if you have a complicated drug regime.

162

"The doctor and I spent ages working out the doses and timing of my tablets. Then I went into hospital and they took them all away. They just brought them round on the trolley about every 4 hours. When I don't have my tablets on time my Parkinson's is terrible."

Going into hospital

Try to take into hospital all the things that will make your stay as comfortable as possible. Take all your medication, together with a list of the doses and times that you take them, and any portable aids or equipment that you use at home. When you are admitted a nurse and then a doctor will take your full medical history. Tell them you have Parkinson's - whatever the reason for your stay. Tell them about your medication and any particular difficulties or help that you need.

The Parkinson's Disease Society has a leaflet entitled "Going into Hospital or Respite Care" which gives information to hospital staff about Parkinson's and the importance of accurate timing and dosage of medication. Attached to the leaflet is a very helpful form that you or your partner can complete prior to admission:

Information for Use on Admission to Hospital or Respite Care

If you have Parkinson's and are to be admitted to hospital or having respite care, you may find it helpful to complete this form, giving details of your drug regime and other relevant information which you consider would be helpful to the nursing staff responsible for your care.

Details of Personal Care

Name .... Date ....

The following drug(s) have been prescribed. It is important that they are taken at the time indicated.

Doses and time

DRUG NAME	DOSE	TIME

ACTIVITY	ASSISTANCE REQUIRED/AIDS USED
Speech	
Comprehension	
Eating/Drinking	
Walking	
Washing/Bathing	
Dressing	
Turning Over In Bed	
Bowels/Bladder	
Other Information	

Please use the continuation section on the back of this form if necessary

163

Many hospitals now have a named nurse, or a small team of nurses, who care for an individual patient. This ensures that they get to know your special needs. Some hospital wards have a self-medication policy, which means that you can keep control of your tablets and take them when you need them.[1] There is also a growing number of Parkinson's Disease Nurse Specialists throughout the country, some of whom are based in hospitals. If you or your partner have concerns you can ask if there is a Parkinson's Disease Nurse Specialist who could visit you on the ward and liaise with the staff.

Speech and communication difficulties

Some people with Parkinson's have difficulty communicating their thoughts, feelings and needs to others because of speech problems or loss of 'body language'. Going into hospital and being cared for by people who may not understand you, will therefore cause you and you relatives additional concern. Your partner, a relative or friend can discuss your particular needs with the ward staff to ensure you have your medication on time and any other help you require. If you use communication aids at home, for example communication cards or a lightwriter, ensure that you take them with you into hospital. Your relative or partner could also ask for a Speech and Language Therapist to visit you, to assess what help you need and to liaise appropriately with the ward staff.

Surgery and anaesthetics

Some people have reported that anaesthetics, during surgical procedures, adversely affect the symptoms of their Parkinson's. Whether this is so or not is still unclear. It may be that because patients have 'nil by mouth' before surgery, the withdrawal of medication for long periods before an operation is the cause of difficulty. It is important for you or your partner to talk to the staff to confirm how important your medication is for the control of your Parkinson's symptoms. Tablets should be withdrawn for only the shortest period of time possible. However, if severe immobility and muscle rigidity occurs and you are unable to take medication by mouth, an apomorphine injection may act as a short term 'rescue remedy'.[2] If you are already under the care of a Parkinson's Disease Nurse Specialist, or one is based in the hospital, they will be able to liase with the surgical staff.

Drug Trials

If your Parkinson's is not well controlled and you are admitted to hospital under the care of a Neurologist or Physician in Care of the Elderly, you might be asked if you would like to take part in the trial of a new drug. Research to develop new drugs is very important and only when laboratory tests on new substances have been completed will a doctor consider testing the drug on their patients. Before taking part in any drug trial however, you should always be given information (spoken and written) and plenty of time to discuss the possible benefits and adverse effects with the consultant and your family. No one should put pressure on you to take part in or continue a drug trial if you decide not to.[3] For more information see page 29.

Making a Complaint

If you are unhappy with any aspect of the care you receive while in hospital you, or a relative or friend, should first discuss it with the person concerned or your named nurse. It is often possible to resolve misunderstandings in this way, without taking further action. However, if you are not satisfied, or the problem continues, you should make a complaint. Hospitals are obliged to publish their complaints procedure so that they can deal appropriately with problems that are brought to their attention. You shouldn't be afraid to make a complaint - it is in everyone's interest to improve standards of care where necessary.

Some hospitals have a leaflet which explains what you should do and who you should contact if you wish to complain. Your local Community Health Council will also advise you and if necessary will act as your 'friend', preparing correspondence or accompanying you to meetings. If you wish to make a complaint, ideally you should: complain as soon as possible after the incident; always be courteous and provide accurate details of the incident (date, time, place, people involved).[4]

> *"The nurses were really kind - but they didn't understand that he needed his tablets at odd times, or that sometimes he could do things and other times he just couldn't."*

Opportunities to access other professional help

Whatever the reason for your stay in hospital, it can provide you with the opportunity of gaining access to a range of professional help for your Parkinson's. A number of specialists and professionals allied to medicine will be based in the hospital setting. If you have a particular difficulty, and you are not already receiving treatment or help, you or your partner can ask for a visit from the appropriate person. For example:

DIFFICULTY	PROFESSIONAL HELP
Poorly controlled Parkinson's, Adverse Drug Side Effects, Depression, Confusion	Neurologist, Physician in Care of the Elderly, Parkinson's Disease Nurse Specialist
Mobility	Physiotherapist
Speech	Speech and Language Therapist
Swallowing	Speech and Language Therapist, Dietician
Independent living	Occupational Therapist, Social Worker
Constipation, Weight Loss	Dietician

Incontinence	Urologist, Continence Advisor
Financial Help	Social Worker
Leisure activities	Occupational Therapist
Emotional Difficulties, Relationships	Social Worker, Counsellor
Carers' Support	Parkinson's Disease Nurse Specialist, Social Worker

The professional concerned can visit you on the ward and undertake an assessment of your needs. If necessary they may arrange to keep in touch with you as an outpatient, or refer you to the appropriate community-based person for follow-up after your discharge from hospital.

Discharge from Hospital

If you or your relatives are concerned about how you will manage when you are discharged from hospital you should talk to the nursing staff on the ward and ask to see the Social Worker. Since April 1993 all hospitals must have an approved discharge policy which ensures that people are not returned home without the support or services they need. The Social Worker can carry out a full Community Care Assessment which should identify the help you and your carer require. It must also take into account how both you and your carer view the situation and how you feel about the outcome and recommendations of the assessment.

If you normally live alone and/or need full time care, it is possible that your hospital doctor may recommend you are discharged from an acute medical or surgical bed to a nursing or residential care home (see Chapter 22 'Care in a Residential or Nursing Home'). If this is not in line with your, or your relatives' plans for the future you should again insist on a full Community Care Assessment to see if alternative arrangements can be made. No one should put pressure on you to be discharged home or into residential accommodation without the time and information you and your family need to make an informed and appropriate decision.

Patients and Professionals - A Partnership

Many people find that when they go into hospital they take on the *passive* role of 'patient', undergoing treatment from doctors and nurses who are *active* in curing illness and administering care. Research has shown that when patients resign themselves passively to treatment without trying to influence their own situation, it can have a negative effect on their health. When hospital staff involve patients, by giving them information and enabling them to play an active part in decisions about the management of their illness, they cope better, recover more rapidly and have fewer relapses.[5]

Try to remember that you are not just a 'patient' - you are a unique individual, with your own personality, history and achievements. You have a wealth of experience about the way Parkinson's affects you. Form a 'partnership' with the professionals and take an active role in decisions which will influence your health and your well-being.

author: - J. Koops, M.D., physician at the Nieuw
           Unicum Nursing Home, the Netherlands
advisors:- Mrs R. Hayward, Placement Advisor,
           Parkinson's Disease Society , UK
         - F.M. Helmer, Board Member of the
           General Dutch Union of Senior Citizens,
           the Netherlands

22

Care in a residential home or nursing home

Summary

When the complaints become very severe it may become impossible to manage on one's own. Admission to a residential home or nursing home may then be the solution. To some people this may sound disturbing, but is however often the best solution.

You can make your admission easier by preparing as thoroughly as possible for it. You can for example begin by gathering information. Most homes have a brochure with house rules. It is possible to pay a visit beforehand. Agreeing a trial period before making a definite decision might also be a worthwhile option.

When you have finally been admitted, you'll need time to adjust. You're suddenly living in a different environment, with different people and rules that you are not accustomed to. In most homes, much is done to make the residents feel welcome. For example, recreation receives a great deal of attention.

The extent to which costs are reimbursed will depend on your income and capital. If you cannot afford to pay for residence yourself, you can obtain financial assistance from Social Services.

Introduction

Sometimes a person with Parkinson's disease can no longer be cared for at home if they need a great deal of care and they live alone or their family and friends are unable to provide the support needed. It may be necessary for the person to be admitted to a nursing or residential care home for either a short stay or longer.

This chapter covers:
- Information in advance
- What kind of people live in residential or nursing homes?
- What are the choices for non-residential care?
- What happens before you are admitted?

- What care and treatment will you receive?
- Living in a home
- Making your opinions known
- The costs
- Income
- Property

Many people are apprehensive about the thought of going into a care home. It is a major change that means leaving your familiar environment without knowing when or if you will be able to return. It means entering a home that is full of unknown people, where you may have to share a room with another resident. Will you be able to get on with him? You will be cared for by people who do not know you. Will they know what's good for you and understand your special needs?

If you need reassurance on these points, you should discuss them with your doctor, district nurse or Parkinson's Disease Nurse Specialist or with a carer or friend.

"I like it here. The nurses are kind and they work hard. Sometimes the doctor chats to me. The speech therapist has taught me how to improve my speech. I don't have any problems with my roommate and the food's good. It's also easier for my wife. At a certain point it really got too much for her to cope with. She visits me now three times a week, although each time she finds it quite an undertaking. No, I can't complain, but I do miss home".

169

Information in advance

Before you make arrangements to enter a residential or nursing home, you can ask to receive information about the homes in your area. Your local Social Services department or your Health Authority will be able to provide you with information about the homes. The Parkinson's Disease Society also has a database containing information about homes in some parts of the country.

Residential homes offer accommodation for people who are unable to manage everyday tasks (i.e. cooking and housework) or to continue living independently in their own home, but do not need nursing care.

Nursing homes offer 24-hour care with trained nursing staff in attendance.

If you wish to move to another part of the country to be nearer to your family, you will need to make these enquiries in the area you wish to move to. You can contact homes directly in order to gain more detailed information. Most homes provide a booklet that gives information on the services and accommodation they provide.

Before you are admitted you should look around the home in advance. If you are unable to do this yourself, then you can ask someone else to make the visit on your behalf. Often the manager or matron will visit you in your own home.

If you are planning to take up permanent residence in a care home, it is a good idea to stay there for a trial period before making your final decision. This will allow you to experience the quality of care provided by the staff, and assess whether they could cater for your needs if you require additional care in the future.

You might like to find out if the home has a commitment to training or if the staff understand Parkinson's. Training courses for nursing and residential home staff designed to raise awareness about the medical, social and personal needs of people with Parkinson's, are available and the Parkinson's Disease Society has a list of homes where staff have attended training. A training video called 'Just a little more time' and an information document called 'Caring for People with Parkinson's Disease' have been especially produced for nursing and residential home care staff and are available from the Society[1].

Counsel and Care publish a fact sheet that could be useful, entitled 'What to look for in a Care Home'.[2]

"I think I've been lucky with my nursing home. It's close by and not too big. There are even some old acquaintances of mine working there. That makes a difference. Actually, sometimes it is hard for my wife, because she has to organise all kinds of things on her own: visiting me, things at home like my administration and the garden. But she does it perfectly. The people in the home sometimes call her my 'personal manager'!"

What kind of people live in residential or nursing homes?

Mostly elderly people are admitted to a home because they are no longer able to look after themselves due to illness or disability. In circumstances where type or quality of care is more important than location, you may wish to look at particular options. The Leonard Cheshire Foundation has homes that are geared towards younger residents. There is a residential home for people with Parkinson's in Walsall, West Midlands, UK. Nearly all homes for people with specialised needs have waiting lists.[3]

What are the choices for non-residential care?

Not everyone spends their days and nights in a care home. Some people can be treated as outpatients. They stay only during the day or for just a few hours. The treatment and care they receive mean they can continue to live at home.

Sometimes a person with Parkinson's will only need to be admitted to a residential or nursing home for a short period of time (e.g. a week). This will give the carers an opportunity to relax and avoid burnout. This arrangement is called respite care. Ask your Social Services department, your doctor or Health Authority for further information.

What happens before you are admitted?

Choosing an appropriate care home can take time. It is important to consider the options and choices in advance, rather than in a moment of crisis. If you feel you might need residential care you should ask for your care needs to be assessed by your local Social Services department. They will carry out a care assessment of your needs and will consider what sort of help and support you need. Your views and preferences, together with the views of your partner/family should also be taken into account. From all this information Social Services will be able to advise you on what community care services they can offer you in your own home, or whether you need a place in a residential or nursing home.

When the local authority is arranging or providing a place, they are legally bound to carry out a 'means test' of your income and capital to calculate how much you must pay towards the cost. For more information, see 'The costs' later in the chapter.

What care and treatment will you receive?

Before you are admitted to either a nursing or residential care home, you should be consulted about your medical, nursing and specialist needs by the home manager or matron. This discussion with you and your carer/family will result in your own, individual care plan being compiled, to ensure you receive the treatment and care you need.

It is important that you receive your medication at the time you need it and this may not fit in with the standard, routine drug rounds in some homes. Ensure that you take a list of your tablets, and the times you should take them, to the manager or matron. The Parkinson's Disease Society produces a fact sheet 'Going into Hospital or Respite Care' which incudes a very useful form about your drug treatment and other needs. See Chapter 21 *'Care in a Hospital'*. This form would be equally useful to take into a care home.

Most care homes should have access to various forms of therapy, such as physiotherapy, speech therapy and occupational therapy, but you will need to confirm this.

You should be able to remain on your own GP's list, and in contact with your previous consultant or therapists if you remain a resident in your local area. However, sometimes admission to a care home means that the home's doctor will replace your GP. You should check this out with the home and healthcare pro-fessionals involved.

Living in a home

Residential and nursing homes try to make their residents feel as much at home as possible. Generally you will have your own room, or share with one other person. There will be a day room or lounge where you can meet your guests and other residents. You can have visitors at any time of the day. Make sure there is somewhere you can have some privacy, either on your own, or with a guest, if you want it.

It is important that residents can relax and socialise with one another at times. This can be stimulated in some homes by activity leaders, who organise events such as handicraft sessions, games, reading aloud, cooking and baking, videos and reminiscence sessions. Other staff members and possibly volunteers may also be involved.

Activities and outings can vary from shopping trips to a week's holiday in a suitable resort. Many homes encourage visitors to participate in activities and meals, particularly on birthdays and holidays. Sometimes visitors may be able to stay overnight or for weekends.

Making your opinions known

Always remember that you are still in control of everything that happens to you, whether or not you are living in a residential or nursing home. Ensure that the home has an established complaints procedure and a residents committee so that your voice can be heard on matters that are important to you. Discuss any medical procedures and treatments proposed and think about whether you want to undergo them. You have the right to refuse anything you feel is unnecessary although you should also explain your reasons for refusing. Bear in mind, however, that some treatments can only be given after certain tests have been made.

Any information that you give to the manager/matron or any other staff members is strictly confidential. For further information see Chapter 26, 'Patients' and carers' rights'.

The costs

If you can afford to pay your own fees for a place in a residential or nursing home, you are free to make your own arrangements to enter the home. Most people will be expected to pay towards the cost of their care, but some people may have their care paid for by the local authority. If you need financial support from the local authority, you will need to be assessed by the Social Services department. You do not have to choose a home suggested by Social Services; you can choose a different home if they can provide the care you need and will agree a contract with Social Services. Once you choose a home, the local authority will conclude a contract with the home to pay the costs but will means-test your income and savings to assess how much you can pay towards the cost.

Who Pays?

If you cannot afford to pay the full costs, Social Services will pay part of the fees and you will pay the rest. You can get help with this. For information on welfare benefits, see Chapter 25 'Welfare Benefits'. The Health Authority may pay for people who have continuing health care needs, and meet the authority's eligibility criteria.

How much help with funding can you get?

There are no set limits on how much will be paid for each type of care. The local authority should fund you to a level that will pay for the type of care you need in the home where you live. Different local authorities operate differently, however, and pay varying rates. You can choose a more expensive home if you, a relative or friend is willing to pay the extra cost.

How much will you pay towards your care costs?

Social Services financial assessment will show how much you can contribute towards your care. If you are receiving financial help from Social Services, you will be expected to contribute all your income except your personal allowance. You need to know from Social Services what the threshold is on income, savings and capital in order to know how much you need to contribute towards the costs.

Income

The local authority will look at your income as part of the means test and will expect you to claim all the state benefits you are entitled to, including Income Support, to pay your share of the fees. The social worker will help and advise you on this if necessary.

Property

If you have property in which you do not live, its value can be counted as capital. If the value is more than a certain amount you will not be entitled to Income Support.

Your property will be disregarded for six months or longer if you are trying to sell it. You will not be expected to sell your property and it will not count as capital if your partner, or close relative over 60 or sick or disabled relative continues to live in it. However, it is likely that the property will be considered as capital, once the estate is sold.

Respite care

If you want to stay in a home for a brief stay you can arrange your own respite care if you can pay the fees. The local authority is not obliged to help you if your stay is less than eight weeks. However some authorities will help with the costs. You need to ask your local Social Services department about the respite care arrangements in your area.[4]

Further detailed information on local authority charging procedures are available from Counsel and Care[5], and Age Concern.[6]

Addresses

Age Concern
Astral House
1268 London Road
London SW16 4ER

Counsel & Care
Twyman House
16 Bonny Street
London NW1 9PG

author: - E. Ernst, Director, Department of
Complementary Medicine, Postgraduate
Medical School, University of Exeter, UK
advisor: - Mrs R. Brown, UK

23

Complementary therapy for Parkinson's?

Summary

Many people with Parkinson's turn to complementary therapies, despite the fact that there is no complementary therapy that can cure Parkinson's. People have their own individual reasons for this: the therapy may fit in better with their life style, they are disappointed with conventional medical science, they find that it helps to alleviate specific complaints, etc.

This chapter will address the effects of many complementary therapies on Parkinson's: from acupuncture to aromatherapy and from massage to yoga.

If you are considering taking complementary therapy, you should bear the following in mind:
- Use therapists who belong to a credible professional association or society.
- Ensure that there is contact between your regular therapist and your complementary therapists.
- Ask for a clear treatment plan and an estimate of the costs.
- Be suspicious of therapists who claim that they can cure Parkinson's or who want you to dissociate yourself from other therapists or carers.

Introduction

Complementary medicine (CM), sometimes also less aptly called 'alternative medicine', remains a highly controversial issue. Some believe in it almost in a religious sense, others condemn it outright as pure quackery. Notwithstanding this long-standing debate, CM has become immensely popular in recent years. Estimates vary but some suggest that about half of the general population is using some form of CM. Individuals living with chronic diseases like Parkinson's are even more likely to try CM.

This chapter offers information on:
1 Cure versus care
2 Complementary therapies
  a Acupuncture
  b Aromatherapy
  c Healing
  d Herbalism
  e Homoeopathy
  f Massage
  g Reflexology
  h Spinal manipulation
  i Special diets
  j Supplements
  k Yoga
3 Treatments to avoid
4 How to find a therapist

One may well ask, why is it so popular? It seems almost ironic that people are turning away from modern medicine just as it is becoming successful as never before. The reasons for CM's popularity are certainly complex. Maybe people want to try everything possible to get well and many could be disillusioned with mainstream medicine in spite of its powerful drugs. Generally speaking, those individuals with chronic ailments for which mainstream medicine does not offer a cure are most likely to try their luck with CM.

Therefore, if you have Parkinson's disease you are bound to be tempted. Even though exact figures are still missing, we suspect that many people with Parkinson's have tried some form of CM. From a recent survey done by the Parkinson's Disease Society Complementary Therapy Working Group[1], it is clear that about 65% of their members (the questionnaire was returned by 2,274 people with Parkinson's) have an interest in complementary therapies.

In this chapter you will find some simple information about CM in relation to Parkinson's. It will guide you to therapies that might be worth trying.

> *"A person is not just a person plus an illness. A person is a whole thing, and it's inside that whole thing that you've developed an illness. This makes you ask all sorts of questions about yourself, but I'm prepared to work at them. For me, just having a medical specialist is not enough."*

1 Cure versus care

In Britain, CM is practised mostly by non-medically trained practitioners. That is not to say that some CM providers are not competently trained, but many have little training and few will fully understand the complexities of your disease. It is important therefore that you do not abandon prescribed drugs, that you continue to see your doctor and that you tell him/her exactly what form of CM you are using. Unfortunately some CM practitioners might advise otherwise but such advice is not trustworthy. Remember that 'complementary' means that which fills out or makes whole: complementary medicine does not replace orthodox medicine.

Some CM providers might raise your hopes and promise a cure. No form of CM can cure Parkinson's. People who tell you otherwise are either naive or deliberately misleading you. In both cases they are endangering your health.

Nevertheless, CM could still have something to offer you. There is an important difference between cure and care. CM can't cure Parkinson's but, in many cases, it may ease your symptoms and help you to cope with your condition. In Table 1 later in this chapter you will find a list of symptoms that occur often with Parkinson's and which might be amenable to complementary therapies.

2 Complementary therapies
CM comprises a confusing array of treatments.
The following will give you a very brief introduction to the therapies that you are likely to encounter and some indication as to which are worth trying for what symptom, what the scientific evidence for or against tells us, and what costs you may incur.

a) Acupuncture
This ancient form of treatment has been practised in China for over 2000 years. It has become highly popular in the West since the '70s. Traditional acupuncturists believe in a 'life force' called Chi. If it is disturbed, illness will result. To re-balance it, acupuncturists stick thin needles in 'acupoints' which are situated along meridians, the channels for the flow of Chi. Western 'scientific' acupuncturists are not entirely convinced of this, but think that acupuncture operates through definable neurophysiological principles.

The evidence for whether or not acupuncture works better than a placebo is far from straightforward. (A placebo is a harmless, inactive substance or procedure; any positive effect comes from the patient's belief in it.) Optimists would say acupuncture works for chronic pain. If you have pain, you simply want to get rid of it and you don't care whether this is through the help of a placebo effect. Preliminary data from the PDS survey show that the majority of people with Parkinson's (about 60%) experienced at least a slight benefit from acupuncture. In other words, acupuncture is worth a try. It does carry certain risks though. These may be minimal, but you should make sure that your acupuncturist has adequate training and experience and uses only disposable needles. Costs per session can amount to a substantial sum, because the acupuncturist will point out that you need a whole series of treatments. If you do not perceive any benefit after, say the third session, you might consider giving it up.

"I don't usually go in for that sort of thing. I've got Parkinson's and I've got to learn to live with it. But I'm not prepared to accept that I'm as stiff as I am now. That's why I went looking for alternative treatment in addition to what I was getting from the specialist. I went to a magnetiser who tried to pass some of his energy on to me. I have to admit that in the last few weeks I've felt less stiff. But that could also be because I've been using essential oils."

b) Aromatherapy

Aromatherapists use essential oils from plants that are particularly suited to you. They massage (massage therapy is discussed below) them into your skin, put them into your bath or just let you smell them. In any case, the effect can be an intense and most agreeable relaxation. There is no scientific evidence that aromatherapy is specifically effective in treating Parkinson's. In the PDS survey more than 80% of people with Parkinson's thought that aromatherapy had helped them at least slightly. If relaxation is what you need, there is little reason not to try it. Aromatherapy does not have any serious side effects. Some oils are expensive and are charged as extra. You may also gain benefit from buying essential oils and using them at home. This would be much cheaper than seeing an aromatherapist.

c) Healing

Healers plug into a 'source of energy' in order to enhance your body's self-healing. No one (not even the healers) can define this energy. Some patients swear by it. They feel less ill and more relaxed or they can cope better with their problems or they experience a new sense of well-being. In the survey of people with Parkinson's some 80% had experienced at least a slight benefit from healing. Scientifically, however, there is little hard evidence to suggest that healing has specific effects. However, if it helps you, why not? If nothing else, healing is safe. Many healers don't even take money.

d) Herbalism

Plants can provide powerful remedies. Unfortunately, there is no herb that specifically cures Parkinson's. Yet, depending on your main symptom, a herbalist may be able to offer some help. For instance, Ginkgo biloba has been shown to help concentration although there are no trials on Parkinson's patients as yet. Therefore, it is not clear whether it will alleviate lack of concentration if this becomes a problem for you. At the very least, however, Ginkgo biloba is almost entirely free of serious side effects.

Other people with Parkinson's may feel tired and worn out. There are several herbal tonics that might help. Ginseng is perhaps the best known. It is worth a try, but be sure to observe the recommended dosage. Ginseng does have a number of unwanted side effects, particularly as it may be addictive, when you overdose.

Many people with Parkinson's feel depressed. If this becomes a problem, you could try St John's Wort (Hypericum). It has been conclusively shown to ease mild to moderate forms of depression. Unfortunately, there have not been any trials on Parkinson's so far. If used for long periods it may make the skin extra sensitive to sunlight.

All three herbal remedies are available in pharmacies and health food shops without prescription. If you decide to try any such treatment, make sure you tell your doctor about it.

In Britain, herbalism is very much under-rated. However, it is potentially useful for a variety of symptoms. In the PDS survey about 50% of people with Parkinson's experienced at least a slight benefit from herbalism. However, being powerful, many herbs are also associated with side effects. Some of these can be serious. So if you see a herbalist, make sure it is a reputable one and discuss it with your doctor. Some herbal prescriptions are costly and the total expenses can add up quickly.

e) Homoeopathy

Homoeopaths insist that they do not treat diseases but individuals. Thus many would assume that they should be able to help you quite regardless of your condition. Scientifically speaking, it is still an unanswered question whether homoeopathic remedies, which are highly diluted, are more than placebos. The fact is, however, that many patients (in the PDS survey the figure was about 60%) experience at least a slight improvement of their symptoms after consulting a homoeopath. They do not worry whether this is due to a placebo effect. People with Parkinson's often suffer from cramps, and there is some preliminary evidence that the homoeopathic remedy 'Cuprum' helps for this symptom. There is little reason to fear serious side effects from homoeopathic treatments. Since consultations with a homoeopath take a lot of time, therapy is not cheap.

f) Massage

Many people with Parkinson's suffer from stiffness and muscular pain. There is little doubt that massage (there are, of course, many types of massage) can be useful in easing these symptoms. A massage is also uniquely relaxing - both for the muscles and the mind. It is an altogether enjoyable experience. In the PDS survey more than 90% experienced at least a slight benefit. What is more, it is safe.

> *"I was lying there so peacefully and felt so secure because of those massaging hands, that I burst into tears. The masseuse put a warm blanket over me and just stroked my hands until I calmed down a bit. Then we carried on, very carefully, and that gave a sort of calm after the storm. After that I felt all peaceful and light."*

g) Reflexology

Reflexologists believe that your whole body is mapped out on the sole of your foot. By massaging certain areas of your foot, they hope to influence defined inner organs - including the brain. Therefore they might be optimistic about helping your Parkinson's. However, there is no evidence that it has a specific effect on your condition. Maybe there is no benefit other than relaxation. Yet, in the PDS survey about 75% of people with Parkinson's thought it was at least slightly beneficial.

h) Spinal manipulation

Chiropractic and osteopathy are similar in that both manipulate the spine in order to alleviate back- pain or other, mainly musculo-skeletal, problems. There is some evidence to show that spinal manipulation helps for acute low back-pain. For other conditions, the evidence is far less compelling or virtually non-existent.

If you suffer from low back pain, do try spinal manipulation. In the PDS survey about 75% thought it was at least slightly beneficial. However, do not believe practitioners who promise a cure for Parkinson's. We recommend that you check the qualifications of the practitioner first ,because untrained people can damage rather than help you. Some forms of spinal manipulation may be unsuitable for people with osteoporosis, which affects most women after the menopause, but many elderly men as well.

i) Special diets

Dietary treatments are mostly in the realm of mainstream medicine. But there are also some that are frequently advocated by complementary practitioners. They range from whole food to macrobiotic diets. There is no evidence that any of these is really helpful for Parkinson's. Furthermore, some of these diets can lead to serious nutritional deficiencies. This, however, does not mean that a good nutritionist cannot assist you in finding the most suitable diet. In the PDS survey about 85% felt that dietary therapy was at least slightly beneficial.

j) Supplements

The market for supplements is booming - everything from trace elements to vitamins, from herbals to fish oil. There is no compelling evidence that supplements are helpful in treating Parkinson's. Some herbal treatments (see above) may be useful for specific symptoms of Parkinson's but if you are eating a balanced diet there is normally no need for supplements.

k) Yoga

Yoga is a 'treatment package' of various elements including relaxation, breathing techniques and posture. It is conceivable that it might help the postural instability in Parkinson's. In the PDS survey about 95% of people with Parkinson's experienced at least a slight benefit from yoga. In fact, it was rated overall as the most effective of all complementary therapies. However, no hard data on scientifically proven efficacy is available at present. There are no serious side effects to be anticipated and thus yoga too might be worth a try. A practitioner will teach you the basic techniques in a series of supervised sessions.

179

Table 1

Frequent symptoms of Parkinson's that may respond to complementary therapies

Symptom	Therapy
lack of concentration	e.g. Ginkgo biloba
depression	e.g. Hypericum
postural instability	e.g. yoga
tiredness	e.g. various relaxation techniques
muscular stiffness	e.g. massage

180

"I've been getting treatment from an alternative therapist for some time and I have to admit that it's made me feel better. I didn't dare tell the GP. You might think it's silly, but I thought she might get angry with me. But one day I made a slip of the tongue and then I had to tell her. I blushed, and I felt like going to confession. But the funny thing was, she didn't get mad at me. She even told that she had once gone to an alternative therapist for advice. And I'd been worried about it for all those weeks."

3 Treatments to avoid

Understandably, people with Parkinson's often get desperate for a cure or at least some help with their symptoms. Thus you could be tempted to try treatments which, on the basis of the evidence to date, do more harm than good. More information: the PDS.

4 How to find a therapist

There are a few points that are well worth remembering if you have decided to try what CM has to offer you. The first rule should always be to avoid harm. You are well advised therefore to consider the following:

- use therapists who belong to a credible professional association or society
- discuss with your doctor what you might try with what benefit
- tell your doctor what you have opted for
- enquire about the therapist's training, clinical experience and insurance cover
- do not trust therapists who promise a cure for Parkinson's or who try to interfere with your prescribed medications
- insist on a proper treatment plan and cost estimates

Conclusions

Many people with Parkinson's are interested in complementary therapies. Even though no cure is on offer, these treatments may alleviate a variety of Parkinson's symptoms. There is little hard evidence, however. The bottom line is to be cautious yet open-minded. Discuss things with your doctor and, if no harm is conceivable, give it a try.

Recommended reading
- "Which? Guide to Complementary Medicine"
- "Alternative medicine, what works" by A. Fugh-Berman, Odonian Press, Tuscon USA, 1996
- "The alternative medicine handbook, The complete reference guide to alternative and complementary medicine", by B. Cassileth, WW Norton Co., New York, 1998.

Notes

Notes

Notes

author: - J. Bucknall, Welfare & Employment
Rights Advisor, Parkinson's Disease
Society, UK
advisor: - E. Falvey, Care Services Manager,
Parkinson's Disease Society, UK

24

Work

Summary

When you are diagnosed with Parkinson's, it does not mean that you can no longer work. Most people with Parkinson's can continue quite realistically to work for a time. This will of course depend on the severity of your complaints. It also depends on what *you* want; for some people work is very important, for others it is less so.

If the complaints become more severe, it may be necessary to have your work or workplace adapted. There is a variety of possibilities:
• Your workplace can be adapted.
• Your responsibilities can be modified.
• Your working times can be adjusted.
• You may be able to obtain a different role within the company.

You may in time decide to give up working, because the complaints interfere too much. This has far-reaching consequences, some of them financial. It is advisable not to rush this step, first weighing up the pros and cons. To help you with this you can for example talk with your medical specialist and with the Welfare & Employment Rights Officer of the PDS.

Introduction

For many people who are still working when they are diagnosed with Parkinson's disease, one of the big questions is likely to be "Can I continue to work?" Parkinson's need not mean the end of work, although it may mean changes at some point.

This chapter considers a number of options for people with Parkinson's who are still in full or part time employment:
• Parkinson's and work
• Continuing work
• Making the decision to change
• Early retirement
• Useful addresses and further information

"Being able to carry on working was really important to me. At first my Parkinson's made very little difference, but then, gradually, I found it more difficult; especially in meetings and with the journey to and from work each day I got very tired. I talked to my boss and close colleagues and fortunately they've been very understanding. With a bit of flexibility – a bit of 'give and take' – I've still got a lot to contribute."

Parkinson's and work

Most of us value work as an important part of our lives. It gives us a purpose, a feeling of worth and an important source of income. Work also helps us build and maintain social contacts and relationships and enables us to feel part of a team. However, for people coping with work and Parkinson's there may be some difficulties.

Some jobs are less compatible with Parkinson's than others, for example jobs requiring high levels of physical stamina and fast reactions.[1] Jobs which demand regular, long hours, meeting deadlines and achieving objectives, can generate stress and make the symptoms of Parkinson's more difficult to manage. Some people with Parkinson's find they can perform their duties and responsibilities to a high standard but it takes them more time, or travelling to and from work may be a problem. Others have found a lack of awareness amongst colleagues about the symptoms of Parkinson's has resulted in insensitivity and misunderstanding. For some the effort expended in fulfilling work commitments may leave little time or energy for other important aspects of their lives, such as family, friends and leisure activities.

"I've had to take sick leave, but I still work half a day a week. Before that I used to have a full-time job. I got steadily worse because of the Parkinson's so I spent the time well that was still left to me. Worked hard, earned as much as possible and paid off as much of the mortgage as we could. Fortunately we're not badly off financially. And now I only have the half day every week, but it's very important to me. It's not like it used to be, but it's one way of keeping in touch."

186

Each person with Parkinson's is an individual and so the decision to carry on or stop paid employment will depend on your individual circumstances: your age, the length of time you have had Parkinson's and how well the symptoms are controlled, the sort of work you do and your working conditions. Some people continue working for many years, others adjust or change their working situation, others decide to stop and look for new opportunities by developing hobbies or undertaking voluntary work. Whatever your decision you will need information and advice, and time to think through the costs and benefits.

Continuing work

Depending on the sort of work you do, and how well your Parkinson's is controlled you may wish to continue working for as long as possible. We recommend that you maintain good control of your symptoms by:

- regular appointments with a specialist for assessment of your Parkinson's and review of your medication
- assessment from an occupational therapist, who can help you to look at the content and structure of your work and advise you on ways to overcome practical problems
- assessment from a speech and language therapist who can help you maintain good communication skills relevant to your work
- assessment from a physiotherapist who can advise you on efficient ways of coping with the physical activities of your work

Talking about Parkinson's to people at work

Some people are reluctant to tell their employer or colleagues they have Parkinson's because of embarrassment or concerns about job security. You will need to decide the best approach in the light of your particular circumstances. However, it is usually a good idea to confide in a close colleague or your immediate manager as stress can make the symptoms of Parkinson's worse and by not having to 'cover up' you will probably be able to do your job better.[2] By explaining how the symptoms affect you and the possible effects these might, or might not, have on your work, you will avoid misunderstanding and prevent colleagues making assumptions about your abilities, based on the effects of Parkinson's on other people they may have known or read about.

Rights and responsibilities

Remember that you have rights under employment law and that your employer has responsibilities. Under the Disability Discrimination Act (see Further Information at the end of the chapter) it is unlawful for an employer with 20 or more employees to treat disabled employees less favourably than other people without justification. The Act covers every aspect of the job, including selection, promotion, redundancy and dismissal.

If your employer is not very understanding, then it is even more important to get advice on your employment rights. People who work in small organisations, or are self-employed, should seek further information about their rights and status (see Useful Addresses and Further Information at the end of the chapter).

Making the decision to change

If you feel you can no longer continue to do the job for which you were originally employed, there are a number of things you can do:

- talk to you GP or specialist
- telephone the Parkinson's Disease Society or their Helpline and ask to be referred to the Welfare & Employment Rights Advisor
- get advice from the Advisory, Conciliation and Arbitration Service (ACAS)
- get advice from a Citizens' Advice Bureau (CAB) that has an Employment Advisor or Solicitor attached to it
- talk to your personnel officer, manager or employer about the possibility of a redundancy package on medical grounds, or about options to modify your job or working conditions

Modifying your job or working conditions

It may be possible to change certain aspects of your job or conditions. For example:

- modifying your job - colleagues may be able to take over parts of your job in exchange for your taking responsibility for certain of their tasks
- reducing your hours or working flexitime
- working from home - this is no longer uncommon and does not require a great deal of expensive equipment. Home computers can be linked to those in the office.[2]
- transferring to other employment in the company
- arranging extra training

We strongly recommend that you discuss these and other possible options with someone who understands the issues involved, before committing yourself with your employer. It is also advisable to have a third party present to support and help you during your discussion with your employer, and that you ask for the details of possible options to be put in writing for your consideration.

Changing your job

If your current job becomes untenable, it may be worth looking for alternative work within the same organisation, in the first instance. Many good employers will be reluctant to lose the knowledge and experience of an existing employee and may be accommodating in finding another, more appropriate position.

If this is not possible you may decide to apply for alternative work elsewhere. You should be aware that under the Disability Discrimination Act it is unlawful for employers with 20 or more employees to discriminate against prospective employees with disabilities when filling a job. The Act does not deny the right of employers to appoint 'the best person for the job' but this must be judged on a person's knowledge, skills and performance relevant to the post. Employers are not entitled to ask questions concerning your Parkinson's at interview.

188

> *"At first I said in my job applications that I wanted to start work again despite having Parkinson's. But I was turned down every time – though they didn't say it was on health grounds. Later on I just kept quiet about my health unless they asked me straight out. That worked much better. At least I was being assessed on my qualities and not on my illness."*

Early Retirement

Retiring from work is a major change in life and should not be rushed into. You need to consider the costs and benefits very carefully. It may be tempting to opt for early retirement if you are feeling depressed or you are going through a bad patch with your Parkinson's. Take time to see your doctor or specialist, and give any new Parkinson's treatment sufficient time to have an effect before making any decisions.[2] This is not to say that leaving paid employment is the wrong decision, but you need to ensure it is right for you in the long term and that you don't make a hasty decision you might regret. The financial implications of leaving work will be very important and you need to get good advice from a competent person.

> *"After a lot of soul searching I decided to take early retirement on medical grounds. I've never looked back! I've now got the time and the energy to do other important things."*

Making the decision to retire

If you feel that giving up work is the course you wish to follow, ensure that you:

- discuss your feelings about possible early retirement with your partner, family or a trusted friend
- consult your GP or specialist and make sure that you have their support
- get advice on your employment rights (or self-employed status if appropriate)
- find out about the welfare benefits to which you may be entitled (see Chapter 25 'Welfare Benefits')
- spend some time looking at your financial situation - do you still have a mortgage? what sort of mortgage is it? do you have savings? are you getting the best rate of interest on your savings?
- speak to your employer, with a witness or trade union representative present if you have one, to establish the most favourable terms and timing.

Occupational pension and early retirement

An occupational pension may be paid to a person under the normal retirement age if the scheme provides for early retirement on 'health or incapacity' grounds. The Inland Revenue defines incapacity as: 'physical or mental deterioration which makes the individual incapable of his normal employment or which destroys or seriously impairs his earnings capacity.' You should check what you are entitled to receive with your employer.

Preparing for retirement

Some firms encourage their employees to attend courses on preparing for retirement or you may find courses that are being run by a local Further Education college.1 Ensure you are claiming the welfare benefits you are entitled to and think about ways of remaining active and maintaining your social life:

- see Chapter 25 'Welfare Benefits'
- see Chapter 11 'Sports, hobbies and holidays'
- *voluntary work* can provide some of the advantages of paid employment. The law classes you as a volunteer if you do voluntary work for anyone other than a close relative. You must not be paid for the work other than reasonable expenses, i.e. travel, cost of equipment, telephone. You must work for less than 16 hours each week, and if you exceed this limit it can affect your right to benefits. Seek advice if you are in doubt about this.
- *therapeutic work* is paid work for less than 16 hours a week and may be allowed if it helps 'to improve or prevent or delay deterioration in the disease or bodily or mental disablement which causes your incapacity for work.' Ask advice from your GP. There are earning limits to therapeutic work and you should seek appropriate advice.

"Every Wednesday afternoon I do voluntary work in a nursing home, in the library. When we take the book wagon along the patients they all say: 'Here come the library ladies'. I enjoy the work. I like being able to organise something, seeing that things are kept in order. I often talk to the people there. They've usually had interesting lives and can sometimes tell great stories. Sometimes they need to offload their miseries onto you. When I hear what they have to say I tell myself: 'You're not doing so bad, even though you've got problems of your own'."

Useful Addresses and Further Information:

ACAS (Advisory, Conciliation and Arbitration Service)
Midlands Region - Telephone: 0121 6225050
ACAS can advise and, if appropriate liaise on your behalf, in disputes with your employer concerning, for example, unfair dismissal

Business Start-up Scheme - run by the Training and Enterprise Councils (TECs). Contact is through your local Jobcentre (listed under 'Employment Service' in the telephone book). Business Start-up Schemes help unemployed people to set up their own small business.

CAB (Citizens' Advice Bureau) - Telephone number in local directory.
CABs can provide a wide range of information on employment law and welfare benefits. Some CABs have an Employment Advisor or Solicitor attached to them to provide specialist advice.

Disability Discrimination Act - The Act defines disability as 'a physical or mental impairment which has a substantial and long term adverse effect on a person's ability to carry out normal day-to-day activities'. Certain groups of employees are not covered by the provision of the Act and these include prison officers, fire-fighters, members of the police force and the armed forces, people who work wholly or mainly outside of the UK, and those who work on board ships, aircraft or hovercraft.
Free material on the provision of the Act is available from the DDA Information Line: 0345 622633

Law Centre - Telephone number in local directory.
Law Centres provide information and advice on all aspects of the law including employment law.

The Parkinson's Disease Society of the United Kingdom
215 Vauxhall Bridge Road, London, SW1V 1EJ
Telephone: 020 7931 8080; Helpline: freephone 0808 800 0303
The Society employs a Welfare & Employment Rights Advisor who can advise you on all aspects of Parkinson's and employment, and welfare benefits

PACT (Placing, Assessment and Counselling Team) - contact through your local Jobcentre (listed under 'Employment Service' in the telephone book). PACT provides disability employment advisers who can offer a range of services to people with disabilities, including re-training. It can be helpful to be registered as disabled as this will enable you to gain access to other sources of help. To qualify for registration you must be 'a person who, on account of injury, disease or congenital deformity is substantially handicapped in obtaining or keeping employment, or in undertaking work on his(her) own account of a kind which ... would be suited to his(her) age, experience and qualifications'. The disability must be expected to last at least 12 months and the person must already be in, or actively looking for work. Services available to people who are registered include free permanent loan of equipment which will help them to obtain or keep employment, and help with costs of travel to work, where driving or public transport is inappropriate. [2]

Telecottage Association - Freephone: 0800 616008
Provides information and a network of support for people who work from home.

Trade Unions - Local contacts in telephone directory

YAPP&Rs (Young Alert Parkinsonians, Partners & Relatives)
YAPP&Rs is a special interest group of the Parkinson's Disease Society, whose members are of working age. They offer friendship and mutual support through their quarterly magazine, letters, phone calls and a computerised bulleting board. A national weekend conference is held every two years and regional groups meet more frequently.[1]
Contact:
YAPP&RS
c/o Ian Prest, Young Onset Project Development Manager
50 Reedly Road
Reedly
Burnley BB10 2NE
tel.: 01282 611 022
e-mail: iprest@parkinson's.org.uk

author: - J. Bucknall, Welfare & Employment Rights
Advisor, Parkinson's Disease Society, UK

advisor: - E. Falvey, Care Services Manager,
Parkinson's Disease Society, UK

25

Welfare benefits

Summary

Parkinson's can mean incurring extra expenses. These are reimbursed in certain cases. This chapter includes a survey of these welfare benefits.

There are various kinds of benefits. These are frequently intended for particular groups such as people with handicaps or senior citizens. In many cases, the level of benefit is partly determined by income, which includes savings. Hence, applying for benefit can involve having your income investigated.

Other forms of benefit involve checking your handicap rather than your income. For instance, there are benefits for people who become disabled before the age of 65 and for those who have been incapable of work for at least 28 weeks.

This chapter contains brief descriptions of ten kinds of benefit and lists the people who are eligible, the conditions that you must fulfil and how to apply for benefit.

Introduction

There are a number of welfare benefits available, to which people with Parkinson's may be entitled. This chapter provides a brief introduction to them and covers:

1. Disability Living Allowance (DLA)
2. Family Credit
3. Disability Working Allowance
4. Income Support
5. Help with buying your own care
6. Attendance Allowance
7. Severe Disablement Allowance
8. Invalid Care Allowance (ICA)
9. Statutory Sick Pay (SSP)
10. Incapacity Benefit
11. Orange Badge Scheme

The chapter concludes with information on where to get further help.

Disability

Disability inevitably leads to extra costs. It is far more difficult for a disabled person to manage on the same income as someone of the same age who is not disabled. Yet the average disabled person has a much lower income than the average non-disabled person. And despite the range of benefits and other help available to people with disabilities, not all people manage to work their way through the jungle and claim their full legal entitlements. The weekly loss can be substantial.

Even among people who have claimed all they are entitled to there are still anomalies. People who are equally severely disabled can be entitled to different amounts of non-means tested income. How old you were when you first became disabled; how you became disabled, the effects of your disability; how long you have lived in the United Kingdom, and whether you worked and paid the right National Insurance contributions at the right time, they all are considerations that can make a difference to the total amount of benefit you may be entitled to.[1]

"I'm 75 and have never claimed any benefits in my life. I knew nothing at all about Attendance Allowance until the Parkinson's Disease Society sent me information. As a result, I now receive Attendance Allowance and this winter I shall be able to have my central heating on for the whole day for the first time ever."

There are a number of welfare benefits available, to which people with Parkinson's may be entitled. This chapter provides a brief introduction to them.

Types of benefits available

There are two types of benefit available in the UK. These are:
- Means-tested benefits, which are dependent upon Savings and Income
- Non-means tested benefits, not dependent on savings, but on your disability

1 Disability Living Allowance (DLA)

This is a non-means-tested benefit for people who become disabled before the age of 65. From October 1997, all new claimants have to be under 65.

This benefit has two parts: Mobility and Care.

Mobility benefit is to help you get around. You may have difficulty in walking or need someone with you when you are walking outdoors. Mobility benefit may be used in the Motability Scheme.

Motability is a scheme set up for people who are disabled. The money received in the mobility part of the DLA may be used for hiring a car or buying a car or a powered wheelchair through a hire purchase scheme. To qualify you must be in receipt of the higher rate of DLA for Mobility for at least three years still to run.

For further details and an application form on the Motability Scheme contact Motability, Gate House, Westgate, Harlow, Essex. CM20 1HR

Care benefit is for people who because of their disability need help with personal care or supervision, for example with dressing and bathing, using the toilet, going up or down stairs or in taking prescribed medication.

To claim DLA you must have lived in the UK for six months out of the past 12 months.

To apply you need Social Security leaflet DS 704 and claim form DLA 1.

2   Family Credit

This is a tax-free benefit for working families with children. Your right to Family Credit does not depend on National Insurance contributions.

To qualify you must:
- be responsible for at least one child under 16, or under 19 if in full-time education up to and including A level or equivalent standard.
- be working more than 16 hours a week (you or your partner)
- have no more than £ 16,000 in savings (either you, or you and your partner together).

Savings between £ 3,000 and £ 8,000 will affect the amount you get. You do not have to have a very low income to qualify for Family Credit. Family credit is being replaced by Working Families Tax Credit from October, 1999. You do not have to be on a very low income to get Family Credit.

3   Disability Working Allowance

This is a tax-free, non-contributory benefit for disabled people who are working but who have a limited earning capacity due to their disability.

To qualify you must:
- be in paid employment for at least 16 hours a week
- be at a disadvantage in getting a job because of your disability
- be receiving or have recently received one or more of certain disability benefits including Incapacity benefit, Severe Disablement Allowance and Disability Living Allowance
- have no more than £ 16,000 in savings.

If you meet these conditions you may qualify for DWA. How much you receive will depend on your income, savings and your personal situation. DWA is a benefit that supports people with disabilities 'to return to work or to top up low earnings'. From October 1999, DWA will be replaced by the Disabled Person's Tax Credit.

For more information see Social Security leaflet DS 703 and DWA claim pack.

"Luckily I'm a real organiser and like to have everything in order. Because it was quite a job to organise my health insurance and get the right payments when I was forced to work half-days because of my Parkinson's. But it worked out, thanks to a lot of help from a social advisor."

4 Income Support

This is a means-tested benefit that does not depend upon your National Insurance contributions. It is intended to provide basic living essentials for you and your family. It can be paid on its own if you have no other income or as part of the topping up of other benefits or earnings from part-time work, up to the basic amount the law says you need to live on. If you do not have much money coming in, it is always worthwhile checking to see if you qualify for Income Support.

To qualify you must:
- have savings of £ 8,000 or less (£ 16,000 if you live in a residential or nursing home)
- have a low income
- be aged 60 or over or be under 60 but not required to 'sign on' as unemployed due to your illness or disability or because you are a carer.
- not work more than 16 hours a week. If you have a partner, he or she must not work more than 24 hours a week.
- be a habitual resident of the UK.

If you are in receipt of Income Support you may also be eligible for the Social Fund. Seek advice from one of the agencies listed under 'What to do next' at the end of the chapter.

5 Help with buying your own care

Under the Community Care Act, local authorities have the principal responsibility for directly providing or arranging services for disabled people and others who are assessed as being in need of them.

From April 1, 1993, two funds to meet these responsibilities were established: the Independent Living (Extension) Fund and the Independent Living (1993) Fund. Despite being statutory, both are independent discretionary trust funds, managed by a Board of Trustees.

Both funds provide cash payments to enable severely disabled people maintain independence in their own homes.

To qualify you must
- be aged under 66
- be in receipt of the higher care component of Disability Living Allowance (DLA)
- have no more than £ 8,000 in savings
- be in receipt of Income Support

- not be able to afford the care you need from your income and be receiving services from the local authority to the value of at least £ 200 each week.

6 Attendance Allowance

This is a benefit for people who are physically or mentally disabled and need help with personal care. There is no upper age limit for AA but if you become disabled after the age of 65 and have not claimed Disability Living Allowance you should claim AA. You can claim if you live alone or with someone else - what matters is that you need help to live. There are two levels of benefit in AA: one is normally for care during the day, the second and higher rate is for 24-hour care.

This benefit is non-means-tested. To claim it you must have lived in the UK for 6 months out of the past 12 months.

To apply you need Social Security leaflet DS 702 and claim pack DS 2.

7 Severe Disablement Allowance

This is a weekly benefit for people who have been incapable of work for at least 28 weeks, but who do not have enough National Insurance contributions to qualify for Incapacity Benefit. It cannot normally be paid for the first time after you reach the age of 65 (The Government proposes to abolish SDA for new claims from April 2001). To apply you need Social Security leaflet NI 252.

8 Invalid Care Allowance (ICA)

This is a non-means tested benefit and does not depend upon National Insurance contributions. It is taxable.

ICA is a benefit for people who are under the age of 65 and spend 35 hours a week or more caring for a severely disabled person. You do not have to be related or live with the disabled person to receive this benefit. But you must be caring for a person who either gets Attendance Allowance or the Disability Living Allowance care component at the middle or higher rate. ICA gives you Class 1 contribution credits.

To qualify you must:
- be aged between 16 and 65 at the time of your claim
- be living in the UK
- not be in full-time education. You are treated as being in full time education if you attend a course for 21 hours or more each week
- if you work you must not earn more than £50 a week once allowable expenses are deducted

This benefit can only be backdated three months.

9 Statutory Sick Pay (SSP)

This is a taxable benefit. If you are earning in excess of £ 66 per week (1999 figure corresponds with National Insurance contribution) and you are aged under 65, you will probably be entitled to receive SSP if you are away from work for at least four days in a row. This is payable by your employer and can continue for up to 28 weeks. Some employers also have their own scheme for paying sick pay, which relates to terms and conditions of employment. There is no addition for dependants.

At the end of the 28-week period, if you are unable to work because of your illness or disability, you should claim Incapacity Benefit.

> *"I was at a Christmas drinks party last night and people started talking about 'social England'. Somebody said that it's all starting to get out of hand, that there was too much social security being paid out! He was trying to point out that all the hand-outs made it 'too easy' for people, made them 'lazy'. I really saw red, I can tell you. It's easy for him to talk, he happens to have everything going for him. But a lot of other people don't and usually there's not a thing they can do about it. I know for sure that if those benefits weren't available I'd be a lot worse off than I am now, and it's not my fault that I've got Parkinson's. What did I say to him? That he ought to think about the meaning of Christmas again..."*

10 Incapacity Benefit

This was introduced on 13th April 1995. It replaced Sickness Benefit and Invalidity Benefit. It is dependent on National Insurance contributions but is not means-tested.

There are three levels of Incapacity Benefit:
- For the first 28 weeks of incapacity you get the short-term lower rate
- After 28 weeks on the lower rate you move onto the short-term higher rate. This is paid from week 29 to week 52
- After 52 weeks of incapacity you will be entitled to receive the long-term rate.

You are entitled to 364 days short-term benefit, which can include entitlement to SSP, before moving to long-term benefit. The days of incapacity may be consecutive or in 'linked periods of incapacity for work'.

If you are an employee you will normally be entitled to receive SSP for the first 28 weeks of your illness. At the end of the 28-week period you will be transferred onto Incapacity Benefit. Your employer should notify the Benefits Agency and you should receive a claim form for Incapacity Benefit.

11 Orange Badge Scheme

The Orange Badge Scheme is a parking concession designed to help people with severe disability problems by allowing them to park close to shops or public buildings that they wish to visit. Local Authorities have discretion to charge for issuing the badge.

If the disabled person is not, or has not been in the vehicle it is an offence to display the Orange Badge unless the driver is on the way to collect the disabled person or drop them off. You can lose the Orange Badge for abuse of the scheme.

Contact your local Social Services department and request information and an appropriate form.

What to do next: further help

All of the above welfare benefit information can be quite complicated to understand. The Parkinson's Disease Society produces a series of Fact Sheets on all relevant welfare benefits and these can be obtained, free of charge, from the Welfare Benefits Assistant at the National Office Tel: 020 7931 8080. The Society also employs a Welfare and Employment Rights Advisor who offers advice, information and support on welfare benefits.

Alternatively you can contact any of the following organisations whose telephone numbers can be found in your local directory:

- Your local Citizens' Advice Bureau
- A local Welfare Rights Group.
- DIAL (Disability Information and Advice Line)
- Age Concern

You can also get benefits information from:

- Your local Advice Centre (if available)
- The local Authority
- A Benefits Agency - e.g. Disability Benefits Centre, Birmingham

Telephone numbers for all of the above can be found in your local directory.

Do not make hasty decisions without all the relevant information available. Trying to understand what you may be entitled to is time consuming and often quite difficult but it is worthwhile in the long term and will help you get the support that you need.

Even if you do not need any welfare benefits right now, you may at a later date. Any knowledge and information that you have will enable you to make the right decisions.

author: - J. Bucknall, Welfare & Empoyment Rights
Advisor, Parkinsons Disease Society, UK
advisor: - E. Falvey, Care Services Manager,
Parkinson's Disease Society, UK

26

Patients' and carers' rights

Summary

You are a 'patient' once Parkinson's brings you into contact with the care services. Being a patient gives you certain rights. This also applies to carers.

The most important rights are the basic NHS rights. A number of important aspects are:
- your right to medical treatment, regardless of ability to pay
- your right to a clear explanation of all treatments including the risks involved before you agree to undergo those treatments
- your right to view your medical records.

Since 1993 local authorities must assess each person who is considered to be in need of community care services in terms of his or her personal requirements. You can ask your local authority to carry out an assessment if you believe that you need these services.

This assessment can also be applied to carers, as stipulated under the Carers (Recognition and Services) Act.

199

Introduction

Everyone who lives in the UK has a right to certain services. These include health services and social services. Below is a list of basic National Health Service (NHS) rights and over the page some information about social services provided by the local authority.

This chapter introduces the following subjects:
- Basic NHS Rights
- What should you do if your NHS rights are not being met?
- Social services provision for the disabled
- The Chronically Sick and Disabled Person's (CSDP) Act 1970
- Disabled Person's (Services, Consultation & Representation) Act 1986
- What to do if you need help
- What are assessments?
- What rights do carers have?

"I care for my husband because I love him - but I do wish people would recognise my needs as well. Hopefully, now that he is going to be assessed, my needs will be assessed"

The information is to help you get the best possible care to maintain your quality of life. As a person with Parkinson's Disease, you know how you are affected and what your needs are. You should also be aware, however, that standards of care differ between health authorities and local authorities around the country and that the needs of people with Parkinson's and their families are not always met. The information below should give you and your carer, if you have one, support and encouragement.

Basic NHS Rights.
- To receive health care on the basis of clinical need, regardless of ability to pay.
- To be registered with a GP.
- To receive emergency medical care at any time
- To be referred to a consultant, acceptable to you, when your GP thinks it necessary and to be referred for a second opinion if you and your GP think this is desirable.
- To be given a clear explanation of any treatment proposed, including any risks and any alternatives, before you decide whether you will agree to the treatment.
- To have access to your medical records, and to know that those working for the NHS are under a legal duty to keep their contents confidential.
- To choose whether or not you wish to take part in medical research or medical student training.
- To be given detailed information on local services, including quality standards and maximum waiting times
- To be guaranteed admission for treatment by a certain date no later than two years from the day when your consultant places you on a waiting list
- To have any complaint about NHS services (whoever provides those services) investigated and to receive a full and prompt written reply from the chief executive or general manager of the organisation providing the service.

"I had a ghastly specialist. There was always a consultation that had taken too long, always appointments re-scheduled. And once you got into his consulting rooms you were out again in five minutes. I put up with it for some time, because it's not all that easy to go and get another doctor. And my GP had told me that he was a really good specialist. But there came a time when I had enough of it. So I got in touch with the patients' association to help me find another specialist. The old one was pretty shocked when I told him I was going to someone else. But with the new one I feel comfortable."

What should you do if your NHS rights are not being met?

If you feel that you are being, or are likely to be, denied one of the above rights, you should first make representation to your GP's surgery (if fundholding) or to your local Health Authority (if non-fundholding). If, after doing this, the matter is still not resolved, you should write to the Chief Executive of the NHS, who will investigate the matter.

Chief Executive of the NHS
Department of Health
Richmond House
79 Whitehall
LONDON SW1A 2NS.

Social services provision for the disabled

There are two Acts of Parliament that give people who are disabled the right to social services. These are the Chronically Sick and Disabled Person's Act 1970 and the Disabled Person's Act 1986.

The Chronically Sick and Disabled Person's (CSDP) Act 1970

This requires local authorities to make arrangements for providing certain services to chronically sick and disabled people who are normally resident within the local authority area. A local authority only has to provide services if it is proved that those services are necessary to meet the individual needs of the person. These services are:

- provision of practical assistance within the home
- provision of disability aids and equipment
- assistance with adaptations to the home
- provision of meals at home or elsewhere
- provision or help with getting a telephone or any special equipment necessary to use a telephone
- provision of, or assistance in, educational or recreational facilities both within and outside the home, including provision of, or assistance with, transport to and from the relevant facilities
- provision of holidays.

Disabled Person's (Services, Consultation & Representation) Act 1986

If you are disabled you can ask for your needs to be assessed under the Act and you must be provided with services under the Chronically Sick and Disabled Person's Act if they are needed.

People with disabilities as defined under the terms of the Act, are those who are:

- blind or partially sighted
- mentally ill
- mentally handicapped
- substantially or permanently handicapped

These definitions apply to people of all ages.

201

What to do if you need help

Since April 1993 local authorities have had a duty to any person who is considered to be in need of community care services to carry out an assessment of that person's individual need for those services. After the assessment the authority must decide whether those needs call for the provision of such services (National Health Service and Community Care Act 1990 section 47).

If during the course of the assessment it becomes clear that you are disabled, the local authority must assess your need for services under the CSDP Act. Once the need has been proved the authority must provide those services. It cannot use the lack of resources as an excuse for doing nothing. Neither should local authorities put you on a waiting list, which could make you wait a long while for those specific services.

What are assessments?

Since April 1993 local authorities have had the duty under the 1990 NHS and Community Care Act to carry out assessments of people who may need to have services provided for them. These services include meals-on-wheels, home care, home help, respite services and care in either a residential or nursing home. You can ask your local authority to carry out an assessment if you believe you need such services.

Local authorities have to publish information about how to apply for an assessment and about how they will carry out the assessment. They also have to give information about the kind of needs for which they can provide help and the kinds of assessments that they undertake.

If you are disabled the local authority must offer you an assessment under the terms of the Disabled Persons Act 1986, for services specified in section 2 of the CSDP Act 1970.

How the assessment should work

The assessor should explain to you what the purpose of the assessment is. He should also listen to you and your carer, to understand as fully as possible the particular needs that you have. Tell him what you used to do and would like to do, what you cannot do and what you need help with. Make quite certain that you have the opportunity to state all your needs and make sure that the assessor understands and writes down all the stated needs. Ask to see the record and make sure you agree what has been written about you before the assessor leaves.

It is on this evidence that a decision about services to be provided will be made by the local authority.

If you are not satisfied with the assessment or are unhappy about the manner in which is has been carried out, then you have a right to complain. You do this through the local authority's complaints procedure. The assessor should tell you about this procedure at the beginning of the assessment.

If you find it difficult to make your needs known during the assessment you can, if you wish, use the services of an advocate who will speak for you and negotiate on your behalf. There are many advocacy services available. Information on local advocacy services can be found in your local telephone book or from a Citizens' Advice Bureau or a local Carers' Group.

If during an assessment you are found to have a housing or health need then the assessor must contact the appropriate authority if you give your consent. If you have more than one need then you may find that there are a number of people involved in your assessment. For example, if you have severe mobility problems and cannot walk without a stick and you live on the fourth floor of a block of flats, then your needs are complex.

What happens after assessments?

Local authorities have been told that 'a copy of the assessment needs should normally be shared with the potential user... this record will normally be combined with a written care plan.' (Care management and assessment: practitioners' guide. Department of Health 1991).

Disabled people have the right to have a copy of their social services file (Access to Personal Files (Social Services) Regulations 1989).

Welfare benefits available for people with disabilities.
See Chapter 25 'Welfare benefits'.

What rights do carers have?

Carers can ask to be assessed separately. Often assumptions have been made in the past about the role of carers. Under the Carers (Recognition and Services) Act 1995 (section 1), the carer can ask to be assessed separately for his own particular needs.

The Act says that a carer is someone who provides a substantial amount of care on a regular basis. The carer does not have to be living in the same property as the person for whom he cares, neither does he have to be the only carer in order to ask for the separate assessment. Potential carers can also ask for an assessment if they believe that they may be involved in providing care in the near future, for example if a relative is about to be discharged from hospital.

203

What happens when a carer's needs are assessed?

By law the social services assessment has to take into account the needs of the carer. But before the needs of the carer can be assessed the needs of the person cared for must first be assessed.

The assessment of the carer should be private. It should be carried out by an experienced professional worker. The most important things that should be taken into account are the age of the carer, his personal circumstances and the amount of current support available.

In many places the provision of support to carers is under discussion and you need to contact your local social services department to find out what is provided in your local area.

Further information can be obtained from

Carers National Association
20/25 Glasshouse Yard,
London EC1A 4JT
Tel : 020 7490 8818
Helpline: 0808 808 777
Email: info@ukcarers.org

Welfare benefits that may be available for carers
Chapter 25 '*Welfare benefits*' contains information on Invalid Care Allowance.

The Parkinson's Disease Society of the United Kingdom (tel. 020 7931 8080) provides two useful booklets, free of charge, entitled 'Meeting Your Health Care Needs' and 'Meeting Your Social Care Needs'.

author: - E.H. Coene, M.D., September
Foundation, the Netherlands
advisors: - Professor L.J. Findley, T.D., O.L.J., M.D.,
F.R.C.P., F.A.C.P, Consultant Neurologist
"Avenue House", Romford, UK
- Dr C.E. Clarke, Consultant in Neurology
& Honorary Senior Lecturer, Hull Royal
Infirmary, UK
- Dr. J. van Manen, neurologist, advisor to
the Dutch Parkinson's Disease Society,
the Netherlands
- Dr. J.D. Speelman, neurologist, Academic
Medical Centre, University of Amsterdam,
the Netherlands

27

Particular symptoms

Summary

Parkinson's most important symptoms are tremor, stiffness, slowness of movement and tiredness. However, there may also be other symptoms. These are much less common. This chapter includes a summary of these symptoms.

Some examples of these symptoms are bluish-purple discoloration of the skin, constipation, drooling, a dry mouth, pain, problems with urination, eye problems and depression.

These symptoms have an extremely wide variety of causes. Sometimes, as is the case with slower bowel motions, they are due to the disease itself. But they can also be the result of Parkinson's symptoms. For instance: drooling is caused by difficulty initiating movements and by muscle stiffness that makes it hard to swallow saliva in the normal way. In addition, symptoms may be caused by the medication such as the bluish-purple discoloration that occurs through the long-term use of amantadine (Symmetrel).

There is a lot that you can do counter most of these symptoms. For instance: you will be less prone to drooling if you train yourself to swallow consciously and regularly. In addition, many of these symptoms can be treated so that you will be less bothered by them.

Introduction

This chapter contains information on other symptoms that are sometimes experienced by people with Parkinson's. Chapter 2 '*General symptoms*' deals with the symptoms that are most commonly experienced: tremor, stiffness, slowness of movement and tiredness. This chapter covers:

1. skin problems
2. bowel problems
3. drooling or a dry mouth
4. difficulty sleeping
5. pain
6. problems with urination

7. eye problems
8. depression
9. other symptoms.

Mental changes are described in Chapter 28 'Mental changes'.

The information also includes practical advice on dealing with the symptoms. Not everyone will experience all, or indeed any, of these symptoms! So it might be a good idea simply to use the chapter for reference if you have a particular symptom and want to look it up. Reading the chapter right the way through might be disturbing and unnecessary.

We recommend that you consult your GP about *any* symptom. Be certain to seek advice if they change, get worse or if new symptoms appear. A symptom might not have anything to do with Parkinson's and may need further investigation. It might, for example, be a side effect of drug treatment. You could also consult your Parkinson's Disease Nurse Specialist or practice nurse.

The medications mentioned here are given as examples only. Others are available. Medications are covered in more detail in Chapter 3 *Treatment and medication*', Chapter 29 'Medication that contains levodopa*' and Chapter 30 '*Other medication*'. When a medication (often referred to as a treatment drug) is referred to by its trade or brand name, an initial capital letter is used e.g., Madopar. When the generic name is given, a small first letter is used e.g., co-beneldopa.

1. Skin problems
Bedsores (pressure sores) are discussed in Chapter 13 '*Care at home*'.

1a Bluish-purple discolouration
The use of amantadine (Symmetrel) over an extensive period of time can result in a side effect where the skin (particularly on the legs) acquires a bluish-purple discolouration. This discolouration is not serious and will disappear if amantadine is discontinued for a couple of weeks. Always talk to your doctor first before discontinuing any drug treatment for Parkinson's.

1b A greasy skin and perspiration

Symptoms and signs
The skin has glands that produce sebaceous matter (sebum). This keeps the skin supple and protects it. Parkinson's causes the sebaceous glands to produce extra sebum so that the skin becomes greasy and shiny. This is known as seborrhoea. It mainly affects the areas that contain the most sebaceous glands such as the forehead, beside the nostrils and the hairy parts of the scalp. Your hair may become greasy and you may get dandruff. These conditions are often exacerbated by heat.

In severe cases, the skin becomes red and irritated and it may begin to flake and itch. This is known as seborrheic dermatitis (dermatitis = skin inflammation). This complaint can also occur amongst people who do not have Parkinson's.

Parkinson's can also cause the sweat glands to react in a different way, which can lead to perspiration or to an extremely dry skin. Medication for Parkinson's can also affect sweating: some medications can make people sweat too much while some can make people sweat too little.

What can you do to help yourself?

These problems are not usually serious. A skin that produces too much sebum should be washed with a neutral soap such as Sebamed. Clean your skin twice a day with warm water and rinse it with cold water. Use gels that are water based instead of creams that are oil based. If necessary, consult a dermatologist or a beautician. Change your underwear regularly.

Dandruff can be treated with a number of shampoos and lotions, which are available from the chemist. Products that contain selenium or selenium sulphide are particularly effective, although it is claimed that their regular use may increase the risk of baldness. You are well advised, therefore, to consult your doctor if you are using these products regularly.

Perspiration cools you down, so even if you only perspire a little, you must be careful not to get too hot. You should wear thin clothes in warm weather and avoid sport or too much activity on a hot day. It would be better not to visit a sauna. If you perspire a lot, you should take regular lukewarm showers and wear cotton clothes. Make sure that you drink enough. If you perspire a lot at night, you should make sure that your bedroom is well ventilated.

What help is available?

Parkinson's medication can help most of these symptoms, so talk to your GP or specialist. A cream can be prescribed for extreme cases of seborrhea, which may contain sulphur and salicylic acid.

Seborrheic dermatitis can be treated with a number of lotions, which often contain an adrenocorticotropic hormone. A doctor can prescribe these.

Too little perspiration can be a side effect of Parkinson medications such as anticholinergic drugs (see Chapter 30 'Other medication'). Therefore, the dosage of an anticholinergic drug should be reduced during very hot weather. Too much perspiration can be a side effect of Parkinson medications such as levodopa containing agents (see Chapter 29 'Medication that contains levodopa'). Your doctor can decide whether you need to change your medication.

2. Bowel Problems

Everyone has a natural rhythm for their bowel movements. With some people that means once every three days, with others it means twice a day; both are quite normal. In general, bowel movements should take place at least once every three days. It is not always easy to know when one should talk in terms of constipation. Constipation means that the individual deviates from his natural rhythm and that the bowel movements become slower or cease altogether. Constipation is a common complaint with Parkinson's.

Slow bowel movements occur because the movement of the intestines, like all other movements, has been slowed down by Parkinson's. Certain Parkinson's medications such as anticholinergic drugs (See Chapter 30 '*Other medication*') can also cause slow bowel movements.

Symptoms and signs

- A sign that you are suffering from constipation is that your rhythm has changed You find that you are going to the toilet less frequently than you used to, although you are eating the same as usual..
- Your stools are dry and hard and they are difficult to pass.
- Your tummy may rumble and you may also suffer from flatulence or wind.

What can you do to help yourself?

- Many people with Parkinson's have to deal with muscle rigidity and slowness of movement. For them eating can be a slow process and they may experience chewing and swallowing difficulties. It is therefore highly recommended to ensure that enough high quality nutrients are being consumed.
- Make sure that you eat plenty of fibre such as fruit, dried prunes, raisins, bran, raw vegetables and brown bread (see Chapter 10 '*Diet*'). Fibre ensures that your motions are soft and easier to pass.
- Try to keep as mobile as possible because this will stimulate the bowel (see Chapter 9 '*Exercises*'). You can do some exercises even if you are in bed. The fact that Parkinson's may mean that you are moving less could be the cause of bowel problems.
- Go to the toilet as soon as you need to. Do not put it off.
- Constipation may be caused by lack of fluid. Make sure that you drink a lot (at least two litres a day). This will prevent your stools from drying out. Fruit juice stimulates bowel movement.
- It may help to go to the toilet at the same time each day, preferably after a meal. Take your time, and perhaps take something to read, which will relax you.
- Coffee, a glass of warm water and a full stomach will stimulate your bowel. Certain foods, such as pickles, can also help.

Try not to worry too much about going to the toilet, as anxiety will only make it worse. Be patient, it may take some time to work.

What help is available?

If the problem persists, or if you experience discomfort or pain, your doctor can examine you to see if there is any other cause for the problem apart from Parkinson's or can prescribe medication, or a combination of medications. *Laxatives* such as Fybogel, Normacon and Co-danthramer may be used. Senna is an alternative (which is also sold as a tea).

The disadvantage of laxatives is that your digestive system becomes used to them and eventually lacks the vigour to make its own bowel movements. This tends to lead to an increased intake of laxatives so that the digestive system becomes totally dependent upon them. Increased doses are certainly not advisable. Instead you should consult your doctor about whether you need to change laxatives. You can then perhaps return to your original brand.

- Do not chop and change between medications. Mostly, if you can be patient for a few days, your bowel movements will come as a matter of course. Many laxatives are available without a prescription but for the reasons mentioned you should still consult your doctor before using them.
- If these suggestions do not help, then you may be prescribed an enema. This is a laxative which is inserted into the anus.
- If slow bowel movements are being caused by Parkinson medication, then the suggestions mentioned above should be sufficient to restore regularity. Only in exceptional cases should the doctor have to adapt your medications.
- If you experience difficulties passing stools, you may have haemorrhoids around your anus, which can itch and bleed. If you lose blood for more than a week, you should consult your doctor in order to find out whether this bleeding has some other cause.
- A dietician or continence advisor may also be able to advise you.
- The Parkinson's Disease Society publishes a booklet, free of charge, called 'Looking After Your Bladder and Bowels in Parkinson's'.

3. Drooling or a dry mouth

3a Drooling

Symptoms and signs
Parkinson's causes a number of people to drool or dribble. This is not because they produce more saliva, but because difficulty initiating movements and muscle stiffness make it difficult to swallow saliva in the normal way. As a result, saliva begins to pool in the mouth and drool, or dribble from the lips. This can be distressing and embarrassing, but fortunately something can be done about it.

What can you do to help yourself?
- Try to consciously swallow regularly. Perhaps there is someone in your immediate environment who can prompt you by saying 'swallow' calmly and firmly. Chewing gum, or sucking a boiled sweet, will also encourage you to swallow.
- Try to keep your head upright and your lips closed. Swallow before you begin to speak.
- Position yourself as upright as possible, if necessary by using cushions. Your head should be tilted very slightly forwards.
- Use honey instead of sugar. Rinse your mouth with mineral water, carbonated water or stout.

What help is available?
Talk to your doctor, because a side effect of some Parkinson's medications (the anticholinergic agents, Chapter 30 'Other medication') is that they reduce the production of saliva and can therefore be beneficial. A disadvantage of using them is that the mouth can end up being too dry. Atropine tablets are an

alternative, but do not use these without first consulting your doctor. You can also consult a speech and language therapist for further advice on improving your swallow, and a physiotherapist to advise on posture and positioning of your head.

3b Dry mouth

Symptoms and signs
A dry mouth can either be caused by the Parkinson's itself or be the result of particular Parkinson's medications.

What can you do to help yourself?
Chewing gum or sweets will help because they stimulate saliva. Breathe through your nose so your breath is moistened and so that you can keep your mouth closed. This will help to stop it becoming parched.
Avoid eating dry foods such as peanut butter, crackers and biscuits as they dry out the mucus membranes and stick to the mouth and throat. Smoking and drinking alcohol and coffee also dry out your mucus membranes.

Drink plenty of ice cold water or citrus-flavoured drinks that can help to make your mouth feel less dry.[2] You can also dip a cotton swab in olive oil and rub it on the inside of your mouth once an hour. Vaseline will help to keep dry lips moist. As a dry mouth creates a greater risk of dental cavities you should clean your teeth regularly, especially when you use sweets to stimulate saliva.

What help is available?
If a dry mouth is being caused by anticholinergic drugs you can consult your doctor about modifying your medication. However, your mouth will usually become less dry after a few weeks of taking anticholinergics. Artificial saliva products can also be prescribed. A dietitian can give you further hints.

What can you expect?
Drooling can usually be effectively controlled by the suggestions mentioned above.
If there is too much saliva in your mouth, it can irritate your throat and palate which in turn leads to an increased risk of infected mucus membranes.

210

4. Difficulty sleeping

Symptoms and signs
There can be many reasons for people having difficulty sleeping but unfortunately, people with Parkinson's may experience additional problems. Sleeplessness can, for instance, be a side effect of medications such as levodopa and selegiline (see Chapter 29 'Medication that contains levodopa' and Chapter 30 'Other medication'). Also, worrying about the consequences of Parkinson's can cause sleeplessness. In some people, Parkinson's symptoms are particularly pronounced at night, which makes it difficult to sleep. Muscle pain, cramps, restless legs and arms can lead to restless nights. People may also wake up

because of difficulties with turning over in bed. Nightmares and hallucinations can be side effects of levodopa. Frequent visits to the toilet may also interrupt sleep.

Sleeping badly over a long period of time can be extremely unpleasant. It makes you feel drowsy, irritable and dejected during the day which in turn can increase your Parkinson's symptoms. Sleeplessness for you may also cause disturbed nights for your partner.

People with Parkinson's are often less active than they once were and may be less sleepy at night. It is quite normal, too, for older people to need less sleep. So sleeping less, for instance through waking earlier, does not necessarily mean that you are suffering from insomnia. This is quite normal and is not something to be worried about.

What can you do to help yourself?
Here are a number of tips. Not everything will work for you but try a few and pursue those that seem to help.

- The occasional sleepless night will not hurt you so try to accept them. Do not view them as being a problem, because you will simply make it more difficult to fall asleep.
- Consult your GP if you think one of the causes of sleeplessness mentioned above is present. He can investigate this and might come up with a solution.
- Move about as much as you can so that you make yourself tired. For instance: do the housework, go for a walk or do exercises (see Chapter 9 'Exercises').
- If you feel that you need more sleep during the day, it can be tempting to take an afternoon nap. This, however, will make you less tired at night. So if you really have to take an afternoon nap, take it, but preferably no longer than half an hour.
- Make sure that you have a firm mattress and that your pillow is not too hard. Some people prefer lambswool bottom sheets. Slippery bed materials such as silk, satin or nylon sheets can make it easier for you to move around in bed if you are experiencing problems in turning over. If you do have problems, see Chapter 8 'Help with movement' (Turning over in bed).
- Try to relax before you go to sleep: read a book or do some relaxation exercises (see Chapter 32 'Coping with stress'). Do not work too late and avoid watching action films or thrillers if you know that you are easily excited!
- Avoid the following: drinking coffee or tea late at night, long afternoon naps, sleeping late, itchy pyjamas and a bedroom that is either too warm or too cold.
- Home remedies for insomnia can also be helpful, for example a glass of warm milk (possibly with honey), raw salad, herbal tea (for instance with valerian), a strong drink (although too much alcohol can make it difficult to stay asleep), a warm bed, an empty bladder, a snack, lying with your feet slightly raised, rubbing the inside of your wrists with a circular motion (for at least one minute for per wrist, keep repeating) and 'counting sheep'!
- Earplugs (from the chemist's) or sleep masks can also help as do curtains that keep out the light.
- Although it is important to drink enough, make sure that you do not drink too much before you go to sleep: getting out of bed to go to the toilet at night can really wake you up. It may be helpful to have a commode or urinal close at

211

hand at night if you do need to go to the toilet frequently. They can be borrowed from your home nursing service or from a chemist's.

> *"Sometimes I can't sleep. I keep tossing and turning and I start worrying about the most ridiculous things. The doctor says this sleeping difficulty is not only caused by Parkinson's, but that it's also to do with my age. She says that the older you get, the earlier you wake up. That helped a lot and I don't worry about it any more. If I wake up now, I make myself comfortable, I read a good book and eat biscuits. The funny thing is that sometimes I even fall asleep."*

What help is available?

If Parkinson's symptoms are causing your sleeping difficulties, then your drug treatment may need to be altered. Perhaps a 'controlled release' preparation last thing in the evening will help to maintain the levels of dopamine during the night (see Chapter 29 '*Medication that contains levodopa*'). Medication can also be prescribed to help with particular symptoms such as pain.

If your Parkinson's medication is causing the problem, then you will usually find that this will decrease after a couple of weeks. However your dose may have to be modified, for instance by lowering your final dose or by taking it earlier.

Your doctor can also prescribe sedatives or sleeping pills. These are only useful for treating short-term sleeping problems and are harmful in the long run. They have side effects such as daytime drowsiness and can adversely affect memory. The quality of sleep also suffers and there is the risk of addiction. Powerful sedatives also affect people during the day so that they find it more difficult to maintain their balance and there is a greater risk of falling. Some sedatives can also aggravate slowness of movement. Consult your GP, neurologist or chemist.

5. Pain

Symptoms and signs

Pain is generally not a direct consequence of Parkinson's but of its symptoms such as muscular stiffness, cramp and tremors. These symptoms overload the muscles so that they can become painful. Hence stiff back muscles can cause low back pain. This can be aggravated by a stooped posture that also places an extra strain on the muscles. Painful muscles in the neck, shoulders and arms are also common. Painful neck muscles are sometimes experienced as headaches. Pain in the chest muscles can resemble angina.

Cramps in the calves and feet are also common, particularly at night or as you wake up. During the day your feet may assume a cramped position, with bent toes. This can be particularly painful if you are wearing tight shoes. This type of cramp is referred to as dystonia and it is often a long-term side effect of levodopa medication.

What can you do to help yourself?

If you're suffering from pain, talk to your GP, specialist or specialist nurse. A visit to the doctor should certainly not be postponed in the case of chest pains. It is necessary to determine whether the pain is caused by Parkinson's or by something else. Once the cause has been established then the right kind of therapy can be provided. There may also be a number of ways in which you can help yourself.

- Rubbing or applying warmth to the painful area often helps because the surrounding area is being stimulated. So gentle massage, possibly in a warm bath, or massaging the neck, back and calf muscles and placing a hot-water bottle (wrapped in a towel) at the site of the pain may help.
- The exercises described in Chapter 9 '*Exercises*' keep joints supple, so that they don't become stiff. They also maintain your condition which generally seems to decrease the chances of pain. Stretching exercises may help prevent calf cramps. If you suffer from calf cramps at night, you could do your stretching exercises before you go to bed. Raising your legs can also bring relief.
- Pain is aggravated by stress and fear because these cause the muscles to tense. Relaxation can therefore be beneficial. Chapter 32 '*Coping with stress*' describes a relaxing breathing exercise.
- If you focus on the pain, it will feel worse so try distracting yourself by concentrating on music, the radio or TV. Keep yourself as active as possible.

What help is available?

- It is necessary that your doctor establishes the cause of the pain. Treatment for arthritis or rheumatism will not help if the pain is being caused by Parkinson's.
- Parkinson's medications are often effective against Parkinson's pain and it may be that your tablets need to be increased. It is essential, however, to establish the correct dosage in order to avoid other unwanted side effects. Some compromise may be necessary to achieve the optimum benefits and the least possible side effects.
- Because of the long gap between taking your last dose of medication in the evening and your next dose the following morning, calf cramps can be particularly severe in the morning. Altering the timing of your drugs, or introducing a controlled release preparation last thing at night might help. Calf cramps can also be decreased with medications such as baclofen (Lioresal).
- The physiotherapist may be able to advise on pain control. See Chapter 17 '*Physiotherapy*'.
- Some people have found that acupuncture helps alleviate pain. See Chapter 23 '*Complementary Therapies*'.

If the pain is intense and becomes difficult to cope with, you can also be referred to a pain clinic where a number of specialists including anaesthetists, physiotherapists and psychologists work together to alleviate pain.

6. Problems with urination

Some people with Parkinson's have difficulty with bladder control. There may be a number of reasons for this and it is necessary to seek advice from your doctor, a urology specialist or continence advisor, in order to establish the cause and therefore the best treatment.

213

6a Lack of bladder control (incontinence)

Symptoms and signs
- People with Parkinson's occasionally experience difficulties with bladder control. They can feel a sudden urge to pass urine but cannot control it. Sometimes they cannot reach the toilet in time because Parkinson's causes them to walk more slowly and they may consequently leak small quantities of urine, this is called *urge incontinence*.
- People can experience a strong, even painful urge to urinate. Yet once they reach the toilet, little water is passed, sometimes only a few drops. However, the urge returns shortly afterwards, maybe just 30 minutes later.
- Passing water becomes painful.
- Sometimes a person with Parkinson's has to get out of bed several times a night to go to the toilet or may even wet the bed.

What can you do to help yourself?
- If you have problems with bladder control, always consult your doctor within a few days. If you experience symptoms of a bladder infection you should contact your doctor immediately. Symptoms of a bladder infection include the frequent need to pass water, a burning sensation while passing water, pain in the lower abdomen and an unnecessary urge to urinate.
- Try to keep a record of exactly when you pass water, approximately how much you passed, how much you drink and what symptoms you are experiencing (difficulty with passing water, leakage, etc.). This can help the doctor to discover the cause of the problem.
- Drink sufficient fluids (two litres) during the day but little at night. Try to visit the toilet at set times (once every two or three hours) to get into a habit of passing urine. Don't cut down on your fluid intake, because that will increase your chances of developing a bladder infection.
- However, it may be useful to make an exception and drink less on occasions when it is difficult to visit the toilet such as at the theatre, sports, etc.
- Alcohol (particularly beer), coca cola, coffee and tea stimulate the production of urine so that you need to pass water more frequently. If you are experiencing difficulties, you could replace these drinks with others such as fruit juices, water and milk.
- Moving from a warm space to a cold one also often increases the urge to pass water. Warm clothing can counter this tendency.
- Wear clothes that are easy to undo, for instance use Velcro fastenings or zippers instead of buttons.
- Using incontinence pads may be helpful and make you feel more confident.
- When traveling in planes or trains make sure that you sit next to the gangway so that you are within easy reach of the toilet.
- Make sure that your home environment is arranged in such a way that will not prevent you from getting to the toilet quickly. A urinal or commode may also be helpful.
- The Parkinson's Disease Society produces a useful booklet entitled 'Looking after your bladder and bowels in Parkinson's'. This is available free of charge on 020 7931 8080.

214

What help is available?

Your doctor, continence advisor or a urology specialist needs to establish the cause of the bladder problem. There are various causes that are not necessarily associated with Parkinson's and will need to be treated in a different way. To establish the cause, it may be necessary to undertake a number of tests, for instance: a urine test, bladder and kidney X-rays and bladder tests.

A number of Parkinson medications (the anticholinergic agents, see Chapter 30 'Other medication') can be effective in treating urge incontinence.

Other medications, such as diuretic pills, aggravate incontinence. If you need to take these make sure you take them in the morning, so that you do not have to keep going to the toilet during the night. If you are prescribed tranquillisers, these may prevent you from reaching the toilet in time.

Various resources such as special underwear, incontinence pads and waterproof sheets are available. For further information, please contact your continence advisor or district nurse. There is a Continence Advisory Service Help line which is based at The Continence Foundation, 307 Hatton Square, London EC1N 7RJ. Help line: 020 7831 9831. Your chemist will also be able to advise you. A condom catheter can be useful for men. This is a catheter which is attached to the penis by a device resembling a condom.

Difficulties with bladder control probably means that you are having to wash yourself more frequently. It is preferable that you do not use soap, because soap removes skin oils and dries out the skin making it more susceptible to damage. Make sure that you dry yourself thoroughly, to avoid infection and soreness. After washing you can use a protective cream, preferably a neutral one such as a baby cream or a baby lotion. If you apply talcum powder, you should make sure that the skin is completely dry (so it should be applied after any creams or lotions). Only use a little powder.

You or your carer may be able to get help with washing sheets from the community linen service. Consult your continence advisor or district nurse about this.

Regular urination prevents incontinence. On the other hand your bladder may not be completely emptied, and you may be retaining urine (see 6b below). Some people solve this problem by self-catheterisation, which involves inserting a catheter (tube) so that the urine can flow out of the bladder. Consult your urologist or continence advisor.

Consulting your doctor sooner rather than later can limit the problem, even if at the moment you feel that it is hardly worth mentioning. A great deal can be done to help. Meanwhile try to talk to the people you live with about this difficulty, so that it is not something you have to hide.

6b Difficulty emptying the bladder

Difficulty emptying the bladder occurs because the bladder can't contract as quickly and powerfully as it used to do. As a result, urination takes longer and may stop before the bladder is completely empty. If your bladder has not been completely emptied, you will find that you soon need to go to the toilet again. If urine remains in the bladder, there is an increased chance of bacteria spreading and causing a bladder infection. If the bladder is extremely full, the urine may end up being pushed back along the ureter towards the kidneys. This can cause infections that may damage the kidneys. It is vital to prevent these infections.

Symptoms and signs

- Difficulty in starting to pass water.
- Urine is expelled in a thin stream or even in a series of drops and the stream may suddenly be interrupted.
- Some people sense that even after passing water their bladder is not completely empty.
- An overfull bladder can also be painful.
- Urine may leak while laughing, pressing down, coughing or changing position. This occurs because the bladder is too full. Laughing increases pressure on the tummy so the urine is pushed out. This is known as *stress incontinence*.

What can you do to help yourself?

- If you have problems with emptying your bladder, always consult your doctor within a few days. If you experience symptoms of a bladder infection you should contact your doctor immediately. Symptoms of a bladder infection include the frequent need to pass water, a burning sensation while passing water, pain in the lower abdomen and an unnecessary urge to urinate.
- After consulting your doctor, keep a record of when you pass water, the approximate quantity, how much you drink and which symptoms you have experienced (difficulties with urinating, lack of bladder control etc.).
- Tight clothing around the tummy can cause leakage. This can be prevented by wearing looser clothes. The bladder must be emptied on time.
- Slow bowel movements (constipation) aggravate difficulties with emptying the bladder. Try to ensure that your bowel movements are regular (see 2. Bowel problems in this chapter).
- The Parkinson's Disease Society produces a useful booklet entitled 'Looking After Your Bladder and Bowels in Parkinson's'.

What help is available?

Your doctor or specialist can request a number of tests to establish the cause of the symptoms, such as urine tests, bladder and kidney X-rays and bladder tests. Older men may experience difficulties with passing water because of an prostate. Your doctor can treat possible infections.

Certain Parkinson medications (the anticholinergic agents, Chapter 29 *'Medication that contains levodopa'*) make it more difficult to urinate. Your doctor will be able to establish whether the dosage of these medications needs to be modified. Anticholinergics should not be used if there are symptoms of a prostrate condition. Discuss with your doctor any history of prostate problems you may have.

Medications: carbachol can help if the muscles of the bladder have become weakened. In this case, men can also use a condom catheter. This is a catheter which is attached to the penis by a device that resembles a condom.

Where incontinence occurs because of difficulty in emptying the bladder it is possible to purchase various resources such as special underwear, incontinence pads and waterproof sheets. You can get advice from *The Continence Advisory Help line* or *The Continence Foundation*, your local continence advisor or district nurse (307 Hatton Square, London EC1N 7RJ, Help Line: 020 7831 9831).

Ask your doctor, district nurse or continence advisor about bladder training which can help to control your bladder for increasing periods of time. Bladder training can also help you to empty your bladder by tensing your stomach muscles and by tapping at the place where the bladder is located (just above the pubic bone about ten centimetres beneath the navel). Do not press too hard, because you may force the urine back to the kidneys, exposing them to potential infection.

6c Dark urine
A side effect of levodopa medication is, that urine can turn from orange to red, right through to black. This is not serious and will disappear if the levodopa is discontinued. It is not in itself sufficient reason to discontinue levodopa.

7. Eye Problems

7a Dry Eyes
Eyes can become dry and irritated because Parkinson's sometimes causes people to blink less frequently. Blinking is one of the automatic movements that can be affected.

7b Double Vision

Symptoms and signs
This symptom generally only appears in long-term cases of Parkinson's Disease. If you look at an object, both eyes are trained upon a single point. If a distant object is brought closer, then the eyes will begin to converge so that they can remain trained on the same point. Because Parkinson's makes automatic movements more difficult, the eyes fail to converge effectively (weakness of convergence). If an object is located nearby, the eyes will no longer be able to observe the same point and this results in double vision.

What can you do to help yourself?
Mostly there's nothing you need to do because the brain will automatically suppress the double image. Until that happens, you can read with one eye closed. If you use reading glasses then you should cover one of the lenses. It is recommended to alternate between lenses so that first one and then the other is covered up.
You can practice eye convergence as follows: stretch out your arm in front of you. Look at the top of your index finger as you move it slowly towards your nose. Keep looking at your finger.

217

What help is available?

Your doctor or optician can establish whether your double vision is caused by Parkinson's or by something else. In some cases, your doctor may prescribe prism glasses if the double vision persists.

What can you expect?

Double vision can come and go quite spontaneously.

More information

If it becomes difficult to read (for instance, if your vision becomes blurred or your tremors are too severe), you may wish to use books or newspapers recorded on audio tape. Useful contacts are:

Talking Newspapers Association

National Recording Centre,
Heathfield,
East Sussex TN21 8DB
Tel: 01435 866102.

National Listening Library

12 Lant Street
London SE1 1QH
Tel: 020 7407 9417.

8. Depression

Symptoms and signs

Feeling low is a common experience with Parkinson's. This may be a very natural reaction against the losses and changes you are facing. However, at times it can develop into a clinical depression requiring treatment from your doctor. If you feel very depressed, are often tearful, if you suffer from insomnia, loss of appetite and weight, discuss this with your doctor or Parkinson's Disease Nurse Specialist.

What help is available?

Your doctor will assess the severity of the depression. It is possible that by improving your Parkinson's with adjustments to your medication or learning new ways to cope, your depression will also improve. However, with a severe depression it may be necessary to treat the depression itself. For instance: to start with an antidepressant drug (sooner rather than later, as they can take weeks or months to work). Very rarely, you may need to see a psychiatrist if the depression does not respond to the treatment.

It may also help to talk to someone about how you feel, for example, a counsellor, or one of the Help line team at the Parkinson's Disease Society, freephone 0808 800 0303.

9. Other symptoms

The scale of this manual means that we are unable to describe every single symptom. However, we will briefly mention a number of less common symptoms, so that you know they can be associated with Parkinson's and you can seek advice. Your doctor will be able to advise about treatments and referral if appropriate.

Symptoms include:

- *low blood pressure*
- seeing '*spots before the eyes*' when standing up (see Chapter 29 '*Medication that contains levodopa*')
- problems with *swallowing*
- *swollen ankles and feet*
- a *cold* or, more frequently, a *warm or burning sensation* in a particular part of the body such as a hand, a foot, the throat or internally
- a *tingling or numb sensation* in the fingers.

If you experience these or any other new symptoms and you are not sure whether they are connected with Parkinson's, caused by your medication or something entirely different, do not hesitate to seek advice.

author: - A. Nouws, psychologist, Regional Office for Mental Health, the Netherlands

advisors: - Professor L.J. Findley, T.D., O.L.J., M.D., F.R.C.P., F.A.C.P., Consultant Neurologist "Avenue House", Romford, UK
- Dr C.E. Clarke, Consultant in Neurologist & Honorary Senior Lecturer, Hull Royal Infirmary, UK
- F.M. Helmer, Board Member of the General Dutch Union of Senior Citizens, the Netherlands

28

Mental changes

Summary

People with Parkinson's may also experience mental symptoms. The precise cause of this is as yet unclear. Fortunately these symptoms are usually not particularly serious and can also be treated.

The most important mental symptoms are:
- sometimes finding it difficult to switch from one subject to another
- experiencing difficulties with reading and with watching TV
- discovering that holding a conversation is no longer an automatic process
- finding it difficult to do two things at once
- becoming swamped in details and losing the overall picture
- experiencing memory problems

You will find these symptoms easier to deal with if you use a step-by-step approach, make lists, keep your home tidy, and prepare for conversations by making notes.

Introduction

The consequences of Parkinson's are not simply physical. They can also involve mental changes in, for instance, perception, thought and reasoning. These are known as cognitive changes. Memory problems may also occur, but these are not the most important. Depression may be another symptom (see page 218). Not everybody is affected and for many people the physical symptoms will continue to be dominant.

This chapter offers information on:
- The causes of mental changes
- What mental changes can occur?
- What can be done about these mental changes?

220

"The doctor said that Parkinson's meant that something was wrong with my head. I immediately thought that I was going senile. But that turns out not to be the case."

The causes of mental changes

The causes of these mental changes are not completely clear. They may be triggered by the physical changes associated with Parkinson's.

A great many people with Parkinson's are troubled by fatigue. Everything involves more effort. Not just everyday activities such as walking or driving a car, but also the absorbing and processing of information. It's possible that these mental changes are partially a consequence of this lack of energy.

There may be other causes of mental changes in someone with Parkinson's. The side effects of some medications may include confusion and short-term memory loss. Some mental changes are the result of ageing.

What mental changes can occur?

People sometimes find it difficult to switch from one subject to another

One way of understanding this is to recognise that to the person with Parkinson's, some parts of the previous subject may still be in the air. If something new occurs, parts of the previous subject can be included in the new subject. It is as if a blackboard has not been cleaned properly and there are still a few old words amongst the new ones.

This switching problem is difficult for outsiders to understand if the divisions between one subject and another seem obvious to them.

Examples of this problem are:
- A person waiting for a particular phone call can be confused by someone else phoning instead. He or she could find it difficult to switch to this new event as they would still be thinking of the person they originally expected to call.
- It can take time to sink in that the person has left a particular environment such as their home. He or she will react as if they were still at home.
- Images and sounds also hang around for a longer period of time. A dog owner may not notice that her dog is no longer resting against her feet because she feels as if it is.
- The point where the subject of a conversation changes can be tricky. The person with Parkinson's may revert to the previous subject or become confused.
- In a meeting, someone may suddenly realise that he or she is still discussing items that other people finished with minutes ago.

Reading and watching TV becomes more difficult

There are a number of factors here. First, as previously mentioned, people with Parkinson's may experience fatigue. Sitting and holding a book may be tiring. There is also evidence that it takes longer before someone can understand the content of a particular text. Processing information takes more time and involves more effort. This increases according to the difficulty of the book. Problems with reading are not generally due to forgetfulness but are caused by a combination of slowness and fatigue. Many people with Parkinson's therefore prefer to read simpler books and short stories.

Following TV programmes may also become more difficult. People may be distracted by their own thoughts, which causes concentration problems. Adjusting to a rapid succession of images and speech can also be tricky.

Holding a conversation is no longer an automatic process

- It can be difficult for someone with Parkinson's to keep track of the thread of a conversation. They may often increase their difficulties by dragging everything into the story. This is quite understandable: someone who is unclear about what he is getting at, will tend to digress.
- A person may forget what he or she wanted to say. It can be on the tip of their tongue, but they can't pin it down.
- Sometimes a person goes completely blank although he is under no pressure whatsoever. What he wanted to say has simply vanished.

One danger can be that people begin to avoid contact with others, which may result in their becoming withdrawn.

A person may find it difficult to do two things at a time

Sometimes it is no longer possible, either physically or mentally, to do more than one thing at once. For instance, in a conversation you are doing a number of things simultaneously: asking questions, giving answers and in the meantime considering what is being said. This can be difficult for some people with Parkinson's. If they want to understand the conversation, they may be left with the choice of either listening or talking, but not both. Conducting a conversation with a number of people simultaneously is therefore for them no longer a practical possibility.

A person becomes swamped in details and loses the overall picture

Examples of this problem are:

- Instructions for using equipment soon become too difficult to follow.
- Following a simple recipe can cause major problems unless you organise and prepare everything in advance.

222

Memory problems

- Sometimes it can be difficult to access your memory. Everything is still there, but it's a question of getting at it.
- It is possible to remember too much. This has been described above as the blackboard that has not been thoroughly cleaned.

Our memory functions better when we can observe and store things in relation to each other. A person with Parkinson's tends to remember details in isolation but not the overall picture and therefore experiences problems. Remembering details is difficult enough in itself and they can be almost impossible to recall in their original context.

What can be done about these mental changes?

If you notice that you can no longer trust yourself while holding a conversation or if you feel that you are losing the overall picture of what is happening around you, an orderly lifestyle can help a lot. For example, you might:

- take some time during the evening to reflect on the things you have to do the next day
- prepare for important conversations by making a list of keywords,
- use a diary or notebook to write reminders to yourself
- keep everything at home in its place
- make sure your daily life includes helpful routines.

If you think it is possible that any of your problems are related to your medication, you could discuss this with your doctor and see whether this could be adjusted in any way. This might bring about some improvements.

A carer, family and friends can be helpful. They can discuss your mental changes and offer their perspective on them. They might be able to reassure you or they might encourage you to express your fears about mental changes. It can be very helpful to discuss problems rather than keeping them to yourself. (See also Chapter 5 '*Talking about your illness*'). Other people may help you to keep in contact with the outside world and they may also be able to suggest ways to help with memory problems.

223

author: - E.H.Coene, M.D., September Foundation,
the Netherlands

advisors: - Professor L.J. Findley, T.D., O.L.J., M.D.,
F.R.C.P., F.A.C.P., Consultant Neurologist
"Avenue House", Romford, UK
- Dr. C.E. Clarke, Consultant in Neurology
& Honorary Senior Lecturer, Hull Royal
Infirmary, UK
- Dr. J. van Manen, neurologist, advisor to
the Dutch Parkinson's Disease Society,
the Netherlands
- Dr. J.D. Speelman, neurologist, Academic
Medical Centre, University of Amsterdam,
the Netherlands
- Professor J.P.W.F. Lakke, chairperson of
the Medical Advisory Council of the Dutch
Parkinson's Disease Society, the Netherlands

29

Medication that contains levodopa

Summary

This chapter includes a summary of the medication that contains levodopa.

Parkinson's Disease is caused by a shortage of a chemical called dopamine that is made in the brain and controls the co-ordination of movement. Levodopa is a chemical that is converted in the brain into dopamine and which therefore counters the shortage of dopamine. This in turn often causes the symptoms to diminish dramatically.

Levodopa is the most effective of all anti-Parkinson's medication. It often works very well, particularly in the beginning. Unfortunately it becomes less effective as time passes so that the symptoms will again increase. It is not possible to predict when this will occur.

Levodopa can have side effects such as nausea and vomiting, appetite reduction and balance problems. These side effects are rarely serious. If you think that you are experiencing a side effect, you should consult your doctor as soon as possible.

There are a number of more serious side effects. They may occur when a person has been using levodopa for a number of years. These side effects include an unpredictable on-off effect, an end-of-dose deterioration, abnormal movements and cramps.

It is sometimes necessary to stop using levodopa. However, the side effects may disappear once the dosage has been adjusted.

Introduction

There is a general introduction to the subject of medication to treat Parkinson's in Chapter 3 *Treatment and Medication*.

Examples of the medication used to treat the symptoms of Parkinson's are given in Chapters 2 *General symptoms* and 27 *Particular symptoms*.

This chapter contains detailed information about the medication containing levodopa that is used to treat *Parkinson's Disease*. This chapter covers:

- Overview
- How does medication that contains levodopa work?
- What symptoms does the medication relieve?
- Are there different types of levodopa?
- What medication is available?
- Taking the medication
- What are the side effects?
- Serious side effects that can appear when levodopa has been taken for a long time

Overview

The medication used in the treatment of Parkinson's Disease can be divided into six groups:

a. medication that contains levodopa
b. medication that imitates the effect of dopamine: dopamine agonists
c. anti-cholinergics
d. amantadine
e. medication that prolongs the effect of dopamine
f. medication used for other diseases and conditions

This chapter covers medication that contains levodopa; other groups are described in Chapter 30 '*Other medication*'.

The medication affects the levels of certain chemicals in the brain and also the way they work with each other. The effects that the drugs have on brain chemistry help to counteract the various symptoms of Parkinson's. As Parkinson's affects people in different ways, however, it may be necessary to use a variety of drugs over time, at different dosages, depending on the symptoms you are experiencing.

Side effects

The information on medication that follows includes a summary of what each sort of medication does, directions for how it should be taken and a description of its possible side effects and what can be done to counteract these. Try not to be alarmed by the description of the side effects. You may not experience any of them and you certainly won't experience all! You can talk to your doctor about any aspect of your medication and you should keep him informed about how you are getting on.

225

> "I've got to take my medication all the time, even when I feel well. Sometimes I find that difficult. You take medicine if you feel ill, not when you actually feel fine. And even though I know why I've got to take them every day, I sometimes find it hard and then I forget.
> I don't actually realise I'm doing it. It's not as if I think to myself: today I feel OK so I'll forget the medication. I simply don't think about it.

> *Fortunately my wife is very strict and she keeps an eye on me. Recently I caught her making notes in her diary: when I'd taken the medication she made a mark. At first I was angry. I thought: don't be so daft, I'm not a child. But then she got mad. She said: if you forget to take them and suddenly get worse again, I will have to look after things. Well, I think she had a point."*

The rest of this chapter will describe medication that contains levodopa.

How does medication that contains levodopa work?

Parkinson's Disease is caused by a shortage of a chemical called dopamine, which is made in the brain and controls co-ordination of movement. You can't take dopamine as a tablet to make up the shortage because it can't cross the barrier that exists between the blood circulation system and the brain. If you take levodopa medication, however, this can cross the barrier and so enter the brain. Here it is converted into dopamine. This helps to relieve the dopamine shortage and so reduces the symptoms of Parkinson's.

There is a complication to this process, however. The chemical responsible for converting levodopa to dopamine, called dopa decarboxylase, is not only found in the brain but also in the blood and the intestines. As a result, the levodopa is converted to dopamine in places where it isn't needed and where it can cause side effects. To stop this happening, what is called a dopa decarboxylase inhibitor is added to levodopa medication. This stops the conversion of levodopa into dopamine before the levodopa reaches the brain. As the inhibitor cannot cross the blood-brain barrier, though, it doesn't affect the process inside the brain. Dopamine can therefore be made in the brain (where it is needed), but not outside it.

What symptoms does the medication relieve?

Levodopa is the most effective of all anti-Parkinson's medication. It is particularly helpful in counteracting slowness and poverty of movement and is often effective against muscle stiffness. It can also help to reduce shaking. It is least effective against problems with balance, speech and hesitation in starting movements, which are symptoms that tend to appear later in the course of the disease.

When someone begins with levodopa the results are often extremely good. As the disease progresses, however, the effect becomes less and the levodopa works for a shorter time. The dose then has to be increased. It is impossible to predict when this will take place. The dose is kept as low as possible to minimise side effects in the long-term.

When starting treatment with levodopa, the first effects are noticeable after three or four days. They become stronger as time goes on and are complete after about two months. If someone stops taking levodopa, the effect is noticeable after about three days and after two weeks the effect of the drug will have disappeared completely. It is dangerous to stop taking levodopa suddenly. It can be stopped for one to two days to allow an operation to take place but for no longer than that. If you need, or want, to stop taking levodopa, consult your neurologist first.

In the past, levodopa was regularly stopped for a week because it seemed that afterwards the effect of the drug was increased. This was called a drug 'holiday'. This approach is not used nowadays. It is unpleasant and sometimes even dangerous because all the symptoms re-appear.

Are there different types of levodopa?

There are three types of levodopa medication.

I Levodopa alone:

This is not prescribed very often nowadays.

II Levodopa drugs with a dopa decarboxylase inhibitor

In this medication a dopa decarboxylase inhibitor is added to the levodopa, which ensures that the levodopa is only converted into dopamine in the brain. Less dopamine forms outside the brain, so side effects such as nausea and vomiting are rare. Brand names include Madopar and Sinemet.

III Slow-release levodopa drugs

This medication can work for a longer period than ordinary levodopa as the levodopa is taken up in the blood very gradually. It needs to be taken fewer times per day as a result. The advantage can be that side effects such as abnormal movements occur less often, and at night and on waking up there will be fewer problems with stiffness and slowness. It is not actually a 'wonder drug', because the effect is not always as positive as summarised here. The dosage of this drug is higher than with the other levodopa drugs because not all the levodopa is taken up.

What medication is available?

Trade name	Generic name	Sizes available
Sinemet	co-careldopa	110mg, 275 mg
Sinemet-Plus	co-careldopa	125 mg
Sinemet LS	co-careldopa LS	62.5 mg
Sinemet CR	co-careldopa CR	250 mg
Half Sinemet CR	co-careldopa CR	125 mg
Madopar	co-beneldopa	62.5 mg, 125 mg, 250 mg
Madopar dispersible	co-beneldopa	62.5 mg, 125 mg
Madopar CR	co-beneldopa CR	125 mg
Levodopa	levodopa	500 mg

Taking the medication

Levodopa is taken with a glass of water. Its effect is noticeable after about half an hour and lasts up to four to six hours initially. You could take it just after breakfast and then have a wash, shave etc., to take advantage of its effects.

If you take the medication on an empty stomach it works quickly but you may have stomach problems. If you take it with a meal there is less chance of stomach problems but it takes longer to work. If you take it with a meal that contains a lot of protein (meat, cheese, milk etc.), it will take even longer before the drug works because protein is absorbed into the blood in the same way as levodopa. You are therefore advised not to eat too much protein at any single meal, in case it interferes with the working of the medication. See Chapter 9 'Diet' for more detailed instructions on timing your medication and mealtimes.

If you forget to take your pills on one occasion, it is not necessary to take a double dose next time.

What are the side effects?

A number of, mainly slight, side effects can occur shortly after beginning to take levodopa. You can discuss these - and possible remedies - with your doctor who can help you decide whether the problems outweigh the benefits of the medication. He or he will also be willing to discuss dosages with you to help make sure that any side effects are minimised. Possible side effects and remedies are listed below.

Nausea and vomiting

These are the most common side effects of taking levodopa. When the body becomes accustomed to the drug, the nausea becomes less. After half an hour the nausea usually disappears, particularly if you lie down. The nausea also becomes less if levodopa is taken during a meal, for example with unsweetened yoghurt. Make sure you have an adequate breakfast, not simply a drink, and do not drink coffee with it. Changing to a levodopa drug with a decarboxylase inhibitor can help (for example Madopar or Sinemet). If this does not help, special medication for nausea and vomiting can be prescribed - for example domperidone (Motilium). This must be taken at the same time as the levodopa.

Less common side effects from taking levodopa include the following:

Appetite reduction

If you find your appetite is reduced when taking drugs containing levodopa, speak to your doctor or to a dietician. Changes to what or when you eat should help with this problem.

Balance problem

If these are serious you should speak to your doctor.

Confusion or hallucinations

With large doses of levodopa, some people become confused, experience mood swings or hallucinations (seeing things that are not there). Your doctor should be alerted and will decide whether these symptoms are caused by the levodopa. If they are, the dose should be reduced. There is a small group of people who cannot tolerate the drug at all because of these side-effects. Other types of drugs may help them.[1]

Dizziness

If you stand up suddenly, dizziness can result. To prevent this, take your time getting up. If you have been lying down, sit up before you stand, then stand up slowly and hold on to something. Wait for a few seconds before you start to walk.

Drowsiness

The time at which the levodopa is taken can be changed and possibly the dose adjusted.

Increased interest in sex

Levodopa very occasionally has the effect of making a person more interested in sex. This is not usually a problem if people know that it can happen.

Restlessness and sleeplessness

Levodopa can make someone more active mentally and sometimes rather restless. This can occasionally cause sleeplessness, which happens mainly at the start of treatment with levodopa and if the drug is taken before going to bed. These side effects usually get less after a couple of weeks. If levodopa is interfering with sleep, it can help to take the last dose of the day earlier or to adjust the dosage.

Taste problems

Levodopa can leave a nasty taste in the mouth. You cannot do much about this except, perhaps, suck a peppermint. Levodopa can also affect your sense of taste. Some people say that it makes tea and coffee taste metallic. If this is the case, you may need to experiment with different brands or try to find other drinks that taste more pleasant. You might also try using more or less sugar. For more advice, consult a dietician.

Urine: change in colour

The urine can become dark. This is nothing to worry about, see page 217.

Serious side effects that can appear when levodopa has been taken for a long time

There are a number of more serious side effects, described below, that can occur when levodopa is taken. If they appear at all, however, this would only be after levodopa had been taken for *several years*. These include:
1. unpredictable on-off effect
2. end-of-dose deterioration
3. abnormal movements
4. cramps

1. Unpredictable on-off effect

This means that one minute someone can move easily, perhaps with an abnormal movement from time to time. This is the 'on' period when the levodopa is working well. This can suddenly turn into an 'off' period during which the effect of the levodopa is greatly reduced and the Parkinson's symptoms re-appear.

Some people can then suffer a great deal from stiffness and slowness of movement. From one moment to the next they can almost freeze in one position. For this reason, '*freezing*' is the term used to describe this occurrence. It is as if a switch is being turned on and off - hence the term 'on-off'. This can happen several times a day. Freezing is described in more detail in Chapter 8 '*Help with movement*' together with suggestions for preventing it.

To counteract the on-off effect in general, it can help to take the levodopa in smaller quantities more often during the day. In serious cases, the on-off effect occurs so often that people talk of a 'yo-yo' effect. This is difficult to treat. Sometimes a slow release levodopa drug, such as Madopar HBS or Sinemet CR, can be effective. A more common option is to combine the levodopa preparation with one that imitates the effect of dopamine, a dopamine agonist (e.g. Pugolide or Rapnivol,) Information about this type of drug appears in the next section of this chapter.

2. The end-of-dose deterioration (wearing off effect)
After a number of years the effect of levodopa becomes weaker. As each dose is exhausted, the Parkinson's symptoms appear again and stiffness and slowness can occur. This is comparable with the 'off' periods described above. It is at its strongest when waking up in the morning because of the length of time since the levodopa was last taken.

A number of possible remedies can be tried. First of all, an afternoon nap can help. Sometimes a combination of a levodopa drug with a dopamine agonist can give better results. Sometimes the dose of the levodopa drug can be reduced. Taking the levodopa in smaller doses more often during the day may also work. In this way, the first dose is usually left the same and the total dose remains unchanged. If this does not help, levodopa may need to be taken more often during the day, which means that the total dose is increased.

3. Abnormal movements (dyskinesia)
These are jerky movements, mainly grimacing, chewing and licking. To a lesser extent, pulling movements of the arms and legs also occur and perhaps twisting movements of the trunk. These appear at the maximum effect of the levodopa. When Parkinson's starts when someone is young, these movements seem to develop more rapidly.

Dyskinesia seems to occur more often if treatment is started with a high dose. Usually these movements are more of a problem for other people than for the person concerned. They can, however affect that person's self-confidence and make it more difficult for him or her to make or maintain contact with people.

If the movements hinder walking or disturb the balance, something can certainly be done to help. It is usually helpful if levodopa is taken more often during the day but in lower doses. The total quantity taken can remain the same although it sometimes has to be reduced. If that doesn't work, the medication can be changed to a slow-release levodopa drug such as Madopar HBS or Sinemet CR. This is absorbed very gradually and works for longer. It does not always have an effect however.

4. Cramps (dystonia)

People can suffer from cramp in the calves and feet, especially in the morning. This decreases in the course of the day and can be helped by walking about a little. If further help is needed then quinine can be taken as tonic water or in tablet form.

"I got a medicine box for Christmas. The ideal present! I'm hopeless, forgetful, always have been. Artists, you know... Their thoughts are always somewhere else. Anyway, I regularly forgot to take my pills. Very annoying, because sometimes the illness would get worse and I wasn't able to paint any more. So the medicine box is an answer to my prayers. It's in the studio, in among all the paint, so that I can never miss it. I did paint it of course, because it was ugly as sin. Now it's a nice colour of red, with all sorts of different coloured pills painted on."

author: - E.H.Coene, M.D., September Foundation, the Netherlands

advisors: - Professor L.J. Findley, T.D., O.L.J., M.D., F.R.C.P., F.A.C.P., Consultant Neurologist "Avenue House", Romford, UK
- Dr C.E. Clarke, Consultant in Neurology & Honorary Senior Lecturer, Hull Royal Infirmary, UK
- Dr. J. van Manen, neurologist, advisor to the Dutch Parkinson's Disease Society, the Netherlands
- Dr. J.D. Speelman, neurologist, Academic Medical Centre, University of Amsterdam, the Netherlands
- Professor J.P.W.F. Lakke, chairperson of the Medical Advisory Council of the Dutch Parkinson's Disease Society, the Netherlands

30

Other Medication

Summary

Other forms of medication apart from levodopa are also prescribed for Parkinson's. These are described in this chapter.

They consist of:
- Medication that imitates the effect of dopamine: dopamine agonists.
- Anti-cholinergics. These drugs work on another brain chemical called acetylcholine. They inhibit the action of this chemical, and this has the effect of increasing the action of the available dopamine.
- Amantadine. It is not known how this medication works. It is most often used with people who only have mild symptoms and is most effective at treating slowness of movement and muscular stiffness.
- Medication that prolongs the effect of dopamine. These drugs block the effect of certain chemicals in the brain that are involved with the breakdown of dopamine. This means that the dopamine works for a longer period of time.
- Medication used for other diseases and conditions. Some forms of medication that are actually used for other conditions also seem to work for Parkinson's. This concerns medication that is used to treat depression, beta-blockers and domperidone (Motilium), an anti-sickness drug.

Introduction

There is a general introduction to the subject of medication and Parkinson's in Chapter 3 'Treatment and Medication'.

Examples of the medication used to treat the symptoms of Parkinson's are given in Chapters 2 'General symptoms' and 27 'Particular symptoms'.

This chapter contains detailed information about medication that is used to treat *Parkinson's Disease*. This medication can be divided into six groups:

1. medication that imitates the effect of dopamine: dopamine agonists
2. anticholinergics
3. amantadine

4. medication that prolongs the effect of dopamine
5. medication used for other diseases and conditions

6. medication that contains levodopa

The medication containing levodopa is described in the previous chapter (29). This chapter covers the first five groups.

The medication affects the levels of certain chemicals in the brain and also the way they work with each other. The effects that the drugs have on brain chemistry help to counteract the varied symptoms of Parkinson's. As Parkinson's affects people in different ways, however, it may be necessary to use a variety of drugs over time, at different dosages that depend on the symptoms you are experiencing.

Side effects
The information on medication that follows includes a summary of what each sort of medication does, directions for how it should be taken and a description of its possible side effects and what can be done to counteract these. Try not to be alarmed by the description of the side effects. You may not experience any of them and you certainly will not experience all! You can talk to your doctor about any aspect of your medication and you should keep him informed about how you are getting on.

1. Medication that imitates the effect of dopamine : dopamine agonists

How does this medication work?
These medications imitate the effect of dopamine by stimulating the parts of the brain where the dopamine works. They do not provide extra dopamine. The medication stays in the bloodstream for a longer time than medication containing levodopa and so is used by people who have a fluctuating response to these drugs including the on-off effect described above.

What symptoms does the medication relieve?
These medications help to relieve slowness of movement and muscle stiffness and to a lesser extent they can treat tremor. They can also relieve on-off fluctuations and end-of-dose deterioration and problems that occur in the night such as difficulty in turning over in bed. Apomorphine can be used as a rapid 'rescue' treatment for people with extended 'off' periods of half an hour or more.

233

What medications are available?
- bromocriptine (Parlodel)
- lysuride (Revanil)
- pergolide (Celance)
- ropinerole (Requip)
- cabergoline (Cabaser)
- pramipexole (Mirapexin)
- apomorphine (Britaject). This medication can only be administered by means of an injection or an infusion and is less often used.

Taking the medication

Dopamine agonists are often used in conjunction with medications containing levodopa. This enables smaller doses of levodopa to be taken, which produces a reduction in the side effects associated with it, particularly involuntary movements. Some specialists suggest that younger people with Parkinson's be given this type of drug before adding levodopa at a later date.

These medications should be taken after eating, except for Apomorphine which is either injected or administered by a syringe driver (a pump that delivers the drug under the skin continuously). Injections probably need to involve a carer as there may be times when the person with Parkinson's is unable to administer them.

What are the side effects?

These are generally similar to the side effects of medication containing levodopa described above. Confusion and hallucinations can be more serious than with the use of levodopa, especially in older people. Other side effects can include pale fingers and toes in cold conditions and a stuffy nose.

The more common side effects, particularly nausea and vomiting, can usually be prevented or overcome by starting at low dosages and building the dose up gradually over a couple of weeks. Some doctors routinely prescribe domperidone against nausea and vomiting when first introducing any of these drugs.

2. Anticholinergics

How does this medication work?

Anticholinergic drugs work on another brain chemical called acetylcholine. They inhibit the action of this chemical, which has the effect of increasing the action of the dopamine available. This helps to produce better control of movement.

What symptoms does the medication relieve?

Anti-cholinergic drugs have a beneficial effect on tremor, and also on muscle stiffness. They have less effect on problems of balance and posture. Anticholinergic drugs can also be helpful for people who produce a lot of saliva (dribble) or who perspire heavily. They are less effective than levodopa, but have fewer side effects. These drugs are often prescribed to younger patients with mild symptoms.

234

What medications are available?
- orphenadrine (Disipal)
- bipiriden (Akineton)
- benzatropine (Cogentin)
- benzhexol (Artane)
- procyclidine (Kemadrin)

Taking the medication

Take the medication with a glass of water. It works for about four hours.

Anticholinergics are often the first medication to be prescribed, particularly when shaking is pronounced. In the long term, they are often combined with other drugs that are effective in dealing with other symptoms. People who perspire very little must make sure that they do not get overheated in hot weather. They should take care during sport or in a sauna.

What are the side effects?
Most of the side effects are mild and serious ones rarely occur. All are reduced by taking a lower dose.

Blurred vision
This usually disappears.

Confusion and short term memory problems
These side effects can appear in older people and so these drugs are not usually prescribed to people over 75.[2] If they are serious or if hallucinations are experienced, the dose will need to be adjusted or the medication stopped. Short-term memory problems may require changes to normal routines. People might need to make lists or use a diary to remind themselves of things they have to do. They might need to organise their medication so that they are always certain when they took their last dose and when their next one is needed.

Constipation
If constipation occurs, the suggestions in Chapter 10 '*Diet*' should help.

Difficulty in passing urine
This would only be a problem for men with prostate problems. If you have experienced these problems, you should talk to your doctor, see page 216.

A dry mouth
The drugs reduce the amount of saliva produced, which may become more sticky. Taking frequent sips of water or sucking a sweet can help, see page 210.

Raised pressure in the eye
This only occurs at high dosages and might be a problem for people with a family history of glaucoma. You should mention to your doctor if this applies to you and you should have the pressure in your eyes checked regularly at your optician.

Other side effects may include dry skin resulting from reduced perspiration, and palpitations. The latter only occurs if a high dosage is taken.

235

3. Amantadine

How does this medication work?
It is not clear how amantadine (Symmetrel) works.

What symptoms does the medication relieve?

It is most often used with people who have only mild symptoms of Parkinson's and is most effective at treating slowness of movement and muscular stiffness. Occasionally, when added later on, it can reduce dyskinesia, but this does not occur in every case.

Taking the medication

Capsules are taken with a glass of water.

The effect of amantadine is similar to that of levodopa but weaker. Its effect usually decreases after six months to a year although this may improve if treatment with this drug is discontinued for a few months.

What are the side effects?

Side effects are generally uncommon. They include nausea and dizziness when standing up. Remedies for this side effect appear under 'Medications containing levodopa'. Dry mouth, constipation and blurred vision are discussed under 'Anticholinergics'. More serious side effects are confusion and hallucinations, when a doctor's advice should be sought.

Other side effects include:

Sleeplessness
To counteract this, the final dose should be taken at least eight hours before going to bed or in one single dose in the morning.

Swollen ankles and skin discolouration (blue-purple spots or lines)
Neither of these is serious and both will disappear if the drug is discontinued. Wearing elastic stockings can help swollen ankles, which are caused by fluid retention. The use of diuretics is not recommended for people with Parkinson's because they can cause unacceptably low blood pressure and can aggravate tiredness.

4. Medication that prolongs the effects of dopamine

How does this medication work?

There are two types: selegiline (Eldepryl) and entacapone (Comtess).
Selegiline blocks the action of another brain chemical called monoamine oxidase B or MAO-B. This chemical causes the breakdown of dopamine. The use of selegiline itself therefore increases levels of dopamine. Another enzyme, catechol ortho methyltransferase (COMT) also breaks down dopamine and can be blocked by entacapone.

It has been claimed that selegiline is not only effective against Parkinson's symptoms, but can combat the progress of the disease itself. There is some evidence to suggest that it works in such a 'preventive' manner. That is why some doctors immediately prescribe it to treat the first symptoms of Parkinson's. However, at present it is the subject of considerable debate.

In 1995, a paper published in the British Medical Journal reported that people with Parkinson's who took selegiline with levodopa had a higher mortality rate than those on levodopa alone. This study is not consistent with results of many other studies. More research is needed before any firm conclusions can be drawn. Anyone concerned about these findings should contact their medical adviser.[3]

What symptoms do the medications relieve?
They help, when combined with levodopa, to relieve the on-off effect. The dose of levodopa may have to be reduced. Entacapone is a more recent drug that can also boost dopamine levels.

What medications are available?
- selegiline (Eldepryl)
- entacapone (Comtess)

Taking the medication
The tablets should be taken with water after a meal in the morning. Do not chew them. As selegiline is mostly used in combination with levodopa, it is important not to exceed the stated dosage as this can risk lowering the blood pressure to a dangerous extent.

What are the side effects?
When selegiline is combined with levodopa, it will increase the possibility of side effects from the levodopa. You should be particularly aware of any mental side effects. If you need anti-depressant drugs while you are using selegiline, consult your doctor or neurologist, since not all anti-depressant drugs can be used in combination with selegiline.

When a combination of selegiline and levodopa increases the side effects of levodopa, the dose of levodopa should be modified so that the side effects decrease.

More information
Another drug of this type (tolcapone, Tasmar) has been taken off the market in the UK because of the serious side effects.

5. Medication used for other diseases and conditions
Medication used to combat other diseases can also be useful against the symptoms of Parkinson's Disease.

Medications for depression
Certain medications that are used for depression (the tricyclic antidepressants) have to some extent the same effect as the anticholinergics. Examples are imipramine (Tofranil) and amitryptiline (Tryptizol). They become effective after two to four weeks. Their side effects are a dry mouth, slow bowel movements and difficulties with passing water.

Beta-blockers
These medications can partially alleviate tremor. They are particularly effective

at treating the hands and, to a lesser extent, the head and voice. One example is propranolol (Inderal). Side effects are low blood pressure (particularly when standing up quickly), a slow pulse rate and fatigue.

domperidone (Motilium)

This is a anti-sickness drug that can be used in Parkinson's Disease if nausea or vomiting is a problem on anti - Parkinson's drugs. Other anti-sickness drugs such as prochlorperazine (Stemetil) and metoclopramide (Maxolon) cannot be taken in Parkinson's Disease as they make the movement problems worse.

author: - E.H.Coene, M.D., the September Foundation, the Netherlands

advisors: - Professor L.J. Findley, T.D., O.L.J., M.D., F.R.C.P., F.A.C.P., Consultant Neurologist "Avenue House", Romford, UK
- Dr C.E. Clarke, Consultant in Neurology & Honorary Senior Lecturer, Hull Royal Infirmary, UK
- Dr. J. van Manen, Consultant Neurologist, advisor to the Dutch Parkinson's Disease Society, the Netherlands
- Dr. J.D. Speelman, Consultant Neurologist, the Academic Medical Centre, University of Amsterdam, the Netherlands

31

Surgical treatment

Summary

Medication helps most people with Parkinson's reasonably well. However, it does not work for everyone, and surgery may help a small number of people. Operations are not performed very often, and then only as a last resort.

Research is still going on into the effects of surgery. These involve various types of operations, usually consisting of making inactive (or stimulating) the part of the brain which is responsible for the disease. These procedures are known as pallidotomy, thalamotomy, deep brain stimulation and operating on the nucleus subthalamicus. Another type of operation involves the implantation of brain tissue.

Introduction

The symptoms of Parkinson's Disease are usually treated with medication and with various forms of movement therapy. In recent years, however, there has been renewed interest in the surgical treatment of Parkinson's, but operations are performed not very often. But although the operations are performed infrequently, the number of active surgical centres performing surgery for Parkinson's Disease is increasing. Therefore, this chapter includes a summary of these operations.

This chapter offers information on:

- Thalamotomy
- Pallidotomy
- Deep Brain stimulation
- New developments
- Brain implants

239

"My neurologist said that they hardly ever operate as a therapy for people with Parkinson's. Only in special cases. I can well imagine – a brain operation is no joke..."

Thalamotomy

In thalamotomy an electrode is directed to the thalamus, which is the part of the brain that influences the tremor. The technique used is similar to that used in pallidotomy. The electrode is removed after the operation.

This operation can diminish tremor on one side of the body. To a lesser extent, it may also improve the stiffness on that side of the body. These operations, however, are generally not effective against other symptoms such as slowness of movement, speech, etc. If someone is treated for tremor on one side of the body, usually the other side of the body is also affected, but less severely. The tremor on that side of the body can become more serious during the months following the operation. But that is due to the natural course of the disease and is not a consequence of the operation. This operation was frequently performed before the discovery of levodopa. Nowadays it is only resorted to in cases where tremor cannot be treated with medication or where their side effects have become unbearable.

Greater risks are involved when this operation is performed on both sides of the brain (so as to diminish tremors on both sides of the body). These risks especially include disturbance of balance and of speech.

Pallidotomy

Pallidotomy is a form of so-called stereotactic surgery. During these operations, a small area of one side of the brain is made inactive. The operation is performed by drilling a small opening in the skull through which an electrode is introduced. This electrode is placed in the part of the brain called the globus pallidus. This particular area is then made inactive by means of a small electrical current or by freezing. The electrode is then removed. This operation takes place under local anaesthetic and the person with Parkinson's remains conscious throughout. No part of the brain is removed in this operation, but an area with a cross-section of approximately seven millimetres is rendered inactive. The operation is generally successful (in 70 to 80 per cent of all cases). There is a small risk of stroke, speech disorders, paralysis or visual problems.

When applied to the appropriate area, pallidotomy not only relieves the three main symptoms of Parkinson's (slowness, rigidity and tremor), it especially reduces the sudden, involuntary movements that can result from drug therapy. In recent years there has been a revival of interest in pallidotomy. Although immediate benefits have been observed in most people, it is important to determine whether improvement is maintained in the long-term. Here, research has not yet been concluded.

Deep brain stimulation

In this type of operation, an electrode is introduced into the brain and left behind. A small electrical current running through the electrode can temporarily disconnect that part of the brain to stop tremor and dyskinesia. The symptoms may reappear in the course of time, at which point the person with Parkinson's can decide whether or not he wants to disconnect that area again. For instance: when something important has to be done or simply when he wants to go to sleep. This operation is called deep brain stimulation and can be performed on both sides of the brain. It is a fairly recent development and its long-term effects are as yet unclear.

Deep brain stimulation can be performed in the following areas of the brain: thalamus, globus pallidus and the nucleus subthalamicus. The indications and effects of this technique are the same as in thalamotomy and pallidotomy. The advantages are that the operation can be performed on both sides of the brain and there seem to be less permanent complications as a result of this technique.

New developments

For several years now, an operation on another area of the brain also seems to offer possibilities. This part is known as the nucleus subthalamicus.

It can be stimulated through deep brain stimulation (see above). Sometimes this area is made inactive, but this is a controversial technique that is virtually never performed.

Some people are able to take a lower dosage of medication.

Brain implants

During the last 20 years, research has been undertaken into the effects of implanting brain tissue in people with Parkinson's Disease. This tissue is derived from human foetuses. These brain implants are also known as *foetal implants*. The aim of this operation is to supplement the cells which do not produce enough dopamine with young cells that can take over their action. So far, about 200 operations have been performed. The results of these operations have been variable.

For more information on surgical treatment, please consult your specialist or The Parkinson's Disease Society.

Notes

242

Notes

author: - E.H. Coene, M.D., September
Foundation, the Netherlands
advisors - Dr. C. Grainger, Consultant in Public
Health Medicine, NHS Executive West
Midlands, UK
- Professor E. Schadé, the Institute for
General Practice, University of
Amsterdam, the Netherlands
- F.G.P.H. Oyen, psychiatrist,
the Netherlands

32

Coping with stress

Summary

Everyone experiences tension. Tension is not per se unhealthy but too much tension can be a problem. Then it is known as stress.

People with Parkinson's also experience stress. Sometimes they find it more difficult to deal with than other people.
Moreover, suffering from a chronic disease like Parkinson's is stressful in itself. For instance certain situations, such as freezing, can cause a great deal of stress. In addition, a person with Parkinson's may feel that he is constantly being stared at. Speech problems can also be a source of stress.

Because people with Parkinson's can experience a higher level of stress, they may find that it helps to pay more attention to the process of dealing with stress.
The first step is to learn to detect the signs of stress. Examples of these signs include back pain, headaches, gloominess, irritation and fear.
You need to act immediately once you detect these signs. Everyone does this in his or her own way but there are some basic ground rules. For instance: try to discover and remove the cause of the stress, live as healthy a life as possible, make sure that you relax enough, maintain social contacts and avoid sleeping pills.

Many people do relaxation exercises. These often involve breathing because breathing and stress often go together. Practically everyone can learn these breathing exercises.

Introduction

This chapter deals with stress: what it is, its consequences and how you can cope with it. The following subjects re introduced:
- What is stress?
- The stress reaction
- What are the benefits of stress?
- Are we all equally sensitive to stress?
- What are the causes of stress?
- Parkinson's and stress
- The symptoms of stress

- Preventing unhealthy stress
- A relaxation exercise

This chapter is based on two fundamental principles:
First: stress is not necessarily a bad thing. It is the body's natural reaction to pressure and gives you the drive to achieve your goals.
Second: stress cannot be avoided. Everyone experiences pressure sometimes and it is impossible to eradicate stress from your life entirely. Most people can cope with some stress but too much can have adverse consequences. This particularly applies to people with Parkinson's.

> *"I'm naturally excitable. I get upset at the smallest and most insignificant of things. But that's just the way I am. Since I've had Parkinson's, I find it hard not to be angry all the time. Or that's how it feels. But a couple of years ago I learnt some breathing techniques. You sit down quietly, you breathe from your abdomen and let the breath flow deep into your pelvis. It really helps. Nowadays, I first count to ten before I vent my rage."*

What is stress?

The concept of stress has become increasingly prominent over the last few years, yet there is much confusion surrounding it. Each day people experience stress or pressure. This can be for physical reasons (an infection, extremely cold weather), external causes (perhaps an argument at work) or it can come from within (worries or even the individual's natural personality). For most of us, most of the time, it will not be a problem. However it becomes known as unhealthy stress at the point where someone begins to experience pressure as being burdensome; when the amount of stress they are placed under is more than they can tolerate.

The stress reaction

When someone suffers from stress, his body will react to it in a fixed way, known as the stress reaction. This develops in three phases, depending on how long the pressure continues. As an example, suppose you have an argument with someone, perhaps a partner or neighbour and you are upset by this. In the *first phase* of the stress reaction the body enters a state of alertness: the breathing rate is increased, the muscles tense, the throat constricts. If the quarrel is then resolved, the body will relax once more.

If the quarrel is not resolved you may feel upset for days. The *second phase* is when the body is unable to relax and the muscles are still tense. If the problem is sorted out, these symptoms will disappear and the person will return to his or her normal relaxed state.

The *third phase* begins if the problem is not solved. The person might be living under constant pressure and be unable to relax. This may lead to symptoms such as backache, insomnia or the individual becoming increasingly withdrawn. This is known as *unhealthy stress* and is harmful. If nothing is done to alleviate the symptoms, the body will become increasingly exhausted. The individual will suffer from severe strain and will finally enter a state of nervous collapse.

What are the benefits of stress?

There is no harm in a little stress, in fact it is necessary for survival. The first phase of the stress reaction enables you to react effectively to danger, for example by running away from a threatening situation, or fighting it (known as the flight or fight response). A limited amount of stress can also help you to perform well. A bit of stress gives you that extra energy that is needed to do something as well as possible.

Too little stress may be as bad as too much. Too little stress can make life dull, and can lower your level of achievement. So imagine a common situation that people with Parkinson's may encounter: you have to conduct an important conversation in which your interests are at stake, and you have to convince the other person that your arguments are correct. A limited amount of stress will actually enable you to handle the situation more effectively.

Are we all equally sensitive to stress?

Some people are more sensitive to stress than others. What leaves one person unaffected will cause another sleepless nights - one person has a higher tolerance for stress than the other. This is connected with the way in which you view events: some people are easy-going while others take life more seriously.

Research shows that people have more chance of suffering from harmful stress if they show the following sorts of characteristics: always being in a hurry, setting themselves difficult tasks for which they do not allow enough time, being desperate to achieve, tending to see other people as opponents, trying to do two things at a time, being scared of making mistakes, being obsessed by their work, finding it difficult to relax and finding it hard to admit that they are tired.

Do not worry if a couple of these examples sound familiar. They are normal and lots of people have them. If you experience most of them, it means that you are sensitive to stress. In this case, it may be a good idea to keep an eye on yourself!

What are the causes of stress?

Stress is connected with levels of pressure and how much a person can tolerate. Virtually anything can make the level of pressure unbearable, but there are number of general points to remember:
* recurrent stressful situations can be more damaging than single shocks
* positive events such as arranging a wedding can cause as much stress as negative ones
* loss also plays an important role in stress - the loss of a friend or loved one, the loss of your ability to do something
* people become more easily upset if they feel uncertain about their future
* being unable to develop your potential may cause stress
* making too high demands of yourself can be very stressful
* feelings of loneliness may also be stressfull

All of these examples are relevant to Parkinson's.

Parkinson's and stress

Parkinson's can cause increased levels of stress. Research shows that a third of all people with Parkinson's can be diagnosed as anxious. People with Parkinson's experience stress in different ways, for example[1], bodily symptoms, lack of self-control, anxiety and psychological distress. They may also find difficulties with social interaction and with relationships such as those with partners and family. All these symptoms can make a person become increasingly withdrawn, making the feeling of stress worse.

There are many reasons why someone with Parkinson's may feel stressed. For example:

- Suffering from a (chronic) disease is stressful in itself. You may be afraid of the symptoms, and find yourself unable to do things as you used to. You may feel uncertain about the future
- People with Parkinson's experience stress in particular situations. 'Freezing' is an example of this. It is extremely embarrassing to find yourself suddenly rooted to the spot on the street or in a doorway.
- People often notice symptoms such as tremors, drooling and a stooped posture. A person with Parkinson's can begin to feel that he or she is being constantly stared at.
- Speech problems in Parkinson's symptom can result in a lot of stress. If you are difficult to understand, you will find it increasingly difficult to talk to other people. This may lead to you avoiding social contact and perhaps result in loneliness.

In short, people with Parkinson's will regularly encounter stressful situations. This chapter provides information about how to deal with it.

The symptoms of stress

As explained above, the stress reaction comprises three phases. During the first phase your breathing rate increases, muscles become tense, your throat constricts, you feel cold or your hands sweat, your heart pounds. If you notice this happening, it means that you are experiencing stress, and your body is reacting to it. If the cause of the stress goes, then so will the symptoms. However, if these symptoms occur on a regular basis and do not disappear rapidly, it means that you are staying tense, the second phase. If you do not take action, then you will end up entering the third, unhealthy phase of the stress reaction.

Many symptoms are associated with the *third phase*:

Physical symptoms: backache (particularly in the lower back), headaches (a nagging that feels like a vice around your head and which becomes worse during the course of the day), migraine (attacks of throbbing headaches that are sometimes accompanied by nausea), insomnia, heart palpitations (a pounding feeling in the chest), lack of appetite, claustrophobia, dizziness (sometimes due to hyperventilation), intestinal problems (diarrhoea or constipation).

Thinking in a different way: for instance, only seeing the downside of the situation or repetitive patterns of thought.
Changes in feelings: you may feel pressurised, listless, depressed, fearful, uncertain or are easily upset (you become angry or burst into tears).
Changes in behaviour: for instance, consuming a lot of alcohol or medication (sleeping pills), becoming forgetful, becoming irritable, complaining a lot or being easily diverted.

Unhealthy stress can therefore result in many different symptoms. The fact that you are experiencing one of these symptoms does not necessarily mean that it is caused by stress. However, if you are experiencing many of these symptoms you may well be stressed. If you observe the symptoms associated with the third phase, we recommend that you seek professional help, for instance from your GP.

"*I always used to think that the stories about stress were wild exaggerations. It takes very little before everybody starts shouting that they're stressed. I always used to say: don't exaggerate, people used to work harder and they never suffered from stress... So I had to swallow my pride when the doctor told me that I was showing 'symptoms of stress'. My head was full of all sorts of things because I'd been told six months before that I had Parkinson'. Besides, I've got a family and work a couple of days a week. And that was a bit too much.*
There came a time when I had all sorts of symptoms, quite separate from the Parkinson's. Especially headaches. Symptoms of stress – that was the diagnosis.
For a few months after that I had someone come to help in the house every day. Then I took it on myself again, but also arranged that somebody would help me one day a week. One week it would be a paid cleaner, another week a friend would come and help. I don't know if everyone's the same, but I felt a lot better when I was less busy. Sometimes, when I feel very tired or when I'm really tensed up, I take a few days 'off'. I ask them if they can come a bit more often. It makes me feel a bit guilty, but I've no intention of being so stressed again".

Preventing unhealthy stress

We will mention a number of general suggestions on how to prevent unhealthy stress. You can apply them if you are regularly experiencing the symptoms of the first phase.

1. Recognising stress

The first and most important step is that you recognise the symptoms that indicate stress.
Never ignore them; take them seriously.

2. What is the cause?

Try to find out what is causing the stress.

Generally there are a number of simultaneous factors. This can be extremely confusing and can make it difficult to know where to start. Try writing down the causes/problems, as this can make them clearer and allow you to tackle them one at a time.

3. General rules for living

These rules apply to everyone and you are probably already familiar with them. We will mention just a few of them here: eat a healthy diet, do not smoke, drink only in moderation, and make sure that you get enough sleep. This will increase your tolerance for stress. We will briefly discuss a number of other suggestions.

4. What is upsetting you - is it really worth it?

This may sound ridiculous, because you do not get upset about nothing. But different people apparently experience the same event in very different ways. Some people panic while others feel as if nothing untoward has happened. The level of stress something causes depends entirely on how you view a particular event. You cannot change your character but you can try to put things in perspective. One way of doing this is to focus on the good things in life rather than concentrating on the bad.

5. Talk to people

Close contact with other people will help to alleviate the harmful effects of stress. People can support you both emotionally and practically and, most importantly, they can convey warmth and understanding. It seems that the greater the support a person receives, the fewer the symptoms of stress he or she will experience. This is particularly true for people who work. These people need to take the time to initiate non-work activities with friends and acquaintances. Talking to people, however, isn't necessarily easy: it can be difficult to ask for help and also to accept it. There is a discussion of this in Chapter 5 'Talking about your illness'.

6. Avoid tranquillisers and sleeping pills as much as possible

These will calm you down or send you to sleep, but they are also unhealthy when used over a long period of time. You may become addicted and they may make you feel drowsy during the day but adversely affect your quality of sleep at night. They are only useful for tiding you over during a brief spell of insomnia.

7. Make an effort to relax

There can be many ways of preventing unhealthy stress. Movement is one of the best ways of preventing and managing stress. This can take all kinds of forms, for instance swimming, going for walks, gardening etc. Movement is highly recommended even if your Parkinson's symptoms make it difficult. Keep trying because it not only combats unhealthy stress, it's also good for your physical condition. Chapter 9 'Exercises' includes a number of suggestions for different forms of movement.

Yoga exercises can be a very effective way of relaxing. Yoga can help you to use your strength more effectively by means of strenuous exercises, maintaining balance and experiencing your body as a whole. Yoga courses are available in most big towns and cities although not all teachers have experience of people with chronic diseases. The Yoga for Health Foundation will be able to provide you with more information and runs a special holiday with the Parkinson's Disease Society. The Yoga for Health Foundation can be contacted at: Ickwell Bury, Biggleswade, Bedfordshire SG18 9EF. Tel: 01767 27271.

Doing things you enjoy is another way of relaxing. These could be peaceful activities as opposed to the more active ones mentioned above. You might like being in the garden, watching a film, reading or listening to music. The company of favourite people or pets can also help you to relax.

For more suggestions, see Chapter 10 '*Sports, hobbies and holidays*'.

A relaxation exercise

There are a great many relaxation exercises, and we include a breathing exercise here. Do not expect it to work miracles but it can be very helpful when used regularly. It can also be very helpful when used during the symptoms of the first phase of the stress reaction, for example if you are afraid of freezing (you can even do this exercise during freezing) or before visiting people if you are afraid of adverse reactions to your tremors or your unclear speech.

What is the connection between breathing and stress?

Your respiration is connected to both tension and relaxation. When you feel tense, your breathing becomes short, shallow and rapid. Mainly it is your chest that moves because you are raising your shoulders and your ribcage. When you are relaxed, your breathing is very different: you take deeper breaths at a slower rate and you breathe using your abdomen (it moves in and out). This also works the opposite way around: if you breathe slowly, deeply and using your abdomen, you will automatically relax. Breathing and tension therefore influence each other.

The aim of this breathing exercise is that you learn to breathe with your abdomen so that you can then relax.

Preparation

Do the exercise two or three times a day, preferably at the same times: for instance, before you get dressed, in the middle of the afternoon or before you go to bed. The exercise lasts about ten minutes. You can also do this exercise at moments of stress, as described above. Make sure that you won't be disturbed (speak to your family and the people at work, unplug the phone, etc.). Choose a particular place such as your bedroom. Remove tight clothing and shoes, or loosen them. Take your glasses off. You can then lie down or sit in a chair.

The actual exercise

Close your eyes once you are seated or lying down. Try to discard the idea that you have to try hard. Nothing is being expected of you, relaxation is not something you have to work to achieve. It doesn't matter if this exercise does not work immediately because you can always try again later. To get yourself into the right frame of mind, you may find that it helps to spend a few moments imagining being by the sea or in a quiet glade.

Try to breathe as normally as possible. Pay attention to your chest and abdomen, and become aware of your way of breathing. Continue calmly for some minutes.

Once you have gained some idea of how you breathe (shallowly or deeply, quickly or slowly, regularly or irregularly, with your chest or with your abdomen) begin slowly to transfer your breathing to your abdomen. Place both hands on your tummy and feel how they keep rising and falling. Breathe deeply through your nose so that your tummy rises. Hold your breath for a few seconds and then let your breath out, feeling your tummy fall. Breathing out will take longer than breathing in. Keep this up for a few minutes and remain aware of how you breathe. Breathe deeply and regularly from your abdomen. You will notice that you become more and more relaxed. Just continue so that you learn to experience and appreciate this feeling of relaxation. After a few minutes, you can calmly open your eyes, stretch your body and slowly stand up.

You may find that your thoughts wander during the first few times. Do not worry about this; just let those thoughts drift by and concentrate on your breathing. You may even fall asleep, especially when you practise this exercise at night. That does not matter, as it is also a sign that you are relaxing.

Practice
The most important thing about this exercise is that you practice it regularly over a considerable period of time. Only then can you expect results. You can ask someone else to remind you to do it.

Once you have built up a little experience and have learnt the technique well, you will be able to practice it in different positions and at different times. Then you can relax when you need to. If you become aware that you are breathing from your chest, it is a good moment to do the exercise.

Another relaxation exercise on audiotape is available, more info:
The Parkinson's Disease Society

author: - Rev. Dr. P. Bellamy, UK

33

Spiritual Welfare

Summary

A serious condition can cast a very different light on your life. You may begin to consider issues that you never thought about before. Your values and norms can change. Many people start to think about God and the role that faith plays in their life. In other words: Parkinson's can change your spirituality.

Generally going through these changes is not an easy process. You may feel that you are 'living in the shadows'. Therefore, it can be a good idea to ask for help. Perhaps you can talk to your family or friends; your priest or spiritual counsellor may also provide a sympathetic ear.

These experiences can be difficult particularly because they may keep recurring. Yet they can also enrich your life.

Introduction

This chapter looks at another dimension to the experiences of living with Parkinson's disease. It looks beyond the need to cope with the consequences of illness, towards the spiritual needs that people may have at this time. People will respond in different ways that reflect their own experiences.

The chapter covers:
- What do we mean by 'spiritual'?
- How is spirituality expressed?
- What happens spiritually when a diagnosis like Parkinson's has to be faced?
- Living with the illness
- Finding a supportive network and community for the journey
- Helpful agencies

"Why me? Why should it be me who gets Parkinson's? That was the question I often asked myself when the Parkinson's arrived on the scene. I'm not a churchgoer, but I did go and talk to someone from the church and that helped. I didn't get a real answer to my question, but at the moment I'm at peace with it. I've come to realise that I don't need to ask the question."

What do we mean by 'spiritual'?

Everyone has his own spirituality. It is what people most value and believe in. It is what matters most in life, such as your career or family. This can change as you go through life. The birth of a first child, promotion at work, the death of a close family member, personal illness and other experiences can change what matters most at any given time. These changes make up a unique spiritual journey which others may be aware of and share.

It can be a useful exercise to draw your own spiritual journey by putting down chronologically the most important events in your life, both happy and unhappy occasions. Think about the effects they have had on you and the way you see life. Think also about whether the experiences and feelings were shared and with whom, and how far the sharing increased the joy or reduced the pain.

How is spirituality expressed?

People express their spirituality in very different ways. For instance, some of us are 'doers' and find our spirituality in people, in good causes, in events or in the natural world (God outside). Others look inside themselves to find their spirituality in the inner world of the self, at the very core of being (God within).

Many people express their spirituality through religious belief. Some will be practising members of a faith community such as a church, synagogue, mosque or temple. Important events in life can change and deepen religious belief. It may have been such an event that enabled a person to become committed to a particular faith.

Spirituality is more than personal and individual. Groups of people can have a common set of beliefs and spirituality. For instance, members of Round Tables express their beliefs by raising money for charities, and people who work for hospices emphasise the importance of people living actively and fully during their last days.

What happens spiritually when a diagnosis like Parkinson's has to be faced?

After an initial sense of shock, or relief that the problem is recognised and that there is permission to feel unwell, many experience the 'why me?' and 'what have I done to deserve this?' type of question. These questions tend to recur from time to time. The values and beliefs that supported your life in the past may be found wanting. A career or money may not seem so central any more. The picture of God or lack of it that seemed to meet your needs in times of health may not be helpful now. It can be such a shock that many people carry on for a while as if nothing has changed. This may partly be to avoid worrying others, and partly pretending to oneself that everything is still normal in a kind of false hope.

In reality, familiar landmarks have gone or changed. Faith and belief may be lost. It can be an unnerving and spiritually painful experience. People sometimes talk of these times as 'life not being worth living any more', 'being in the shadows', 'the dark night', 'the valley of the shadow of death'. Some will need to talk about it a great deal, while others will need their space to be apart and to come to terms with it. This process can take a lot of energy and may continue on and off over a period of time.

It may be important for you to seek help because in this uncharted territory maps and guides can be vital to prevent the feelings of being lost and without hope. Help can come from people who share and listen with wisdom and humanity, from meeting others who have been there before, and from appropriate leaflets, cards, books and video programmes. It is essential to choose what is personally helpful, i.e. right for you, at this moment and to refuse inappropriate advice whoever it is from. If unsure, then check it out with someone trustworthy.

The journey, though difficult, can be strengthening and even fulfilling. New ways of being and doing may emerge. Relationships can grow and deepen. New friendships can be made. New understandings of yourself, of the world, of the meaning of life, and of things beyond life. Looking back people sometimes recognise the presence of something beyond themselves in the darkness, and have a sense of having been carried through the crisis, even if it did not feel like it at the time. Each person will have his own story to tell as he comes to terms with the diagnosis.

"I wasn't brought up religious, but at the moment I enjoy being in a church. Churches have a spiritual effect on me. And – to my great surprise – I've started to pray. Somehow it gave me a lot of support. It's as if I can find the right words and that gives me a lot of strength. I pray on the quiet, because if I tell anyone about it they don't understand. And in any case, I think that praying is a very personal thing."

Living with the illness

There may be times of loss of energy, problems of concentration and a sense of not being able to do everything you used to do in the past. It may be possible to prepare for ongoing changes by talking things through with your partner, carer, or a friend. If you are by nature disorganised and chaotic the illness can accentuate this so it can be important to introduce some order and milestones into the day and the week. If on the other hand you are a very orderly person then the illness can raise anxieties by lapses of concentration. Rather than feeling helpless and out of control, disorganised thinking can be the opportunity for spontaneity of action or for just resting and letting go the need to control.

It is important to maintain your identity apart from the illness. Many professionals and others will relate to you in terms of the different problems that you are experiencing. This can lead to your feeling that you *are* a 'problem' with the accompanying loss of confidence, powerlessness, vulnerability and over-dependence. Even voluntary groups can use well-meaning but negative images associated with particular conditions as a means of raising profile and awareness. The crucial factor is to create an environment that enables you to be fully informed and fully involved in all decisions concerning you. It can be useful to ask yourself a checklist of questions from time to time such as:

- Have I got all the information I need?
- What questions do I need to ask at my next medical appointment?
- What practical things do I require to maintain my dignity and autonomy?
- Are there new areas of life, interests that I want to explore?
- Can I plan any activities and treats that will be memorable?

Finding a supportive network and community for the journey

Far from walking alone across a desolate country it will soon become apparent that others around you are catching up as they too come to terms with your situation. You will also find travellers ahead who have covered some of the same and some different ground before you. Joining a group of them is an occasion to share stories, and the company may be pleasant. Some may seem to have a 'know it all' attitude which makes it feel important to find your own way. More exploring of the way ahead will prove to you that some of what the group says is true, but some of the details may be different for you. When meeting the group it can be an advantage if people don't try to convert others to their point of view, but share experiences, ask questions, and learn from each other.

Sharing your journey more fully with family, neighbours, friends at work will help to develop a network of people with different gifts, which might be called upon as need arises. Some people are glad to do practical things such as collecting a prescription or meeting children from school to cover you for a hospital appointment, while others will be there at the end of the phone when everything feels as though it's falling apart. It does mean being courageous enough to ask for help and being open to receive it. Healthy support has a sense of giving and receiving and does not add to a sense of dependence. But some help that is offered by odd individuals and quirky groups can exploit feelings of vulnerability and result in much hurt.

As the journey continues some people with an ongoing condition like Parkinson's find that there is an important role in caring for the people around them who can be over-anxious, over-protective and confused by events. With good support and spiritual resources, you as the person at the centre of the crisis may develop a spiritual strength that enables not only you yourself to cope more effectively and find fulfilment on the journey but also enables others to do so far into the future. It results in a very special way of binding people together so that out of a very painful experience new strengths are discovered and the sense of community grows.

Spirituality on the journey can often be expressed without words, for instance through music and pictures, someone's smile and touch. Think, for instance, of the ways in which hands can express feelings and bring mutual comfort and support in a crisis; how holding someone wracked with pain and fear can soothe and reassure; how tensions can be massaged away; how warmth and energy can be expressed through linking hands; how hands can express the growth of love, happiness and peace in relationships with each other; how much religious language reflects this experience of being held in love within the everlasting friendship of God.

Helpful agencies with spiritual resources
1 National and local self-help groups
2 Counsellors: may be based in hospitals, in health centres, or working in local counselling organisations
3 Religious organisations: local churches, synagogues, mosques and temples; the Humanist Society (hospital chaplains normally have contact names and phone numbers for these groups).

Notes

authors: - Prof. A. Williams, UK
- M. Oxtoby, UK

34

Glossary

Terms in *italics* in these definitions refer to other terms in the glossary.

A

acetylcholine - A chemical messenger found in the body that transmits messages between nerve cells or between nerve cells and muscles. These messages can affect the way muscles behave, or the amount of saliva produced. Because the actions of acctylcholine are called cholinergic actions, the drugs that block these actions are called *anticholinergic drugs*.

advocate - A person who intercedes on behalf of another; someone who helps vulnerable or distressed people to make their voices heard.

agonists - A term used for drugs which have a positive stimulating effect on particular cells in the body.

Alzheimer's disease - The most common type of *dementia*.

anticholinergics - A group of drugs used to treat Parkinson's, which work by reducing the amount of acetylcholine in the body, and so facilitate the function of dopamine cells.

anti-depressants - Drugs given to treat depression.

apomorphine - A *dopamine agonist* drug which is usually given by injection.

aromatherapy - A *complementary therapy* involving treatment with *essential oils* often involving massage, but the oils can also be inhaled or added to baths.

B

benign essential tremor - Another name for essential tremor.

bradykinesia - Slowness of movement

C

carbohydrate - A class of food which consists of starchy and sugary foods - examples include rice, bread, pasta, potatoes and dried beans.

cardiologist - A doctor who specialises in the care and treatment of heart conditions.

care manager - A person from a *Social Services department* (or sometimes from *Community Health Services*) who is given the task of putting together, monitoring and reviewing the plan of care agreed after a *community care assessment*.

carer - In the broadest sense, a carer is anyone who provides help and support of any kind to a relative or friend. More specifically, a carer is a person who is

259

regularly looking after someone w ho needs help with daily living (perhaps because of age or long-term illness) and who would not be able to live independently at home without this care and support.

choreiform movements - Another name for *involuntary movements*.

clinical trials - Closely-supervised scientific studies into treatments for diseases. A clinical trial may investigate a new treatment for a disease, or a different way of giving an existing treatment, or may compare a new treatment with the best treatment currently available.

communication aid - Equipment which helps someone who has difficulty with speaking and/or writing to communicate more easily. Communication aids can very from the very simple, such as alphabet boards or cards with messages already written on them, to the very complex, such as computers.

community care - The provision of professional care and support to allow people who need help with daily living (perhaps because of age or long-term illness) to live as full and independent lives as possible (often in their own homes). The amount of care provided will depend on the needs and wishes of the person concerned (which must be taken into account) and on the resources which are available locally.

community care assessment - The way in which professional staff from a *Social Services department* work out which *community care* services someone needs. The views of the person concerned and of their *carers* must be taken into account in making the assessment.

Community Health Councils or CHCs - Each Health Authority has its own Community Health Council which is an independent voice on health care and is responsible for representing the interests of users of local health care services. CHC services range from providing information on what services are available locally to helping individuals who are unhappy with the service which they have received.

Community Health Services or Community Health Trusts - The parts of the NHS which provide health care in people's own homes or in local clinics and health centres rather than in hospitals.

complementary therapies - Non-medical treatments which may be used in addition to conventional medical treatments. Popular complementary therapies include *aromatherapy* and *homeopathy*. Some of these therapies are available through the NHS, but this is unusual, and depends on individual hospitals and GPs.

continuous care beds - Beds, usually within hospitals but sometimes in *nursing homes*, which are funded by the NHS for people who need permanent medical care.

controlled release - Special formulations of drugs that release the drug into the body slowly and steadily rather than all at once. They keep the amount of drug in the blood stream at a steadier level than the 'ordinary' version of the same drug.

corticobasal degeneration - Also known as Steele-Richardson syndrome, progressive supra-nuclear palsy or striatonigral degeneration, this is one of the *Parkinson's Plus syndromes*.

counselling - Counsellors are trained to listen carefully to what someone is saying about a particular problem or experience, and then to respond in a way which helps that person to explore and understand more clearly what they are thinking and feeling about that situation. Counselling therefore provides an opportunity for talking openly and fully about feelings without the worry of upsetting close friends or family members. It is always private and confidential.

D

dribbling - Another word for *drooling*.

driving assessment - A test, which takes place at a specially staffed and equipped centre, of someone's ability and fitness to drive a car (with or without special adaptations).

drooling - Having saliva overflowing from the mouth.

drug-induced Parkinson's - Parkinson's-type symptoms caused by taking certain types of drugs, usually those used for severe psychiatric problems or dizziness. The symptoms wear off with time when the drugs are stopped. The term can also refer to the Parkinson's-like symptoms caused by drugs of abuse containing *MPTP*.

dyskinesias - Another name for *involuntary movements*.

dystonia - An involuntary contraction of the muscles which causes the affected part of the body to go into a spasm (i.e. to twist or tighten). Such spasms can be painful and can produce abnormal movements, postures, or positions of the affected parts of the body.

E

encephalitis lethargica - Encephalitis means inflammation of the brain and this particular type, which is caused by a virus, makes people very slow and tired (lethargic). It is rarely, if ever, seen now, but there was an epidemic of it after World War I. It often led to a particular type of a Parkinson's called 'post-encephalitic Parkinson's'.

epidemiology - A branch of medical research which tries to establish the frequency with which diseases occur. For example, it might be used to try to find out how many people in a population of 100,000 have Parkinson's, how many of these people are male and how many female, and how the people with Parkinson's are distributed among different age groups.

essential oils - Aromatic (scented) oils extracted from the roots, flowers or leaves of plants by distillation. The complex chemicals in the oils can affect the nervous and circulatory systems of the body and so are considered to have therapeutic properties.

essential tremor - A type of *tremor* which often runs in families and which is different from the tremor found in Parkinson's. Essential tremor is at its worst with the arms outstretched or when holding a cup or tea or writing, whereas the tremor of Parkinson's is usually most obvious when the arm is doing nothing and at rest.

F

familial tremor - Another name for *essential tremor*.

foetal cell implants or **foetal implants** - A much-publicised experimental technique involving implanting cells from aborted foetuses (unborn babies) into the brain of someone with Parkinson's in the hope of repairing the damage that the Parkinson's has caused. Although the technique has been quite successful in animals its application to people with Parkinson's is still at the experimental stage.

free radicals - High active chemical units which can be produced by the body or absorbed from outside sources (such as cigarette smoke or polluted air). They only last for very short periods of time, but have the potential to do damage to the body's cells during that time. The body has defence mechanisms against free radicals, but if it is unable to dispose of them fast enough then cell damage results.

freezing - The symptom, quite common in Parkinson's, which causes the person affected to stop suddenly while walking and to be unable to move forward for several seconds or minutes. It makes people feel that their feet are frozen to the ground.

G

genes - The 'units' of heredity that determine our inherited characteristics, such as eye colour.

geriatrician - A doctor who specialises in the care and treatment of elderly people.

glaucoma - A disease affecting the eyes, usually found in older people. In glaucoma, the pressure of the fluid in the eye becomes so high that it causes damage and the field of vision becomes progressively narrower and shallower. If left untreated, it can lead to blindness.

growth factors - Natural substances produced in the body which help cells to grow in embryos and foetuses (unborn babies) and which also help adult cells to remain healthy. It is hoped that research into growth factors and the way they work may lead eventually to discovering ways of using these substances to help damaged cells in the brain and the rest of the central nervous system to regenerate (repair themselves and grow again). Conditions such as Parkinson's which affect the brain and the rest of the central nervous system are difficult to treat because, cells in these parts of the body have very limited capacities for repair and regeneration. It might be possible in the future to use growth factors to make these cells behave more like cells in some other parts of the body (e.g. the skin) which already have the ability to regenerate.

H

home care worker - Usually a person who provides help with personal care, such as getting washed and dressed, and with preparing meals. *Social Services departments* normally provide home care workers and there is usually a charge for their services.

homeopathy - *A complementary therapy* based on the principle that 'like can be cured by like' (the word homeopathy comes from two Greek words that mean 'similar' and suffering). The remedies used (which are completely safe) contain very dilute amounts of a substance which in larger quantities would produce similar symptoms to the illness being treated. Although there is as yet no scientific explanation for why homeopathy works, it is available through the NHS, although provision is limited.

I

idiopathic - A word used before the name of an illness or medical condition which means that its cause is not known.

impotence - Failure of erection of the penis.

inhibitors - A terms used for drugs which have a blocking effect on particular cells or chemical reactions in the body.

involuntary movements - Movements, other than *tremor*, which are not willed or intended by the person affected. They tend to occur in people who have had Parkinson's for many years and to be related, often in complex and variable ways, to the timing of medication.

L

L-dopa - A substance one step removed from *dopamine*. It is not possible for dopamine to pass from the blood stream to the brain, so the problem is solved by giving drugs containing L-dopa. The L-dopa can reach the brain from the blood stream, and when it gets there it is converted into dopamine.

levodopa - Another name for *L-dopa*.

Lewy body - A microscopic structure seen in the brains of people with Parkinson's.

local ethics committee - A group of doctors, researchers and lay people who check the plans of medical researchers to make sure that the interests of people who take part in research projects are protected. Each Health Authority has its own local ethics committee.

M

mask face - Another name for *poker face*.

micrographia - The technical name for small handwriting. It comes from two Greek words, 'mikros' meaning little and 'graphein' meaning to write.

mitochondria - A part of each cell in the body. It is the 'power pack' of the cell and if it is damaged the cell dies.

monoamine oxidase B - A naturally-occurring chemical found in the body which causes the breakdown of *dopamine*.

MPTP - poisonous chemical contained in some drugs of abused used by young American drug addicts in the early 1980s. It produced an illness with symptoms very similar to those found in Parkinson's.

multidisciplinary assessment - An assessment, involving medical nursing, therapy and Social Services personnel, of the medical and social care/support someone needs. It is called multidisciplinary simply because professionals from several different disciplines or specialities are involved.

multiple system atrophy - Also known as Shy-Drager syndrome, this is one of the *Parkinson's Plus syndromes*.

music therapy - The use, by trained professionals, of music as treatment for certain physical and mental illnesses. The music can be used to improve mobility and speech and to enable people to relax or to express feelings and ideas. Music therapists often work with *physical therapists*.

N

neurological conditions - Conditions affecting the body's nervous system (i.e. the brain and associated nerves).

neurologist - A doctor who specialises in the diagnosis, care and treatment of diseases of the nervous system (i.e. the brain and associated nerves).

nursing homes - *Residential homes* which offer continuous 24-hour nursing care.

O

occupational therapists - Trained professionals who use specific, selected tasks and activities to enable people who have difficulty with control and co-ordination of movement to attain maximum function and independence. The also assess people's homes and places of work and suggest ways of making them safer and more manageable. Occupational therapists aids and gadgets to help with the practical problems of daily living, and on leisure activities to help improve the quality of daily life.

on/off phenomenon - This phenomenon is characteristic of some people with long-standing Parkinson's. It can cause them to change from being 'on' and able to move to being 'off' and virtually immobile, all within a very brief period of time - minutes or even seconds.

osteopathy - A *complementary therapy* involving manipulation of the bones and muscles. It is most commonly used for back pain, joint pain and stiffness, and similar conditions.

oxygen free radicals - *Free radicals* of oxygen.

P

pallidotomy - An operation on the pallidum, which is a part of the brain concerned with movement. This type of stereotactic surgery was originally developed in the 1950s but fell out of favour during the next 30 years. It is now attracting renewed interest and research.

Parkinsonism - or Parkinsonian Syndrome, is not another name for Parkinson's Disease. It is an 'umbrella term' for all conditions which present with the three symptoms of tremor, stiffness and slow, reduced movements. The most common form of Parkinsonism is idiopathic (i.e. cause unknown) Parkinson's Disease, but it is not the only one.

Other rarer, forms of Parkinsonism are:
- manganese poisoning (of manganese miners)
- carbon monoxide poisoning (from a leaking exhaust pipe, or a faulty outlet for a water heater or a coal fire)
- hardening of the arteries in the head
- repeated blows on the head (in the case of boxers)
- multiple systems atrophy
- systems atrophy
- progressive supranuclear palsy

Parkinsonism can also be caused by the long-term use of some medications, for example neuroleptic drugs used in psychiatry to treat psychosis.

The correst differentiation of Parkinson's Disease from these other conditions requires considerable experience. If you want confirmation of the diagnosis you could ask to see a hospital specialist with a particular interest in the condition. This specialist might be a neurologist or a geriatrician. Many Movement Disorder Clinics have been established in the UK over the last 10 to 15 years. You could also look for confirmation of the diagnosis and for continuing care in one of these highly specialised clinics.

A fact sheet on Parkinsonism and the Parkinsonian Syndromes is available from The Parkinson's Disease Society.

Parkinson's Plus syndromes - Rare conditions whose early symptoms look like Parkinson's, but later develop in rather different ways.

pavement vehicle - A motorised wheelchair or scooter suitable for use outdoors.

Penject - A type of small portable syringe which looks rather like a pen (hence the name), used for apomorphine injections. The syringe delivers a pre-measured dose when a button it is pressed.

PET scans - The only type of scan that can 'show' Parkinson's. As yet it is only available in some research centre.

physiotherapy - Physical treatments (including exercises) which are used to prevent or reduce stiffness in joints and to restore muscle strength.

placebo - The name given in *double blind trials* to the non-active substance with which an active drug is being compared. It is a 'dummy' version of the drug, identical in appearance to the drug being tested.

poker face - Lack of the facial expressions that indicate emotions, for example frowning and smiling.

progressive supra-nuclear palsy - Also know as Steele-Richardson syndrome, striatonigral degeneration or corbicobasal degeneration, this is one of the *Parkinson's Plus syndromes*.

protein - A class of food that is necessary for the growth and repair of the body's tissues - examples include fish, meat, eggs and milk.

R

residential homes - Accommodation for people who are no longer able or who no longer wish to manage everyday domestic tasks (such as cooking , shopping, housework and so on) or to maintain an independent home of their own, but who do not need nursing care.

respite care - Any facility or resource which allows those who care for sick, frail, elderly or disabled relatives or friends to have a break from their caring tasks. Respite care may be provided in residential or nursing homes, in the person's own home, or with another family.

resting tremor - A name sometimes used for the type of *tremor* found in Parkinson's.

restless leg syndrome - Legs that regularly burn, prickle or ache, especially in bed at night. The cause is not known.

rigidity - The name given to the special type of stiffness which is one of the main symptoms of Parkinson's. The muscles tend to pull against each other instead of working smoothly together.

S

season ticket - Shorthand name for a prepayment certificate for NHS prescriptions.

self referral - Going direct to a therapist for treatment rather than through a GP or other health professional.

sheltered housing - Accommodation which is purpose-built for people who need a certain amount of supervision because of old age or disability, but who wish to maintain a home of their own. The amount of supervision available can vary from a warden on site who can be contacted in an emergency to high-dependency units where there is still a degree of privacy and independence, but where higher staffing levels allow assistance with meals and personal care.

Shy-Drager syndrome - Also known as multiple system atrophy, this is one of the *Parkinson's Plus syndromes*.

side effects - Almost all drugs affect the body in ways beyond their intended therapeutic actions. These unwanted 'extra' effects are called side effects. Side effects vary in their severity from person to person, and often disappear when the body becomes used to a particular drug.

sleeping sickness - In this text, another name for *encephalitis lethargica*.

senile tremor - Another name for *essential tremor*.

Social Services departments - The department of local authorities responsible for non-medical welfare care for children and adults who need such help.

speech and language therapists - Trained professionals who help with problems concerning speech, communication or swallowing.

Steele-Richardson syndrome - Also known as progressive supra-nuclear palsy, striatonigral degeneration or corticobasal degeneration, this is one of the *Parkinson's Plus syndromes*.

stereotactic or **stereotaxic surgery** - Type of brain surgery which involves inserting delicate instruments through a specially created small hole in the skull, and then using these instruments to operate on deep structures in the brain which are concerned with the control of movement. The forms of stereotactic surgery which are very occasionally used in Parkinson's are *pallidotomy* and *thalamotomy*.

subcutaneous - Under the skin

substantia nigra - So-called because of its dark colour (the name literally means 'black substance'), this part of the brain co-ordinates movement and contains cells that make *dopamine*. It is cells from the substantia nigra which are lost or damaged in Parkinson's.

syringe driver - A small, battery driven pump which can deliver a continuous dose of medication through a flexible line (fine tube) which ends in a needle which is inserted under the skin. It allows people with serious *on/off* Parkinson's to receive a continuous infusion of *apomorphine* and to top this up with occasional booster doses as necessary.

T

thalamus - A part of the brain (located near the *substantia nigra*) which is responsible for relaying information from the sense organs about what is going on in the body to the various parts of the brain.

thalamotomy - A type of *stereotactic surgery* performed on the *thalamus*. It was used quite extensively in the past (before the advent of *L-dopa* and *dopamine replacement therapy*) in the treatment of one sided *tremor*, but is rarely used nowadays.

tissue ban - A collection of body tissues which can be used for research purposes. People interested in supporting a tissue bank sign and agreement during their lifetime; the tissue is then donated to the bank after their death. Tissue banks are very important research resources, and the Parkinson's Disease Society has its own Brain Tissue Bank.

tremor - Involuntary shaking, trembling or quivering movements of the muscles. It is caused by muscles alternately contracting and relaxing at a rapid rate.

W

wearing off phenomenon - In this phenomenon, which is characteristic of some people with long-standing Parkinson's, the effectiveness of the drug treatment is substantially reduced, so that it 'wears off' some time before the next dose is due.

Y

yo-yoing - Another name for the on/off phenomenon.

author: - Mrs B. Cormie, Publications Manager,
Parkinson's Disease Society, UK

35

Further reading

Introduction

This chapter offers an overview of educational materials on Parkinson's Disease: brochures, books, videotapes etc.

It is the publications list of the Parkinson's Disease Society of the UK (see page 124).

The chapter concludes with some Internet addresses where more information on Parkinson's Disease is available. Unfortunately not all the information on the Internet is of high quality. If you have any doubts, please consult your GP, your neurologist or the PDS.

How to obtain the products

N.B. All PDS products and publications are available via the PDS's distributor, Sharward Services.

To obtain any of the items listed below, please contact them.

N.B. Although many items are free, postage must be paid. Postage charges are as follows: £1 for 1-5 items; £2 for 6-10 items; £3 for 11-16 items, £4 for 17-24 items.

If you have any queries about ordering or postage, please contact Sharward Services directly: Sharward Services, Westerfield Business Centre, Main Road, Westerfield, Ipswich, Suffolk IP6 9AB, United Kingdom. Tel: 01473 212115; e-mail: services@sharward.co.uk

General publications

P21 **Facing the Future** - free (also available on tape, P21c)

An introductory guide to Parkinson's and the PDS with information such as 'What is Parkinson's?', 'Living with Parkinson's,' and the different activities of the Society.

B1 **Moving On** - free

A sequel to Facing the Future, Moving On covers aspects of Parkinson's which may affect those who have lived with the condition for some time. Written in an A-Z format.

B42 **Parkinson's At Your Fingertips** (second edition) - £14.99
Clear and helpful information on Parkinson's written in a very accessible question and answer format. (Published by Class Publishing, available via PDS.)

B6 **The Parkinson** - sample copy free (also available on tape, B6c)
The quarterly magazine of the PDS contains features on living with Parkinson's, medical updates, welfare information, education, news and views. (Free to PDS Members.)

B9 **An Essay on the Shaking Palsy,** by James Parkinson - £7.50
First published in 1817, this is recognised globally as the classic description of the condition.

Personal accounts

B18 **Parkinson's Disease and Employment** - £2.50
Personal accounts from 43 people on how the condition has affected their working lives.

B19 **Parkinson's Disease, Doctors as Patients** - £2.50
Eleven doctors describe how their diagnosis affected them personally and professionally.

B20 **An Old Age Pensioner at 18** - £2.50
By Helen Rose, a women in her 30s who has had Parkinson's since she was 18. The book gives a moving account of Helen and her family's experiences of living with Parkinson's.

Publications for children and young people

(Codes on order form) **Gramps has Parkinson's/Grandma has Parkinson's** - free
Two fully illustrated booklets for young children, explaining how the condition will affect their grandparent. As well as the versions in English, there are also Grandad/Granny has Parkinson's aimed at Afro Caribbean children and versions in Urdu, Gujerati and Punjabi.

B43 **Understanding Parkinson's: A Guide for Young People** - £4.00
A more in depth guide for c10-15 year-olds which explains Parkinson's causes and treatment, how it affects people, and how they can help. Personal experiences are given. Fully illustrated.

Health publications (see also general)

B49 **Meeting Your Health and Social Care Needs** - free
This aims to help people with Parkinson's and their families get the best from their various social and health care providers. It outlines people's basic rights and gives the PDS minimum standards of care. Can be used to highlight specific services you need or to promote the care of people with Parkinson's in your area.

B3 **Living with Parkinson's Disease** - £2.50
An illustrated handbook of exercises divided into three sections: physiotherapy, speech therapy and occupational therapy. (See also Audio Tapes section.)

B60 **Looking after your Bladder and Bowels in Parkinsonism** - free
A thorough and practical guide to bladder and bowel care for people with Parkinsonism.

B45 **Parkinson's and Dental Health** - free
Written by a dentist for people who have had Parkinson's for some time, this booklet will also be useful for those who work in dental health. It contains information on the common concerns raised and offers practical advice.

B65 **Parkinson's and Diet** - free
Commonly asked questions are answered along with general guidelines on diet. The booklet also includes tips on shopping, cooking and eating.

B13 **The Drug Treatment of Parkinson's Disease** - free (also available in large print, B13b)
The various medications currently available to those with Parkinson's, listing their effects and side effects.

B34 **Parkinson's Disease and Sex** - free
A leaflet on the problems some people with Parkinson's and their partners can experience with sex, the possible solutions and sources of further advice.

Welfare publications (see also general)

B49 **Meeting Your Health and Social Care Needs** - free
See above under Health Publications for details.

B47 **Occupational Therapy and Parkinson's** - free
A leaflet about the role of occupational therapy in Parkinson's.

B66 **Respite Care & Holidays** - free, via PDS National Office ONLY
This booklet gives respite care advice and information including details of places which cater for people with Parkinson's and their families, and Parkinson's-friendly holiday accommodation. A new edition is produced each year.

B64 **Parkinson's and Driving** - £2.00
People with Parkinson's' rights and obligations as drivers. Answers to commonly asked questions and sources of further help and advice.

L3 **Clothing Leaflet** - free
Advice on clothing and footwear issues. Includes a list of stockists.

Information fact sheets

Free fact sheets on a variety of topics. Contact the PDS Information Department (see page 130) for details.

270

Arts publications

B2 **Dancing Till Dawn Broke** - £7.99
A collection of poetry and prose by people with Parkinson's and carers.

M3 **My Favourite Betjeman** - £2.00
Poems by the late Sir John Betjeman, who had Parkinson's, selected by celebrities including Sir Kingsley Amis, Sir John Gielgud, Daphne du Maurier and Dame Thora Hird.

Mali Jenkins Prize and research

The Mali Jenkins Prize was set up in memory of the PDS's founder. Two prizes are awarded, Medical and Welfare, for an account of a project developed to improve medical or welfare services for people affected by Parkinson's. For details call the PDS Research Department.

B35 **Research Booklet** - free
Details the medical and welfare research projects currently being funded by the PDS.

B10 **Parkinson's Disease: Studies in Psychological and Social Care** - £12.95 (£11.65 to PDS members)
Published with the British Psychological Society, this book contains highlights of PDS-sponsored welfare research over the last 10 years, with reports of key projects carried out to improve the lives of people with Parkinson's and provide better standards of care.

B5 **Survey of Members of the Parkinson's Disease Society** - £7.50
Results and analysis of a survey carried out in 1998, which looks at the lives and needs of those with Parkinson's and carers. Results are compared with a similar survey of 1979.

Forms and cards

L1 **The Parkinson's Disease Society Leaflet** - free
Introductory leaflet about the Parkinson's Disease Society of the UK and its work.

B52 **Drug Times Postcard** - free
Stresses the importance of each person with Parkinson's getting their drugs at the right time for them. Can be used by people with Parkinson's and professionals to promote awareness.

B48 **Hospital/Respite Care Drug Information Form** - free
Form which people with Parkinson's and their carers can use to give hospital/respite care staff information about their medication and other aspects of their care. Contains general information about the problems some people have experienced in hospital/respite care.

M1 **Parkinson's Disease Medication Card** - free
A card people can keep with them to record their drug treatment and doctor's details.

M14 **Parkinson's Disease Alert Card** - free
A card for people with Parkinson's to carry with them in case of emergencies, or when experiencing difficulties with movement or communication.

Audio tapes

T1 **Speech Exercises Audio Tape** - £5.00

Contains exercises to help with the speech problems which some people with Parkinson's experience. Can also be used with the PDS booklet Living with Parkinson's (B3) as a guide.

T2 **Physiotherapy Exercises Audio Tape** - £5.00

Contains physiotherapy exercises to help people with Parkinson's keep fit and mobile. The exercises are done to music. The tape is best used with the PDS booklet Living with Parkinson's (B3) as a guide.

T7 **Relaxation Audio Tape** - £5.00

Contains advice and exercises to aid relaxation - very important with Parkinson's as stress can make symptoms worse.

Video tapes

V3 **Face to Face** - £16.00

The video and booklet contain exercises to help improve facial expressions, a vital part of communication sometimes lost when people have Parkinson's.

V6 **Living with Parkinson's Disease** - £16.00

For those newly diagnosed. The video and accompanying booklet provide a comprehensive guide to Parkinson's and its treatment, including three case studies.

V7 **No More Secrets** - £20.00

For carers of those recently diagnosed. Contains practical advice from professionals and interviews with carers about how they cope. Includes a booklet with further information.

V8 **The Uninvited Guest: Young Onset Parkinson's** - £20.00

Using drama and interviews, this provides an insight into living with Parkinson's as a younger person. Also describes the support available from the PDS and its special interest group YAPPR&S (Young Alert Parkinson's, Partners and Relatives). Accompanied by a booklet.

PDS Merchandise and utensils

C8 **T-shirts white with dark blue PDS logo** (small, medium, large, x-large) - £5.00

C22 **Sweatshirts dark blue with white PDS logo** (small, medium, large, x-large) - £15.00

C11 **Baseball Caps dark blue with white PDS logo** (one size) - £5.00

C13 **Ties dark blue with dark blue embossed PDS logo** - £7.00

C14 **Clip-on Ties dark blue with dark blue embossed PDS logo** - £7.00

C16 **Car Stickers PDS logo** - £0.35 (also available at £3.00 for 10)

C17 **Pens retractable white pens with PDS logo** - £0.35 (also available at £3.00 for 10)

C18 **Coffee Mugs white with dark blue PDS logo** - £3.80

C19 **Tumble-not Mugs blue and white patterned mugs with extra-wide bases** - £5.00

C23a, C23b, C23c **Cut-away Mugs blue & white patterned mugs with cut-away necks for easier use** (right, left or double-handled) - £7.00-7.75

FR1 PDS **Lapel Badges both butterfly and broach fastening available** - £1.00

M12 **Tulip Notelets** (10 cards with envelopes) - £1.00

Internet

On the Internet you can find a lot of information about Parkinson's Disease. Unfortunately not all the information is of high quality. If you have any doubts, please consult your GP, your neurologist or the PDS.

Parkinson's Disease Society

www.shef.ac.uk/misc/groups/epda/parkuk.htm
The website of the Parkinson's Disease Society is of course a good starting point for your search on the Internet.

Awakenings

www.parkinsonsdisease.com
Awakenings is an open forum, designed and written for all with an interest in Parkinsons' Disease. It aims to improve understanding and management of the condition. The website is supported and guided bij Mary Baker, president of the EPDA.

Parkinsons' Diseae Webring

www.pdring.com
A webring is a thematical series of websites, in this case websites about Parkinson's Disease.

Mayo Clinic Parkinson's Research Group

www.mayo.edu/fdp
This website from the famous Mayo Clinic provides a lot of information.

The Parkinson's Web

neuro-chief-e.mgh.harvard.edu/parkinsonsweb/Main/main html
Here you will find many links to relevant organisations in the US. Many of them give useful information about Parkinson's Disease.

Parkinson's Information

www.parkinsonsinfo.com
This site gives a lot of practical information.

The Michael J. Fox Foundation for Parkinson's Disease
www.michaeljfox.org
The American actor Michael J. Fox was diagnosed with Parkinson's Disease a couple of years ago. Het set up a foundation to collect money for research. On the website, among other things, you can read in Michael's journal how he copes with his disease.

Parkinson's Disease Caregiver's Information
www.parkinsonscare.com
This site is especially interesting for caregiver's.

The Parkinson's Disease Index at Wake Forest University
www.bgsm.edu/bgsm/surg-sci/ns/pd3.html
This website gives links to many articles and othe websites on Parkinson's Disease. There is special emphasis on surgical treatments such as pallidotomy and deep brain stimulators.

More information on this project

This manual is the result of a project that was financed by the NHS Executive West Midlands in the context of the *Partners in Care Programme*.

The aims of Partners in Care:

To contribute to the improvement of the quality of health services by making them more *responsive* to the needs and preferences of those who use them.
To empower users through giving them skills and knowledge to:

- become *active partners* with professionals
- *make informed decisions* and choices about their own treatment and care
- enable them (as individuals or communities) to *exert influence* on NHS service policy and planning
- to promote user *involvement in their own care* to contribute to therapeutic goals and processes.

One way of achieving these aims is:

- the production and dissemination of *information* for health service users and their representatives, which can contribute to their empowerment and improve partnership in the treatment and care process.

Dutch self-care manuals

This English Self-care Manual is based on an existing Dutch self-care manual which was produced by the September Foundation in co-operation with the Dutch Parkinson's Disease Society. The Dutch manual was originally published in 1993 and has been kept up-to-date by a series of subsequent editions.

For some years now, there has been a tradition in the Netherlands of publishing illness-specific self-care manuals that focus on a number of chronic disorders. These manuals have proved to be remarkably effective in the Netherlands. Both patients and professional carers make use of them and they appreciate both the contents and this particular way of keeping patients informed.

An English self-care manual on Parkinson's Disease

The NHS Executive West Midlands discovered this initiative and had the vision to develop an English version on the basis of the existing and successful Dutch manual.

Through the European Parkinson's Disease Association contact was made between the Dutch and the English Parkinson's Disease Associations. It was partly because of this fertile basis for collaboration that the NHS Executive West Midlands decided to opt for the subject of Parkinson's Disease.

The Dutch texts have been translated and then edited by a great many English experts to make the manual relevant to the situation in the UK. The concept was then judged both by a Consumers' Panel consisting of people with Parkinson's and their partners, and by an Expert Panel consisting of professional experts. This has resulted in a text that is suitable for the specific situation in England and contains also information that is state-of-the-art.

Collaboration

This manual has been realized through the collaboration of the NHS Executive West Midlands and the September Foundation. It was also made in close consultation with the Parkinson's Disease Association of the UK and the EPDA.

CD-ROM

The information has been published not only in the form of a manual, but also on a CD-ROM. Here, in order to reach a larger audience, full use has been made of the possibilities that multimedia has to offer: sound, animations, photographs and video; for more information contact the Parkinson's Disease Society of the United Kingdom, tel. 020 7931 8080, or the NHS Executive, West Midlands, tel. 0121 224 4676.

More information on the National Health Service (NHS) Executive & Regional Office

The purpose of the NHS is to secure, through the resources available, the greatest possible improvement to the physical and mental health of people in England by promoting health, preventing ill health, diagnosing and treating illness and injury, and caring for those with long-term illness and disability who require the services of the NHS: a service available to all on the basis of clinical need, regardless of the ability to pay.

The NHS Executive is part of the Department of Health with offices in Leeds and London and eight regions across the country. It supports Ministers and provides leadership and a range of central management functions to the NHS, while the regional offices make sure national policy is developed in their own particular areas.

The NHS Executive's main responsibilities lie in:

- Formulating policies for improving health care, including research
- Securing resources and allocating funds to health authorities
- Setting guidelines for performance expected by purchasers and providers and monitoring their achievement.

The NHS Executive West Midlands is one of the eight regional offices of the NHS Executive responsible for strategic management of the NHS in each region. In addition the Regional Office with other relevant agencies aims to:

- contribute actively to the development of health strategy and health service policies nationally and locally;
- manage the integration of research and development, education training and service strategies;
- ensure the effective performance and development of the NHS at local level.

West Midlands region covers Birmingham, Coventry, Dudley, Herefordshire, North Staffordshire, Sandwell, Shropshire, Solihull, South Staffordshire, Walsall, Warwickshire, Wolverhampton and Worcester and has a population of 5.6 million.

The Priorities and Planning Guidelines for the NHS sets the overall direction for the work of the NHS as a whole. Including:

- Work to improve the public's health and tackling health inequalities.
- Promoting fairness and equity through reducing variations in access and use of services.
- An integral programme of action and measures in relation to quality.
- Working in partnership and co-operation for the development of an efficient, effective and responsive service, removing the artificial barriers between the NHS and personal social services.
- Effective commissioning and provision of comprehensive mental health services.
- Improved clinical and cost effectiveness of services throughout the NHS, supporting R&D and formulating decisions on the basis of appropriate evidence about clinical effectiveness.
- Greater voice and influence for users of NHS Services and their carers in NHS Executives care (*a key aim of this manual*).
- Ensure that people with continuing health care needs are enabled through the NHS to live as independently as possible.
- Developing NHS organisations and the staff who work within them to meet the challenges of a new NHS.
- Ensuring a prompt and effective emergency service appropriate to the needs of the people, improved care for the critically ill, improved access for cancer services.

More information:
NHS Executive West Midlands
Department of Public Health
Bartholomew House
142 Hagley Road
Birmingham B16 9PA
Tel: 0121 224 4676
Fax: 0121 224 4601

More information on the September Foundation

The September Foundation is a non-profit organisation. It is based in Amsterdam, the Netherlands and specialises in the implementation of self-care projects.

The September Foundation and its sister organisation The Augustus Foundation work in close co-operation with:
- The Dutch Ministry of Health, Welfare and Sports
- The Dutch National Committee for Chronically Ill People

Activities

The September Foundation specialises in developing books, manuals and CD-ROMs that provide information on health and health care for different diseases.
The Foundation is responsible for all the Dutch national self-care manual projects.

Target groups

The materials are primarily written for patients and their families. However, due to the quality of the information provided, these books, manuals and CD-ROMs are also widely used by health care professionals.

Basics

All the materials are written in close co-operation with leading specialists in the field; this results in *state of the art* information.
The character of the information is *practical*: it focuses on what patients and health care workers can do to alleviate the condition.
The information is *integral*: it deals with every aspect of a disease (medical, psychological, social, legal, etc.).
The information can be *easily understood* by people with different levels of education.

Different types of materials

September produces several types of materials:

1. Self-care manuals

Self-care manuals consist of 225 pages, large-format books in a loose-leaf system. They provide extensive information about an illness.

2. Self-care books (paperback, large format)

Self-care books provide extensive, integral information about an illness. However, they are not available in a loose-leaf system.

3. Equipment and Adaptations books

These books aim at providing complete information about equipment and adaptations regarding specific illnesses: which, why, when, where to buy them, prices, funding etc.

4. CD-ROMs (TREE-D-ROM's)

CD-ROMs provide extensive, integral information about an illness. They draw on multimedia's full potential: text, sound, video, photographs, cross-linking and animations.

What materials are available?

Self-care manuals
- AIDS
- Multiple Sclerosis
- Parkinson's Disease
- Dementia
- Epilepsy
- Home Care
- Kidney Disease

Self-care books
- Depression
- Pain
- Diabetes
- Rheumatoid Arthritis
- Cystic Fibrosis
- Celiac Disease
- Food Allergy and Intolerance
- Hirschsprung's Disease
- Urine incontinence
- Arthrosis

Equipment and Adaptations books
- Decubitus (bedsores)
- Rheumatoid Arthritis

CD-ROMs
- Parkinson's Disease

The following titles will be published in the near future eg.:
- Asthma/COPD
- Breast Cancer
- Life after a heart attack

Free updates on the Internet

Information changes quickly. All the Foundation's manuals, books and CD-ROM's are updated on a regular basis on the Foundation's website.
This service is *free*.

The Foundation's activities

The September Foundation undertakes complete projects:
- Fund raising
- Assessment of the needs of the people involved
- Collection of existing materials
- Co-ordination of the writers/advisors/animators/photographers etc.
- Editing
- Co-ordination of the production (printing, lay-out, illustrations, shooting of video etc.)
- Designing the distribution strategy, co-ordinating the distribution
- Promotion
- Evaluation
- Updating the manuals, books and CD-ROMs

Although September is capable of undertaking complete projects, our working process can be adjusted according to the wishes and possibilities of the participating organisations.

The projects are implemented in co-operation with all involved parties such as: government, patients' organisations, professional health care workers, volunteer organisations and hospitals.

Our activities are largely financed by grants from the Dutch government, the European Commission, sponsoring and endowments by funding organizations for patiens and the disabled.

International experience

The September Foundation has considerable experience of international projects. For instance:
- The Dutch Aids self-care manual has been translated and rewritten to meet the needs of people with Aids in many other European countries (e.g. France, Germany, Italy, Spain, Sweden, Finland, Denmark, Belgium, Austria, Greece, Portugal and Ireland).
- The self-care manual and CD-ROM on Parkinson's Disease are being published in the United Kingdom.
- Books and manuals on Food Allergy and Intolerance, Diabetes and Aids are being published in Russia.
- A manual is being published in Slovenia.

For further information, please contact:

The September Foundation:

E.H. Coene, M.D., Director
Nieuwpoortkade 2 A
1055 RX AMSTERDAM
The Netherlands

Phone: +31 20 60 60 745
Fax: +31 20 60 60 798
E-mail: info@stichtingseptember.nl
website: www.boekenoverziekten.nl

European Parkinson's Disease Association (EPDA)

The Association is a non-political, religiously neutral and non-profit making, organisation concerned only with the health and welfare of people living with Parkinson's Disease and their families.

The European Parkinson's Disease Association was formed in Munich in June 1992 with a membership of 10 European Parkinson's Organisations. We now have a membership of 31 European organisations and 5 Associate member organisations.

Aim

To promote international understanding of Parkinson's Disease, enabling people living with Parkinson's and their families to draw on best caring practice world-wide, to access the latest medical and surgical advice and thus make informed choices to achieve the best quality of life possible.

To this end, the EPDA seeks to:
- Establish the extent of Parkinson's Disease in Europe
- Provide and continually update medical and caring best practice
- Make this information readily available to patients and carers of all walks of life throughout Europe
- Offer people with Parkinson's and their families, through information technology and international networking, a community of information and assistance
- Promote and encourage co-operation between scientific and other professional groups enabling advancement of health
- Motivate, promote and support new and existing national organisations to provide optimum care and rehabilitation
- Promote co-operation and exchange of experiences between the member associations

Initiatives

Through collaboration, partnership and commitment we have developed many initiatives which have helped to achieve our aim e.g.:
- Medical Advisory Board consisting of representatives from each organisation
- Magazine, 4 editions per year
- Express News, 4 editions per year
- Euroyapp&rs Network
- Promoted holidays in France and Germany
- Shared literature, videos and information, some translated into various languages
- Collected Parkinson's drugs from throughout Europe for distribution in Bosnia/Croatia

- Produced a leaflet identifying the most commonly prescribed medicines for Parkinson's available in most of the countries in Europe and the United States.
- Set-up WorldWideWeb Site containing validated information on Parkinson's medication, activities, etc., which encourage sharing of knowledge and expertise.
- Conferences and study days.

On 11 April 1997 the first ever World Parkinson's Disease Day was held which would not have been possible without joint collaboration with the World Health Organisation, voluntary organisations, medical profession, health organisations and the pharmaceutical industry. As a result of this great partnership it has been possible to:

- Produce the first WHO Fact Sheet on Parkinson's Disease
- Form a Global Working Group on Parkinson's Disease comprising of health-care professionals, representatives from voluntary organisations and people with Parkinson's, to develop recommendations for guidelines to assist the WHO in their international efforts to manage Parkinson's throughout the global community to look at Epidemiology, Management and Organisation of Services, Education, Training and Information and the Emotional and Economic Cost of Care.
- Set-up a Global Parkinson's Disease Survey (GPDS) involving the participation of Canada, Italy, Japan, Spain, the UK and the USA.
- Set-up a Study on the 'Economic and Emotional cost of Care' which involves a partnership of 5 European countries
- Set-up an evaluation of Physical Therapies designed to unwrap the complexities of management and treatment in Europe
- Set-up a Drug Profiling pilot multi-centre observational registry
- Participated in the development of this Self-Care Manual and a CD-ROM based on this manual, which offers integrated multimedia information on Parkinson's.

Despite what has been achieved in 8 short years, we are very aware that some countries benefit from greater wealth thereby enabling growth, education and expertise. We want to share this knowledge with other cultures and ethnic backgrounds. Some of the ways we can do this is by developing a programme consisting of:

1. Eppnet (European Parkinson's Peoples' Network). Providing validated information on Parkinson's Disease using Information Technology
2. Distance Learning (training modules on Parkinson's which can be a template for other neurological conditions)
3. Animated Video on Parkinson's Disease which will transcend culture and language barriers
4. A Healthy Eating Publication
5. Setting up an exchange neurology scheme whereby newly qualified doctors can spend part of their time with the under-served population who need neurologists with a real driving interest in Parkinson's and its management. This would be a vehicle for introducing drug management into new territories.

Members

Austrian Parkinson Patients Association
Association Parkinson Belge
JeePees, Belgium
Bulgaria Fondazia Parkinsonism
Czech Republic Parkinson's Disease Society
Dansk Parkinson Forening
Estonian Parkinson's Society
Faeroe Islands Parkinsonfelagid
Finlands Parkinson-forbrund
Federation des Groupements de Parkinsoniens, France
The Parkinson Association in Iceland
Parkinson's Association of Ireland
Israel Parkinson Group
Azione Parkinson, Italy
Confederazione Italiana tra Associazioni de Parkinson (CONFIAP)
Association Luxembourgeoise de la Maladie de Parkinson
Parkinson Patienten Vereniging, the Netherlands
Norges Parkinsonforbund
Kracow Parkinson's Disease Association, Poland
Parkinson's Disease Patients Association, Warsaw, Poland
Associacao Portugesa de Doentes de Parkinson's
Parkinson's Disease Society of Slovenia
Parkinson España, Barcelona
Association Parkinson Madrid
Swedish Association of Neurologically Disabled
Swedish Parkinson's Disease Association
Schweizerische Parkinsonvereinigung, Switzerland
Parkinson's Disease Society, Istanbul, Turkey
Association for Parkinsonian Disabled of Ukraine
Parkinson's Disease Society of the United Kingdom
Serbian Association against Parkinson's Disease, Yugoslavia

Associate Members

Atalantic-Euro-Mediterranean Academy of Medical Sciences
Division of Movement Disorders of the Russian Society of Neurologists
European Federation of Neurological Societies (EFNS)
Movement Disorder Society
National Tremor Foundation, UK

Administration Board

PRESIDENT	Mary G. Baker, MBE	(UK)
VICE PRESIDENT	Brita Nybom	(Finland)
SECRETARY	Louise van der Valk	(Holland)
TREASURER	Lars Tallroth	(Sweden)
EDUCATION	Dr Irena Rektrova	(Czech Republic)
MEMBER	Bruno Dupont	(Belgium)
LIAISON	Liz Graham	(UK)

More information:

Mrs Lizzie Graham
Projects Development Manager (PDS UK)
Liaison for European Parkinson's Disease Association
Parkinson's Disease Society of the United Kingdom
215 Vauxhall Bridge Road
LONDON SW1V 1EJ
tel. : D/L ++ 44 20 7932 1304
fax:: D/L ++ 44 20 7233 9226
mobile no.: 077 9940 7501
Home tel./fax: ++ 44 1732 457 683
e-mail: Lizzie@epda.demon.co.uk (home)
e-mail: lgraham@parkinsons.org.uk (work)
web: http://www.shef.ac.uk/misc/groups/epda/home.html

Notes

Chapter 1, What is Parkinson's Disease
1 Taken from: 'Parkinson's and the Occupational Therapist', Parkinson's Disease Society
2 A fact sheet on Parkinsonism and the Parkinsonian Syndromes is available from the Parkinson's Disease Society

Chapter 2, General Symptoms
1 Taken from: 'Parkinson's and the Occupational Therapist', Parkinson's Disease Society
2 Ibidem
3 Taken from: 'Advice notes for People with Parkinson's Disease', Parkinson's Disease Society
4 Taken from: 'Coping with Parkinson's', Parkinson's Disease Society

Chapter 3, Treatment and medication
1 Taken from: 'Parkinson's and the Occupational Therapist', Parkinson's Disease Society

Chapter 6, Information for partners, families and friends
1 Nancy Kohner, Caring at Home, published by the National Extension College in Association with the King's Fund Centre Carers Unit, 1988
2 Lucille Carlton, Surviving as a Caregiver, European Parkinson's Magazine, Issue 6, Winter 1996

Chapter 7, Tips for everyday living
1, 3 - 15 Taken from: Advice notes for People with Parkinson's Disease, Parkinson's Disease Society
2　　　　　Taken from: Parkinson's at Your Fingertips, M. Oxtoby, A. Williams page 73, 128

Chapter 8, Help with movement
1 Taken from: 'Parkinson's and the Occupational Therapist', Parkinson's Disease Society
2 Taken from: 'Parkinson's and the Occupational Therapist', Parkinson's Disease Society
3 Taken from: 'Living with Parkinson's Disease', D. Carrol, p.152 et seq.
4 Taken from: Parkinson's and the Occupational Therapist, Parkinson's Disease Society

Chapter 10, Diet

1, 2, 10   Taken from: 'Parkinson's Disease and the Nurse', Parkinson's Disease Society

5   Taken from: 'Advice Notes for People with Parkinson's Disease', Parkinson's Disease Society

3, 6   Taken from: 'Parkinson's and the Occupational Therapist', Parkinson's Disease Society

4, 8   Taken from: 'Parkinson's at your Fingertips', M Oxtoby & A Williams

7   Taken from: 'Parkinson's Disease and the Nurse', Parkinson's Disease Society

9   Taken from: 'Caring for People with Parkinson's Disease', Parkinson's Disease Society

Chapter 11, Sports, hobbies and holidays

1, 2   Taken from: 'Parkinson's Disease and The Occupational Therapist', The Parkinson's Disease Society

3, 4   Part of this information was taken from: 'Parkinson's at your Fingertips', M. Oxtoby & A. Williams, and from 'Parkinson's Disease and the Occupational Therapist'

Chapter 12, Relationships

1   Taken form: 'Cuddles and Parkinson's', Val Kirby, Parkinson's Disease Society

2   Taken from: 'Changing Relationships', P. Smith, Parkinson's Disease Society

Chapter 16, Outline of professional help

1   This chapter is partly based om information taken from Parkinson's Disease Society publications: 'Moving on ..... an A-Z guide for people who have had Parkinson's for some time' (1998), 'Meeting Your Health Care Needs' (1997), 'Meeting Your Social Care Needs' (1998)

Chapter 19, Speech and language therapy

1   The Parkinson's Disease Society produce a video and accompanying booklet entitled 'Face to Face', which contains useful exercises to help maintain and improve facial expression

2   The Parkinson's Disease Society produce a very useful pack for speech and language therapists who are treating people with Parkinson's entitled 'Parkinson's and the Speech & Language Therapist'

3   Your nearest communication aid centre will be listed in your local telephone directory. British Telecom have advisors to help with telephone modifications where appropriate. Information is under 'Help for customers with special needs' in the 'Useful Information' section at the front of your telephone directory

4   Some Helpful Hints taken from 'Speech & Language Therapy' *The Parkinson* (Spring 1998), Parkinson's Disease Society

5   Some Helpful Hints taken from 'Expressions - Understanding the Language of Parkinson's' (1998), Parkinson's Disease Society

Chapter 20, Parkinson's Disease Nurse Specialists

1   Taken from 'Value of the Carer, PD and the PDNS', Parkinson's Disease Society, Information Pack

Chapter 21, Care in a hospital

1 Bernadette Porter - Mali Jenkins Prize Essay, Parkinson's Disease Society.
2 Taken from 'Parkinson's at your Fingertips' M. Oxtoby and A. Williams (1995)
3 Taken from 'The Drug Treatment of Parkinson's Disease' Parkinson's Disease Society
4 Taken from 'Parkinson's at your Fingertips' M. Oxtoby and A. Williams (1995)
5 Taken from 'The New Role of the Patient' Svend Anderson, European Parkinson's Disease Association Magazine

Chapter 22, Care in a residential home or nursing home

1 Parkinson's Disease Society training resources for nursing and residential care staff in 'Just a little more time' - training video; 'Caring for people with Parkinson's Disease' - booklet.
2 Counsel and Care *Factsheet No.5* 'What to look for in a Care Home'
3 'Parkinson's at your Fingertips', M. Oxtoby & A. Williams, page 171-173.
4 Age Concern *Factsheet No. 37* 'Hospital discharge arrangements, and NHS Continuing Health Care Services'.
5 Counsel and Care *Factsheet No.19* 'Paying the fees of a registered or voluntary home'
6 Age Concern *Factsheet No.10* 'Local authority charging procedures for residential and nursing home care'.

Chapter 23, Complementary therapy for Parkinson's?

1 Parkinson's Disease Society: Complementary Therapy Survey 1997

Chapter 24, Work

1 Taken from 'Moving On ....' (an A-Z guide for people who have had Parkinson's for some time), Parkinson's Disease Society
2 Taken from 'Parkinson's at your Fingertips' M. Oxtoby and A. Williams (1995)

Chapter 25, Welfare benefits

1 Disability Rights Handbook. 22nd Edition. April 1997 - April 1998. page 7. Disability Alliance ERA.

Chapter 27, Particular symptoms

1 Taken from: 'Living with Parkinson's', D. Carroll
2 Taken from: 'Parkinson's at your Fingertips', M. Oxtoby & A. Williams, page 50, 61
3 Taken from: 'Parkinson's and the Occupational Therapist', Parkinson's Disease Society

Chapter 29, Medication that contains levodopa

1-3 Taken from: 'The drug treatment of Parkinson's Disease', Parkinson's Disease Society

Chapter 30, Other medication

1-3 Taken from: 'The drug treatment of Parkinson's Disease', Parkinson's Disease Society

Chapter 31, Surgical treatment

1 Taken from: 'Parkinson's Disease and the Occupational Therapist', Parkinson's Disease Society.

Chapter 32, Coping with stress

1 Taken from: 'Parkinson's and the Occupational Therapist', Parkinson's Disease Society.

Index

It is possible that you may not find particular terms in the index.
This means that we have not used these terms in the text.
In some cases, you may be able to find the meaning of a term in the Glossary
(see page 259).

Notes

295

WITHDRAWN